# Work without Wages

# Work without Wages

Russia's Nonpayment
Crisis

Padma Desai and Todd Idson

The MIT Press
Cambridge, Massachusetts
London, England

This book was set in Palatino by Wellington Graphics.
Printed and bound in the United States of America.

Library of Congress Cataloging-in-Publication Data

Desai, Padma.
   Work without wages : Russia's nonpayment crisis / Padma Desai and Todd Idson.
      p. cm.
   Includes bibliographical references and index.
   ISBN 0-262-04184-7 (alk. paper)
   1. Wages—Russia (Federation)   2. Debt—Russia (Federation)   3. Russia
(Federation)—Economic conditions—1991–   I. Idson, Todd. II. Title.

HD5047.2 .D47 2001  2000
331.2'947—dc21                                                          00-056846

For Jagdish and Lorraine

# Contents

# Acknowledgments

This book could not have been written without the generous financial support provided by the office of Executive Vice Provost Michael Crow of Columbia University; nor could it have taken its final shape without the helpful comments and occasional criticisms by analysts and colleagues at numerous seminars where we presented our initial results.

Padma Desai discussed them at St. Antony's College, Oxford University; the London School of Economics; the EBRD in London; the OECD in Paris; Yegor Gaidar's Institute of Transition Economies; the New School of Economics; the Carnegie Endowment; and before a World Bank group, the latter four meetings held in Moscow. Todd Idson presented them at an Economics Department seminar at the University of Kentucky. Desai and Idson jointly participated in seminars in the Economics Department at Yale University, at the Davis Center for Russian Studies at Harvard University, and at the January 2000 panel discussion of the American Economic Association meetings in Boston. Perhaps our revisions would have been fewer without the give and take, but the final version of the book has gained enormously from the frequent exchanges.

We thank Anna Demidova for her help in translating Russian material, Masoud Anjomshoa for programming assistance, Emil Czechowski for his expertise in converting lifeless numbers into lively charts, and Elena Kondratieva for putting together coal industry data while battling several weeks of Siberian cold. We acknowledge grateful thanks to Anatoly Kandel, who tracked down Russian sources for us, clarified their definitional ambiguities, and plugged occasional gaps in our understanding of Russian wage nonpayment practices.

Most of our data originate from the Russian Longitudinal Monitoring Survey (RLMS) project of the Carolina Population Center (CPC) at the University of North Carolina at Chapel Hill, financed by the

United States Agency for International Development and continuously sustained and monitored by the dedicated group of researchers led by Barry Popkin. In particular, we would like to thank Laura Henderson and Karin Gleiter for expediting and facilitating the availability of the data and Namvar Zohoori for helping us resolve numerous questions relating to RLMS.

We have also generously drawn upon the policy and institutional material translated from scores of original Russian sources by the Current Digest of the Post-Soviet Press, to which we would like to draw the attention of the international financial institutions, among them the World Bank, whose analysts routinely avoid this gold mine of information.

Despite much help from a variety of sources and utmost effort on our part, we acknowledge that Russian data pose serious problems, testing a researcher's patience and skills to the hilt. The definitions tend to be ambiguous; old series are abruptly terminated and new series introduced without sufficient explanation. Politically sensitive information—for example, time series of pension and military wage payment arrears—is difficult to track down. We draw our readers' attention to the introduction of the new ruble on January 1, 1998, which exchanged for 1,000 old rubles; we have noted the change when necessary. While battling numerous handicaps, we have sought to introduce technical rigor and policy insights in our treatment of Russia's nonpayment crisis in the hope that our work will promote further research in areas where our endeavor is less than complete.

# 1 Introduction

The seventy-year old Soviet tradition of "wages without work" turned all too soon into "work without wages" as the Stalinist planned economy began switching to a market system in 1992. The lack of budget discipline surrounding unrealistic budgets, combined with the breakdown of contractual obligations at all levels and the failure of state agencies to enforce businesses laws (described in chapter 2), led to pervasive wage nonpayment to workers in the budget sector and privatized industry.

At the same time, as we argue in chapter 3, the cash-flow problems persisted in both sectors as bankruptcies, which could have trimmed the workforce and the wage bill, were avoided. Bankruptcy enforcement, however, was slowed not only by the inherited industrial structure, changing bankruptcy laws, and inadequate infrastructure, but also by unstable relative prices that complicated the assessment of enterprise profitability and insolvency rating.

In chapter 4, we analyze wage nonpayment patterns across demographic groups defined by gender, age, and education, and in various occupations, industries, and regions of Russia. In chapter 5, we focus on an in-depth analysis of the divergent regional pattern of wage arrears. We conclude that the economic viability of a region defined in terms of its per capita GDP, unemployment rate, and the median wage influenced variations in per capita regional wage arrears.

We pose the issue of nonpayment to Russia's servicemen in chapter 6 in the wider context of a disintegrating military lacking leadership, political clout, and organization, and subjected to massive and haphazard financial cutbacks. By contrast, as we argue in chapters 7 and 8, the pension system and the coal sector escaped overhaul. Russia's pensioners, a united and committed electorate, managed to get repeated pension hikes from the president and the legislators that bankrupted the

Pension Fund. Plans to reform the arrangements were shelved in 1998. The coal industry, plagued by trade union militancy and controlled by the Soviet-era management company Rosugol, also held at bay the structural changes demanded by the World Bank, which provided funding for the purpose.

Having avoided bankruptcies and substantial worker layoffs, Russia's Soviet-era managers resorted to wage nonpayment, barter, and cash nonpayment as survival mechanisms. We conclude in chapter 9 that, having opted for reduced wages via wage withholding rather than explicit contract renegotiation, managers withheld wages more frequently, in larger amounts, and for longer periods for the relatively low-paid workers. We also find in chapter 10 that women with similar demographic and job market attributes as men were more likely to be subjected to wage nonpayment. The prevalence of barter among enterprises and between employers and workers, seems to have been exaggerated, as we show in chapter 11. The extreme measure of barter at 51 percent of enterprise sales toward the end of 1998 included non–cash-clearing arrangements involving financial planning among a chain of enterprises that, in the revised view of Russian analysts, did not constitute barter. Similarly, despite mounting anecdotal evidence, although employers did pay workers in goods, the payments, according to our calculations, were insufficient to counter the adverse impact of accumulated wage nonpayment.

Did wage denial push people below the poverty line, defined in terms of a minimum living standard? How did families survive when they were denied wages for months at a time? Did strikes lead to reduced wage arrears? We explore these issues in chapters 12 and 13.

In chapter 12, we argue that workers' recourse to laws for extracting back wages was ineffective, and strikes were largely uncoordinated over time and territory. Our statistical results show that although wage arrears led to increased strike activity, strikes did not result in a lowering of wage arrears.

However, wage denial increased the likelihood of families falling into poverty. Russian families, according to our analysis in chapter 13, engaged in a variety of survival strategies to compensate for nonpayment by undertaking informal paid activity, selling family assets, engaging in home production for consumption and sale, and receiving cash from relatives.

Our findings, based on a careful application of statistical methods to the available data, are also supported by a mass of qualitative evidence from Russian sources. We believe, however, that our treatment of the topics relating to Russia's nonpayment crisis is by no means exhaustive. We hope that, while proving of interest to readers, our analysis of the crisis will open up new directions of research for scholars engaged in this challenging and exceptional feature of Russia's transition to a market economy.

In conclusion, Russia's policymakers in the budget sector and managers in privatized industry devised strategies, tainted with corruption and lawbreaking, to battle the onslaught of the markets. The public, driven to impoverishment, reacted with a survival mechanism that seemed peculiarly Russian in its vigor and variety. A rational, efficiency-oriented response, which could have led to the speedy emergence of a healthy budget sector and thriving "value-creating" enterprises, was instead at best a miscalculation and at worst, a gamble.

# 2          Why Wage Arrears?

Wage nonpayment to working men and women has been an exceptional and persistent feature of Russia's market transition, defying a credible solution. From 1994 to 1998, wage arrears were on the rise, continually spreading to more economic sectors, occupations, regions, and demographic groups.

The arrears in the budget sector and privatized industry—the former approximately 15 to 20 percent of the total—arose from cash-flow problems in both that, in turn, resulted from five factors:

• The government, unable to collect taxes, failed to pay its suppliers in industry and the energy and transport sectors that, in response, withheld tax payments to the treasury.

• Tight monetary policy firmly in place from 1995 contributed to a cash shortage in the economy. But the shortage in the privatized sector also resulted from its inability to streamline production activity along competitive lines.

• Managers converted cash into foreign exchange for depositing abroad, diverted it for private enrichment, and used it for gainful financial transactions rather than to pay taxes and wages.

• The government accommodated nonpayment among enterprises, between enterprises and the treasury, and ultimately from the budget sector and enterprises to workers via permissive policies. Despite these policies aimed at easing the liquidity shortage, the nonpayment crisis continued unabated.

• Russian wage nonpayment represented a crisis of state power. The state instruments of authority had become inactive at various levels, even powerless battling industrial bosses, regional governors, a defiant Duma (lower house of parliament), and a vacillating president.

Attempts to augment budgetary or enterprise funds, target them for wage disbursement, and ensure that wages were actually paid turned out to be ad hoc at best and futile at worst.

Wage nonpayment to employees of the budget sector and workers in the privatized economy was thus part of a larger, labyrinthine problem attributable to these failings. Clearly, institutional failure to pay employees was but one component of a wider nonpayment crisis that included tax and inter-enterprise arrears. The various elements of the Russian nonpayment crisis were interconnected: Inter-enterprise arrears arising from liquidity constraints contributed to enterprises failing to pay their workers on time; tax arrears similarly led to wage arrears indirectly as the government failed to pay suppliers on time, and directly as it failed to pay employees in the budget sector (funded by local and federal government budgets). In this chapter, we do not measure the impact, direct and indirect, of the government's lagging tax collection on wage arrears nor of the massive inter-enterprise accumulated liabilities on wage withholding to the workforce. Rather, we analyze the factors leading to the cash-flow problems in both, beginning with the lapses in government fiscal management.

### Arrears in the Budget Sector

The government failed to collect projected tax revenues. Only 16 percent of the 2.6 million enterprises registered in the country paid their taxes in full and on time. Eight hundred thousand enterprises, targets of tax authority surveillance, had failed to submit reporting documents to the state. The rest were defaulters.[1]

There was also a vicious circle in place. Enterprises did not pay taxes to the treasury because they were not being paid by major consumers of industrial services and energy—the army, the Ministry of Internal Affairs, educational institutions, housing authorities, and public utilities. These delinquents had no money because they were maintained by the budget, which was not receiving taxes.

Could the treasury have acquired cash by borrowing from the central bank, the Russian public, and foreigners? The budget deficit targets specified by the International Monetary Fund (IMF) and approved by the Duma increasingly lowered and, by the end of 1995, ruled out government borrowing from the central bank. Subsequently, foreign short-term capital inflows, encouraged by capital account convertibility and attracted by the interest rate differential in Russia, became a major source of budgetary funding along with domestic borrowing and receipts from the sale of government stock in privatized companies. The annualized rate of interest on government short-term treasury bills toward the end of 1997 was around 20 to 25 percent. With annual inflation running close to 15 percent at the time, banks, enterprises, and local governments invested available cash in treasury bonds to earn positive real interest income rather than using it to pay employees. (Details of the macroeconomic and exchange rate policies are in Desai, 2000.)

With disbursements from the budget exceeding revenue receipts, the budget sector emerged as a nonpayer par excellence. Sloppy management marked budget planning: The government placed orders for weaponry, for example, that it could not pay for. No one was held responsible for placing an order for which funds were not appropriated.

**Tight Monetary Policy**

Every time monetary control became effective (as in the first half of 1992 during the brief shock therapy phase, and after 1995), inflation dropped, the production slump worsened, and nonpayments accumulated. Nonpayments and slump were thus connected, creating in turn the preconditions for structural changes and labor layoffs that were not carried out. Enterprise managers facing price decontrol, cutbacks of budgetary subsidies, and cash shortage in early 1992 jacked up prices instead of cutting costs and creating market networks with customers. When they ran into problems of selling their outputs or recovering payments, they demanded financial support from the government to bail them out of debts with clients and suppliers. The year was marked by a mountain of inter-enterprise overdue payments amounting to half of GDP, with the ratio coming down to 10 to 15 percent of GDP by the end of 1993.[2]

As budgetary support diminished and monetary control intensified, leading to diminished liquidity, enterprises resorted to barter exchanges with one another and with the goverment, such as offers of construction services to local governments in lieu of construction companies' tax payments—arrangements that could neither generate taxes nor create cash to pay wages. These barter practices and offset arrangements among enterprises and between governments and enterprises created economywide arrears to workers.

In the process, enterprise managers continuously juggled options involving product lines to be trimmed or discontinued, different groups of workers to be denied wages or put on forced leave or unpaid vacation, and suppliers and clients to be sought out for barter deals at market-determined rates. Managers who succeeded in keeping their factories afloat via barter deals and wage nonpayment, however, acquired short- term, interest-free credits that could be used for personal gain, a topic to which we now turn.

## Unruly Enterprise Directors

Nonpayments proliferated because managers who failed to pay wages to workers or charges for goods and services shipped by suppliers did not have to worry about legal penalties or shareholder sanctions.

### Poor Law Enforcement

Laws supplemented by presidential decrees were aimed at penalizing managers who withheld wages from workers or undertook shady deals for diverting cash. Article 138 of the Russian Federation Criminal Code laid down that enterprise executives who held up wage payment could not only be dismissed and fined up to 500 times the minimum monthly wage, but also be subjected to one year's corrective labor.[3] A presidential decree of January 1996 prescribed procedures for prosecuting directors of state and privatized companies. The labor and tax inspectorates and tax police agencies were authorized to ensure that organizations complied with wage legislation "irrespective of their ownership form, jurisdictional subordination, or institutional affiliation." The Supreme Court was drawn in to consider cases involving violations of wage legislation.[4] (Details of labor laws and Russia's civil code safeguarding workers' employment and earnings—and trade union participation in enforcing them—are discussed in chapter 12.)

Enterprise managers ignored presidential decrees and Duma legislation because these could not be enforced. For example, the Tulaugol (Tula Coal Association) in the central region was unable to recover its claims against the Ryazan' State Regional Power Station for coal shipments despite a court ruling because of the absence of an established mechanism and court officers for the purpose.

## Absence of Regulatory Control

Managers had acquired decision-making powers and the right to manage money without facing penalties from higher authorities, banks, or shareholders for mismanagement. As a result, they sold goods to clients without working up contracts or demanding prepayment. Such deals were especially frequent in oil refining: Clients often managed to extract gasoline from refineries without payment or a proper contract. A buyer would approach the manager of an oil refinery and say: Sell me 100,000 tons of gasoline. The manager would want prepayment, but the potential buyer would offer a briefcase full of cash, which varied from 3 to 5 percent of the transaction. According to the bankruptcy administration's investigation, such de facto trade credit averaged as much as five times the monthly output of the refineries. The refiners kept their operations going by borrowing oil from the oil producers. Less cash in the entire chain resulted in delayed or withheld wage payment to workers.[5]

Inter-enterprise barter deals leading to wage arrears became widespread because unscrupulous managers were not regulated by shareholders as in a market economy. The Duma passed a law on June 4, 1997 seeking to impose sanctions on managers via shareholders. It held the head of an organization (whether privatized or state-owned) financially liable, to the full extent of his assets, for losses caused to the unit. He was required to declare his annual income to the shareholders. A rank-and-file employee could be fired only on grounds stated in the Code of Labor Laws. A chief executive could be fired by shareholders.[6]

Thereupon managers proceeded to remove outside shareholders, Russian and foreign, from company lists in order to escape shareholder monitoring. Thus the director of the Krasnoyarsk Aluminum Plant (KAP) removed representatives of the Mortgage Bank and the Russian Capital Company from KAP's board of directors by deleting computerized entries of share ownership without court proceedings. The managers of the Moscow Likhachov Automobile Plant (ZIL) locked out the Mikrodin Company, removing 22 percent of the company's ZIL shares from the registry. The director of the Lebedinsky Mining and Ore-Dressing Combine (LMODC) removed the Russian Credit Company, which owned 22 percent of the company, from its board of directors and prepared to float new shares to dilute the credit company's role. The managers were usually protected by politicians. The ZIL manager

successfully appealed to President Boris Yeltsin. KAP and LMODC
contributed substantially to their cities' budgets.[7]

### Barter, Wage Nonpayment, and the Resulting Cash Windfall

As insolvent enterprises accumulated debts, they also acquired working capital they would have lost had they paid their suppliers.
One-fourth of the liquidity was reportedly used for production activity; one-fifth was deposited into foreign accounts. But more than half
was used elsewhere for financial transactions that enriched enterprise
directors who had, in effect, obtained interest-free loans.[8]

The transactions also enriched creditors who shipped items to clients
known to be unreliable or insolvent or both. As a result, the creditor enterprises got ruined, but the executives who got cash under the table
from the client managers for the deals became rich. Such transactions,
in which the clients did not have to pay supplier enterprises in advance, took place in export activities because the contracts enabled
supplier managers to receive cash. Occasionally, such deals arose because factories could not sell what they had produced, but a taker
could be found if the supplier did not insist on immediate payment.
Nonpayment on a massive scale could not have arisen if the players
did not have a stake in the activity.

In fact, nonpayment proliferated because cash transactions were discouraged by the government via a variety of policy maneuvers,
financial and administrative.

### The Policy Failures

In early 1994, the financial devices of short-term debt instruments and
debt write-offs were implemented to help enterprise managers tide
over cash shortages, straighten out their finances, undertake cost-
saving measures, and streamline their production routines. They totally backfired.

### Financial Maneuvers

Even during the planned economy days, nonpayment existed, requiring debt offsetting between branches of the economy. Payments by customers for products were registered as credits in enterprise accounts by
the Central Bank of Russia. The bank also debited the accounts of customer enterprises by the appropriate amounts. Persistent negative

accounts were periodically cleared up via cash infusions from the ministry overseeing enterprise finances. Everyone survived under this "squatter's rights paradise."

But the debt write-offs of the Soviet days slackened the enforcement of market discipline and delayed the Schumpeterian "creative destruction" in the new reform regime. How could automatic debt cancellations distinguish between debts owed for shipment of nonsaleable items and for receipt of exportable oil? 'At the same time, the emission of liquidity in the form of short-term debt instruments for facilitating the movement of potatoes from trading warehouse to store shelves was counterproductive if the public wanted to buy onions instead of potatoes. From this perspective, inter-enterprise nonpayments and wage arrears were a structural problem. Entire branches in the economy turned out to be noncompetitive when faced with real prices, inadequate demand, and marketing problems. The crisis required the closure of noncompetitive production units and the sale of salvageable units. (The role of correct relative prices including a suitable exchange rate policy in the decision making is highlighted in chapter 3 on bankruptcies.)

In practice, the government deliberately avoided confronting the nonpayment crisis by letting enterprises use short-term debt instruments for facilitating inter-enterprise payments, and by allowing write-offs.

### Issuing Short-Term Debt Instruments

A government resolution of August 26, 1994 allowed suppliers to settle customer accounts via standardized, transferable interest-bearing notes. Creditors issued these ninety-day notes valued at 100 million rubles each when they shipped goods to clients. Ideally, they were short-term credits extended by suppliers for facilitating purchases by clients who were short of working capital. In principle, the central bank would rediscount notes issued by a solvent supplier enterprise and by an enterprise to a commercial bank provided the bank took responsibility for the marketability of a note presented for rediscounting. The debt would be finally recovered from the debtor enterprise's account or from its physical assets when the note fell due.

Interest-bearing notes, intended for financing current transactions, were subsequently extended for the settlement of accumulated inter-enterprise and agricultural debts. The treasury issued special notes for settling the state sector's debts for purchases of defense items. The market economy's trusted device of short-term credits, which would eventually be cleared by borrowers, became a reckless free-for-all that participants used for accommodating their financial mismanagement. At the same time, mutual payment offsets between the budget and the taxpayers, between the center and the regions, and among enterprises were becoming pervasive.

## Offsets

The system, starting with small amounts and approved by former finance Minister Alexandr Livshits, allowed enterprises and regions to clear their liabilities by offsetting them against the center's liabilities to them. A convenient device for canceling tax obligations of enterprises to the federal budget, they were practiced more avidly by regional authorities for canceling their payment liabilities to the center until they were finally abolished in 1997. Offsets deprived the budget of hard cash. In 1996, cash amounted to only 10 percent of total tax payments by large enterprises.[9]

The Ministry of finance began disallowing offsets in 1997. The railways, listed as major debtors to the federal budget, had hauled coal and defense ministry freight for years on government instructions without getting a kopeck. The demand from the railways that the amount should be credited as taxes paid or the railways would stop hauling freight for the government was brushed aside by the finance ministry. Communications and construction enterprises were denied similar offsets by the ministry and the Central Bank of Russia. The ministry also denied a tax write-off to the fuel and energy complex that provided rural areas with commodity credits. The demands for offsets arose in these cases because the government had failed to pay suppliers for services rendered. In mid-November 1997, the president issued a decree barring the use of offsets for settling debts to the federal budget from January 1, 1998.

The crisis of nonpayments among enterprises, between enterprises and the government, and from the budget sector and enterprises to the workers worsened over time because rather than systematically enforcing bankruptcies, the government accommodated nonpayments via fixed-term, interest-bearing notes (including special state treasury notes for purchases of defense items) and mutual offsetting of debts. In fact, the finance ministry, the economics ministry, the State Property Committee, and the Central Bank of Russia maintained a safe distance from confronting the enterprise restructuring issue while the government issued directives, passed resolutions, and called upon the relevant agencies to take charge of the problem.

The government also resorted to administrative measures, among them the appointment of monitoring commissions and voluntary price setting by major monopoly suppliers, for easing the payment problem of client enterprises.

### Recourse to Administrative Measures

Prime Minister Viktor Chernomyrdin suggested an array of measures containing a heavy dose of government monitoring, sanctions, and bailouts reminiscent of a planned economy, at the same time ruling out the Soviet practice of automatically rescuing loss-making enterprises. Among these were a systematic monitoring of enterprise accounts, compulsory debt payment from their foreign currency accounts, enforcement of punitive sanctions on enterprises for concealing accounts, replenishment of enterprise working capital via interest-bearing notes, mutual agreements among executives of railroads, power, coal, and metallurgy industries on power and freight charges without government intervention, and participation of trade unions in wage setting.[10] What better way to address this set of issues than to appoint a commission?

### *Soskovets Commission*

On August 5, 1994 the government, evidently realizing that the nonpayment problem was becoming unmanageable, appointed a Commission on Improving the System of Payments and Settlements with emergency powers under the chairmanship of first Deputy Prime Minister Oleg Soskovets, an ardent advocate of state support of defense and heavy industry enterprises. The commission intended tackling the problem by writing laws based on twenty-four top-priority drafts of presidential decrees and government resolutions submitted by various ministries and departments for enforcing discipline in the tax and accounting systems and in bankruptcy procedures. The commission, the chairman asserted, had the political will to act "without drowning in paperwork." The network of the Agency for Insolvency and Bankruptcy was ready to investigate the finances of loss-making production units, separate the essential from the nonessential, and liquidate those that had no future.[11] The resolve, however, was not translated into action.

Soon after, the government proposed introducing new procedures for harmonizing prices and fees in the basic industries with a view to avoiding nonpayment accumulation in their balance sheets. The Ministry of Railways, the Ministry of Fuel and Power, the Russian Federation Committee on Metallurgy, and Rosugol (the Russian Coal Company) pledged to coordinate price and rate policies in the winter of 1995, and facilitated the mutual offsetting of debts between sectors by signing the General Agreement on Joint Actions to Stabilize Prices and Reduce Mutual Nonpayments, approved by the government on September 12, 1994. The government instructed the Ministry of Fuel and Power to draw up proposals by the end of September for coordinating and revising charges for natural gas, electricity, heat, and railroad shipping. By the end of 1995, electric power rates for the general public and for the agricultural sector were to be brought in line with the real cost of heat and electricity, with the needy to be compensated via a special support fund. At the same time, the Ministry of finance was instructed to issue treasury securities up to the amount of the federal budget's indebtedness to enterprises participating in the agreement to settle the ministry's debt. Enterprises participating in the agreement were to be given priority for deferring their taxes to the budget.[12] In the end, there was no getting away from old practices

Exasperated by mounting enterprise debts to the treasury, the government passed a resolution in March 1997 giving enterprise directors a choice of either paying their current taxes, in which case all accumulated debts before January 1, 1997 would qualify for a five-year deferred payment plan, or letting the state acquire a controlling block of shares in their companies in exchange for debt settlement. A later resolution consolidated the defaulters' debts to the federal and regional treasuries and proposed assigning 51 percent of the enterprise shares to the Federal Property Fund as collateral against their accumulated debts. The plan did not succeed. Enterprise directors refused to surrender controlling blocks of shares to the government.[13]

Collecting taxes from corporate tax dodgers remained a problem. The government's policy stance hardened from administrative measures, monitoring devices, and enterprise managers' voluntary acceptance of concessions (for example, swapping shares for clearing tax liabilities) to active arm-twisting of big businesses that held back tax payments to the treasury. It sought to bolster its revenue collecting authority by challenging the Duma in a complex legal battle over the issue of managerial accountability with respect to tax payment versus wage payment. Its bargaining capability was stretched to the limit in negotiating nonpayment issues with the monopoly suppliers, among them the fuel and energy complex, that held disproportionately large claims on the rest of the economy, including government customers. finally, it found itself pitted against unruly regional administrators who were responsible for paying wages to budget sector employees from funds provided by the center. In all these respects, the government came across as either weak and accommodating or heavy-handed, unable to collect taxes or settle nonpayment issues via statutory means.

## Crumbling State Authority

Measures to collect taxes and unlock the wage arrears crisis in the budget sector via unorthodox means were launched by Anatoly Chubais, chairman of the government's payment commission that succeeded the Soskovets commission. Tax collection under his leadership unfolded as an exercise in rule bending, muscle flexing, and deal making among tax authorities, company directors, and regional political bosses in which the Russian president occasionally participated.

In a move that simultaneously angered the president and the Duma, Chubais sought larger corporate tax payments in the budget in late 1995 by abolishing the 30:70 requirement, according to which 30 percent of balances in enterprise accounts was reserved for wages and salaries. On the eve of the December 1995 Duma elections, the president, fearing a political fallout, restored the 30:70 requirement that ensured wages to workers, thereby crippling the mandate of the Chubais commission to ensure a flow of tax resources from companies into the budget.

### Should Wages Be Paid before Taxes?

Not to be outdone by the president in its concern for worker welfare, the Duma enacted legislation in the summer of 1996 that locked horns with the government on the issue of tax payment versus wage payment by enterprises.

The Duma amended Article 855 of the Civil Code legislating that enterprises should clear their debts with employees before paying taxes to the budget. The government objected to the Duma's use of the Civil Code for regulating tax matters: The State Tax Service, the finance ministry, and the Central Bank of Russia instructed banks to follow the old rules (giving priority to tax payment) and pay taxes to the budget from company accounts before making any other payments. They cited Article 15 of the law "On the Principles of the Tax System" under which payments into budgets and off-budget funds had first priority.[14] Not to be held back, the Duma deputies restored Article 855 and instructed the banks to ignore the directive of the government troika.

Commercial banks were caught in the middle. If they followed the civil code and paid wages from enterprise accounts ahead of tax payments, they faced fines from the State Tax Service and risked sanctions from the Central Bank of Russia, their supervisory agency. If they obeyed the instructions of the financial trio, they violated the law of the land and risked potential lawsuits from enterprises. Faced with the options of breaking the law and displeasing the government, most banks continued paying taxes.

On November 11, 1996, the justice ministry filed an inquiry with the Russian Constitutional Court regarding the interpretation of various provisions of civil, tax, and budget legislation. The dispute between the government and the Duma involving commercial banks had turned even more contentious. On December 23, 1997, the constitutional court ruled that enterprises must pay their taxes to the federal budget before paying their employees' wages and salaries: The provision of the Russian Civil Code requiring that obligations to employees be cleared before taxes were paid was unconstitutional. The sequence established by this provision could, in the court's view, violate the constitutional duty of enterprises to pay legally established and assessed taxes. Taxes, the ruling affirmed, were the primary source of budget revenues that provided resources to the state for maintaining and defending the rights and freedoms of citizens and for carrying out its social functions.[15]

While the highest court of the land ruled in favor of the government, the State Tax Service's record of tax collection remained woeful, with revenue flows trailing behind projections. In fact, the majority of company directors remained a law unto themselves, manipulating company resources and accounts to their advantage without facing legal action.

*Tax Collection Chubais-Style*

Commission chairman Chubais swung into action, systematically identifying tax delinquents, alternatively offering them deals or threatening them with loss of assets if they failed to comply.

In early 1996, the commission identified fifty large enterprises that accounted for half the tax arrears in the federal budget. Evidently 80 percent of enterprise indebtedness resulted from the machinations of directors of industrial giants who deliberately delayed the settling of accounts with clients, banks, and the state treasury. If the big tax defaulters could be handled, the entire chain of nonpayment could be disentangled.

On October 14, 1996, six dominant debtors received notices to the effect that unless they paid their current debt, in the amount of 1.3 trillion rubles, within a week, their cases would be turned over to a court of arbitration with a view to starting bankruptcy proceedings against them.[16] The "magnificent six" were Tatneft (Tatar Petroleum Company) in the Volga region, Permeftegaz (Perm Petroleum and Gas Company), in the Urals region, the Moskvich car factory, Krasnodarnefteorgsintez (Krasnodar Petroleum Organic Synthesis Company) in North Caucasus, the Achinsk Alumina Combine in Eastern Siberia, and KAMAZ (Kama Automative Plant) in Tatarstan.

Additionally, 185 enterprises, most of them profitable companies, owed 25 trillion rubles to the budget in mid-October 1996, which amounted to half the budgetary arrears. Notices were dispatched to ten more debtor enterprises, that like the first six, had cleared less than 10 percent of their obligations to the budget in the past six months.

In response, the commission was pressured by a number of operatives. The Union of Petroleum Industrialists appealed to the president, the government, and the parliament that forcing Nizhnevartovskneftegaz (Nizhnevartovsk Oil and Gas Company) in Western Siberia to clear tax arrears would ruin the company. Irkutsk Province governor Yuri Nozhikov countered a government resolution and postponed by two months the tax payments by four main enterprises into all budgets and the federal off-budget funds. But Vagit Alekperov, Chairman of Lukoil, Russia's largest oil company, paid 1 trillion rubles in back taxes by selling a block of state shares with Chubais's consent. Chubais also allowed Vladimir Bogdanov, the head of Surgutneftegaz (Surgut Oil and Gas Company) in Western Siberia to clear tax arrears in the budget by acquiring state shares in the company at a collateral-based auction.[17]

In reality, the Chubais Commission's authority was modest. It lacked the legal means to investigate company accounts even in cases when tax manipulation by enterprise directors smacked of criminal activity. Hundreds of cases got stuck in agencies of the Ministry of Internal Affairs and the prosecutors' offices. The Civil Code also contained few legal means of extracting tax payments from delinquent directors, forcing the tax authorities to resort to scare tactics and accommodating deals rather than legal procedures.

On May 31, 1997, the government adopted a plan, approved by Chubais, that levied stiff penalties on persistent defaulters to the budget who nevertheless paid dividends to shareholders, gave large salaries to directors, and made financial investments. The plan guaranteed oil-export pipeline access to oil producers who were clear in their payment obligations to the budget or the off-budget funds or who promised to pay off such debts within a short period.[18]

The most sensational confrontation on the tax issue arose in July 1998, when the government threatened to seize the assets of Gazprom, Russia's giant gas monopoly, and terminate its agreement with Chairman Rem Vyakhirev, who managed the 40 percent government stake in the company. But Gazprom had the potential of humbling the Russian state.

The government's aim was to pry open the company's accounts and collect taxes without granting it special privileges or getting involved in its day-to-day management. The June tax collection figure of 1.9 billion (new) rubles in company records differed widely from the 800 million rubles recorded in the ledgers of the State Tax Service. The government backed down from its threat of seizing company assets after Gazprom agreed to restructure its tax liability to the state budget and pay its taxes in full from July 1.[19]

The Chubais Commission-Gazprom confrontation had repercussions beyond the job of collecting taxes from Russia's largest company, which contributed up to 20 percent of tax revenues. Evidently in solidarity with Gazprom, on July 3 the Duma threw out the government's anticrisis program presented by Prime Minister Sergei Kiriyenko to contain the mounting threats to the stability of the ruble. Political heavyweights and leaders of the major financial-industrial groups rallied around the company. The episode nevertheless revealed the existence of Gazprom's vast banking and media empire, a Moscow skyscraper, countryside villas, planes, yachts, and fitness centers that set Vyakhirev apart from other oligarchs. Gazprom's outlays on this paraphernalia vastly exceeded its debt to the federal budget.

In a show of strength, humiliating to the government in mid-July, Gazprom threatened to suspend gas deliveries to power companies in twenty regions, forcing a massive electric power cutoff to cities and enterprises across the country. Pressured by the government in Moscow, the regional governors, and Chubais, now Chairman of Unified Power System, Gazprom withdrew its threat.

The lopsided accumulation of nonpayments in the economy, whereby monopoly enterprises in the fuel and energy sector (Gazprom among them) had emerged as massive creditors of the remaining industrial sectors, agriculture, the state, CIS customers, and households, ruled out a straightforward clearing of arrears. Political and social considerations outweighed economic calculations of balancing debits against credits.

By early October 1993, half the inter-enterprise debt of 11 trillion rubles was owed by Russian enterprises to the fuel and energy sector. In early April 1995, debt to the sector, at 75 trillion rubles, was half the national budget. The CIS states, among them Ukraine and Belarus, owed substantial amounts to Russian gas suppliers. Domestic customers, including local governments and households, refused payment as well. In the first five months of 1998, Russian customers had paid cash for only 14 percent of the gas supplied to them by Gazprom, their performance marking a slight improvement over the 8.1 percent cash payment for their purchases by CIS customers. As a result, the company was owed 100 trillion rubles, implying that Russian consumers had withheld payment to the company for fifteen months.[20]

## The Fuel and Energy Sector: The Critical Link in the Nonpayment Crisis

The fuel and energy complex took the major share of the nonpayment load because it was technically difficult for oil, gas, and power companies to "turn off the spigot" and stop delivery. The mounting arrears also resulted from the government's decision in October 1995 to enforce continued power supply to strategic consumers in the metallurgical, chemical, and machinery manufacturing sectors. Again, the Ministry of Defense and Ministry of Internal Affairs installations and defense industry enterprises, all classified as strategic, accounted for a sizeable chunk of accumulated debt.

Occasionally the players indulged in tit-for-tat. On the other hand, the Minister of Fuel and Power, Yuri Shafranik, recommended issuing currency and reviving offsets to clear the mountain of debt to the complex. During his brief tenure (from March 23, 1998 to August 23, 1998), Prime Minister Kiriyenko proposed Soviet-style ceilings on power and gas consumption by government users.

The blow-counter-blow approach was tried in Urengoi Province. The province's gas producers threatened to cut off the supply to the mayor's office, which in turn intended filing a lawsuit against Urengoigazprom (the Urengoi Gas Industry Production Association) in Western Siberia for tax nonpayment into the city budget. Gazprom intermittently closed the valve, shutting off deliveries to Ukraine, Belarus, and Kazakhstan. In mid-November, 1994, the supply of electric power to all industrial enterprises in Arkhangel'sk and Severodvinsk Provinces in the north was cut off because the local heat and electric power plants had run out of fuel to generate electricity. In October, Pavel Balakshin, the governor of Arkhangel'sk Province, procured credits from the federal government in the form of treasury bonds, which the middlemen suppliers of electricity refused to accept. Balakshin turned for help to Oleg Soskovets, who in turn signed a request asking the general director of Rosneft, the oil supplier, to release fuel to Arkhangel'sk Province. The general director of Rosneft declared that the signature of the deputy prime minister of the Russian federation would not compel him to release fuel.[21]

Shafranik's plea for currency emission and offset revival for unlocking the gridlock of enterprise debts to the fuel and energy sector was motivated by the sector's continuing deterioration. Nonpayment by consumers to Tyumen' province gas suppliers affected their investments in prospecting, drilling, and pipeline expansion. They regarded interest-bearing notes as a nuisance obliging them to extract cash from the debtors when the notes expired. They demanded instant cash, urging the central bank to print currency. Viktor Gerashchenko, the chairman of the Central Bank of Russia, was more popular in Tyumen' than Boris Fyodorov, the minister of finance, who had floated interest-bearing notes.[22]

In Shafranik's opinion, the central bank's restriction on currency emission exacerbated the fuel and power complex's financial situation. The industry was the last "oxygen tank" providing interest-free credit to an unreformed housing and public utilities system and inefficient state-owned enterprises. The complex, he argued, was decisive for the country's economy, providing more than half the budget revenues and 70 percent of foreign exchange earnings. Nonpayment, in his view, should be addressed via mutual offsetting of debts and provision of inflationary credits to the fuel and power complex's subcontractors and customers.[23]

Much to the minister's disappointment, the cancellation of the practice of mutual offsetting of debts, was enforced under IMF pressure in December 1997. Prime Minister Kiriyenko's plan to impose gas and power consumption ceilings on government users was soundly rejected by them. Nor was the policy option of pumping cash into the economy for replenishing enterprise working capital and activating wage payment—a plan promoted by a group of Russian Academy of

Science economists during former Prime Minister Yevgenii Primakov's tenure in office (August 24, 1998 to May 11, 1999)—actively pursued by the Central Bank of Russia.

The nonpayment crisis pitted the government against tax dodgers in industry and nonpaying customers to the fuel and energy complex, prompting solutions, noted above, that were counterproductive. Equally aggravating was the opposition that the center encountered from regional administrators in its attempts to hold the crisis at bay.

## The Regional Factor

Russia's regions that paid wages and salaries to state-sector employees—among them teachers, doctors, judges, and police—from funds transferred for the purpose by the center violated payment agreements, raising troublesome issues of center-periphery relations. Regional administrators from governors to local mayors diverted funds allotted by the center for a specific purpose (for example, to pay coal miners in the privatized coal mines or teachers and doctors in the budget sector) to other uses. During the heating season, regional chief administrators diverted cash flows from the payment of wages to the housing and municipal services sector.

Occasionally the Russian president followed a decree with stern action to set an example. In early 1996, he dismissed two governors for nonpayment of wages, salaries, and pensions and initiated criminal proceedings against a third—all members of the Council of Federation—without the council's knowledge or consent. The chairman of the council's budget committee, Samara Province Governor Konstantin Titov, pointed out that the required funds were not received by the regions, laying the blame on the Ministry of finance.[24]

For a long time, as already noted, the government promoted the development of artificial money, with regional budgets getting 60 percent of their revenues in the form of debt offsets rather than hard cash. At the same time, wages and salaries to employees of the budget sector were to be paid by regions from retained tax revenues collected by them for the center, constituting implicit transfers from the federal budget. The budget sector wage arrears were therefore owed by the regions, not by Moscow. In habitually diverting the funds to other uses and not paying wages, the regions counted on Moscow to follow the established tradition of coming up with extra cash for avoiding strikes; in December 1997, several governors used this method forcing the government to clear their local debts.

Following the presidential decree that all debts in the budget-financed sphere be cleared by January 1, 1998, the Ministry of finance started transferring money to the regions in early November, 1997. The regions were to raise a ruble for every ruble transferred from the center. Despite colossal efforts from Moscow, the regional governments managed to pay off only part of the wage arrears to employees of budget-financed organizations. fifteen trillion rubles went out to the regions before the first of the year. However, total arrears for various payments in the amount of 21 trillion rubles (including debts owed to servicemen and to Chernobyl victims, and benefits to children owed by local budgets) remained outstanding. The 1997 experience of splitting the payments to employees of the budget-financed organizations between the center and the regions did not work.[25]

Making emergency payments to teachers and doctors produced one significant result: January 1998 passed without strikes. In February, debts to employees in the budget-funded organizations shot up 21 percent and continued climbing.[26]

Given the prevailing reporting procedures, the government became aware of the financial situation in the regions only a month or more after the fact. It was almost March 1998 by the time the government learned how the governors had disposed of the funds sent to them the previous December. The system of monitoring the transfer of funds from the center to the regions needed strict enforcement and transparent reporting. Nineteen ninety-eight had passed without progress on that front. At the same time, with 1999 parliamentary elections drawing closer, some governors, facing the end of their terms, had already raised official wages while huge arrears remained.[27]

During the December 1993 Duma election campaign, Grigory Yavlinsky, leader of the Yabloko Party, was asked in a crowded hall: "Grigory Alekseyevich, we're ready to vote for you, but we haven't been paid for three months. If we elect you to the Duma on the 12th, will you guarantee that we'll be paid on the 13th?" Yavlinsky began by explaining that the Duma was not the Ministry of finance—that it was elected to make laws. He was shouted down by the audience.

Vladimir Zhirinovsky, the flamboyant leader of Russia's National-Liberal Democratic Party, promised a radical solution to the nonpayment problem when he spoke before the same group in the same hall a few days later. Someone asked him the same question about wages, again saying that they were all ready to vote for anyone who would pay them.

"Look," Zhirinovsky answered, "all of you vote for our party on the 12th, and on the 13th those who aren't paying your wages—Gaidar, Chubais and all the others—will be swinging from that lamppost."

There was a storm of cheers and applause.[28]

Rather than provide such a dramatic solution, Yeltsin stuck to explaining the origins of the crisis in terms of budgetary mismanagement. In his message to the Federal Assembly on March 6, 1997, the president summed up the nonpayment situation as follows: The government started out with unrealistic plans and ended up with poor budget discipline. An unrealistic budget became one of the main sources of mutual nonpayment. Tax receipts fell, and the treasury ran short of cash, which delayed wages, pensions, and benefits. Enterprises were thrown into disarray. The vicious circle must be broken.[29]

## Conclusions

The Russian president put the lack of budget discipline surrounding unrealistic budgets at the center of the crisis of wage arrears. Restoring budget discipline, however, was only a partial solution. The resolution of the crisis called for the enforcement of contractual obligations that had collapsed at all levels. Presidential decrees and parliamentary laws aimed at extracting taxes, disciplining enterprise business activity, and regulating center-state cooperation with a view to restoring payments to working men and women were disregarded. Equally ignored were bankruptcy laws designed to rein in wage arrears by enforcing factory restructuring and workforce downsizing, the subject of our analysis in the next chapter.

# 3

# Where Are the Bankruptcies?

Wage arrears in Russia could have declined and disappeared over time if nonviable units were identified, declared bankrupt, and folded or reorganized, resulting in a smaller workforce and wage bill. The adoption of suitable bankruptcy laws and their enforcement by appropriate agencies were necessary for initiating the process.

Soviet-era traditions, however, weighed heavily in the formulation and application of bankruptcy rules. The transition from an arrangement in which all productive units were owned by the state and managed under planners' rules, guaranteeing automatic bailout of farms and factories and full employment of workers, to a system in which the former could be folded and the latter could be given pink slips, marked a seismic change. The structure of the Russian economy—geared toward heavy industry, including the defense sector (discussed in the appendix to this chapter), and huge, mechanized farms—required time and resources for their overhaul, rendering widespread bankruptcy implementation a formidable challenge and an impractical solution in the short run.

Russia's bankruptcy problem also extended beyond its privatized factories. Legally enforceable rules were required to compel Russian state agencies to pay wages and pensions while targeting them for restructuring. Again, Russia's collective farms, all converted into joint stock companies, could technically be covered by bankruptcy laws. In actual practice, however, the farms, sacrosanct in history and society, would more readily be spared bankruptcy rulings.

While the social and political implications of enforcing bankruptcies resulting in factory shutdown and worker job loss are paramount everywhere, the separation of viable from nonviable units in terms of stable economic norms presented additional headaches to policymakers in Russia's continuing transition. Problems arose because inflation control was shaky and relative prices were in a state of flux. The pricing policies of monopoly suppliers of fuel, energy, and railroad freight worked to the disadvantage of Russia's manufacturing sector, which continued facing unfavorable relative prices. The handicap arising from an overvalued real exchange rate also confronted suppliers who were outcompeted by cheap, better-quality imports.

Given this background, Russian bankruptcy procedures were hobbled by changing bankruptcy laws, inadequate infrastructure, meddlesome regional and local politicians who often rescued sick units in their orbit, and unsettled relative prices that complicated the selection of unprofitable units. Overall, a deliberate "hasten slowly" attitude evident in a series of cumbersome bankruptcy laws and presidential decrees, and an accommodating stance by the government that continued providing financial surrogates to insolvent units (described in the previous chapter), contributed to the delay. Wage nonpayment resulting in lower effective wages rather than worker layoffs, implying plant overhaul or closure, and barter practices continued to be the preferred option of decision makers in privatized industry.

In this chapter, we address the complex issue of Russian wage arrears from the perspective of bankruptcy laws and their enforcement, the inadequate infrastructure (including the fragile market-oriented institutionalization), and the unstable relative prices, beginning with a discussion of the bankruptcy legislation.

## Bankruptcy Law of 1993

A bankruptcy mechanism that could systematically implement industrial restructuring and break the chain of nonpayments was missing in Russia until March 1993. The first Law on Bankruptcy that went into effect on March 1, 1993 was followed five years later by the Law on Insolvency of Enterprises, which became operational on March 1, 1998.

The 1993 law empowered a court of arbitration to initiate a bankruptcy on appeal from the insolvent enterprise, its creditors, or a prosecutor. The court could liquidate the enterprise or reorganize it by sorting out its finances. If reorganization was ruled out as an option, the enterprise could be pronounced insolvent and liquidated after a lapse of two to two-and-half years.[1]

Soon after, the State Committee on Industrial Policy was reportedly working up a list of money-losing enterprises as candidates for instructive bankruptcies. But no such list could be located in the intractable files of the committee.[2]

This provoked an outburst from Prime Minister Chernomyrdin, who complained of the lack of a functioning mechanism for implementing bankruptcies; he singled out the State Property Committee, the Ministry of Economics, and the Ministry of finance for their lethargy in defining a bankrupt, working up a list of candidates, and providing clear guidelines. Foot dragging on the issue, in his view, imposed great damage to the economy.[3] At the same time, while renouncing centralized planning and resource distribution, he suggested that priority areas, among them the fuel and energy complex, food and defense-industry conversion, science, and the social sphere, would be monitored and regulated. The rest must adapt to the laws of the market.[4]

Responding to the president's concern over the need to reorganize a number of enterprises via bankruptcy procedures for resolving the nonpayment issue, the prime minister charged Deputy Prime Minister Aleksandr Shokhin with implementing the president's instructions and the Ministry of Economics with coordinating the task. Three plans, which focused on devices to shore up government finances with a view to easing the the cash-flow problems in the budget sector, were floated in response.

The Ministry of Economics proposed settling the government's debts to supplier enterprises with funds borrowed from the central bank. The central bank in turn concentrated on the mounting tax payment arrears by enterprises that cut back budgetary cash for paying suppliers to government. It suggested a calendar-based debt settlement with enterprises by having the State Tax Service unlock enterprise deposits and foreign currency accounts with banks. Taking a cue from the president's decree of October 19, 1993, the finance ministry released interest-bearing notes for converting government debt.[5]

The multipronged approach, however, bypassed the issue of bankruptcy enforcement. Policymakers distinguished between state units and privatized enterprises and, of the former, between essential and nonessential providers, creating opportunities for exceptions to the application of bankruptcy rules by the relevant agencies.

## The State Sector, Presidential Decrees, and Government Resolutions

Since the Bankruptcy Law of 1993 provided for state assistance to state units in the priority sector, an interagency commission was set up to extend financial help to insolvent state enterprises (those with at least 25 percent state ownership) that were "key to the economy." Enterprises in basic, light, and food industries, sole producers of essential outputs, and infrastructure units strategic to a region fitted the bill.[6]

The presidential decree "On the Sale of State Debtor Enterprises" of June 3, 1994 sought to deal with nonpriority, insolvent units in the state sector that did not, in the view of the Federal Administration on Bankruptcy, qualify for financial assistance. The decree took a bold leap by providing for their sale (rather than self-liquidation through bankruptcy) in commercial competition to new owner-managers who would be required to settle the enterprise debts, undertake minimum investments, and rejuvenate the units.[7]

In this nonpriority category, 1,500 of 100,000 units, each with more than 1,000 employees and the state holding more than 25 percent authorized capital, were insolvent. Most were in the textile and machine-building industries and in transport. As of July 1, 1994, thirty enterprises (twenty in Moscow) were officially declared insolvent. Should they be reorganized or folded? A special commission would decide their fate after consulting with branch ministries and regional authorities and judging the "social realities" of enterprises that provided a critical share of a city's infrastructure.[8]

The failure to advance the sale of bankrupt state units to prospective buyers led to a government resolution of May 5, 1995 "On Additional Measures to Implement Russian Federation Legislation on the Bankruptcy of Enterprises and Organizations" which allowed subsidies from the federal budget to the insolvent units. Private capital preferred investing in high-yield state bonds rather than buying bankrupt companies.[9]

The process in the essential and nonessential state units thus went forward pell-mell: Some enterprises continued receiving state subsidies to finance their reorganization; a few were sold to the highest bidders. Elsewhere, the most unpromising sections were folded and the remaining recreated as new legal entities. In sum, the logic of the situation pointed to keeping to a minimum the number of units that would be pushed into court proceedings.

### Privatized Industry and Bankruptcy

As for privatized enterprises, arbitration courts had initiated proceedings in about fifty cases, with only ten of these subjected to bankruptcy declaration or initiation of receivership. Unfamiliar with court action, Russian managers reckoned that if their client factory was bolted up, nobody would buy their output. The preferred option was amicable settlement without court action. Ambiguous legislative provisions also played a role.

Sensing the need for a frontal assault on the lagging bankruptcies and advancing nonpayments by enterprises to the state budget and the workforce, the president issued another decree on February 15, 1996, allowing government agencies to confiscate property of companies that were in debt to the budget (except those that had bankruptcy cases under review in an arbitration court). According to the decree, items not directly involved in the production process were to be seized first, among them securities, cash, and hard currency in the debtors' accounts, autos, and office furnishings. finished products would be auctioned next, followed by real estate, material inventories, and production-related fixed equipment. The presidential decree was redundant, however, because tax authorities had the right to seize property as debt payment by defaulters. The decree demonstrated the desperation of the executive branch to solve the nonpayment problem.[10] The task of seizing an insolvent company's assets was occasionally risky: Arbitration court agents encountered a worker at the factory gate carrying an assault rifle.[11]

The 1993 bankruptcy law, presidential decrees, and government resolutions were constrained by a string of provisions and accompanied by a series of addenda, occasionally subject to discussion by the parliament. The procedures were equally cumbersome and time consuming: They vacillated between requiring the debtor to pay the creditor by selling enterprise assets and selling the entire debtor enterprise in a closed-bid auction to a new owner, who would pay the debt. Debts of a primary employer in a city were generally converted into future obligations. In practice, stalling was the name of the game.[12]

## The Record

Bankruptcies, based on the 1993 law, moved exceedingly slowly in privatized industry. Bankruptcy proceedings had increased from 9 in 1993 to 300 in 1994; 1,108 in 1995; 2,800 in 1996; and 3,700 in 1997. Of Russia's 2 million privatized enterprises, 800,000 were in dire straits.[13]

The performance in the state sector under the jurisdiction of the Bankruptcy Administration of the Russian Federation State Property

Commission (hereafter the bankruptcy administration) was no better. The agency, founded in 1993, supervised 38,500 enterprises, some fully state owned, others with state ownership of up to 25 percent.

Turning first to units with less than 25 percent state ownership: By mid-April 1996, the bankruptcy administration had investigated 15,000 units that were experiencing financial difficulties on the basis of information provided by Goskomstat (the state statistical agency). Of the 3,700 declared insolvent on the basis of the Property Commission's criteria, 265 became solvent under the commission's bankruptcy mandate, suggesting that even insolvent enterprises had potential for turning around if managers who were incompetent or dishonest (or both) were compelled to straighten out their operations under an effective threat of dissolution. Sixty enterprises had to be dissolved.[14]

Among those with federal ownership of more than 25 percent, more than 1,200 enterprises with a workforce of 1.8 million were declared insolvent by the bankruptcy administration in December 1994. In addition, more than 4,500 state enterprises on the verge of bankruptcy were located in the fuel and power, agro-industrial, defense, and extractive sectors. Of the 122 units put through bankruptcy procedures in 1994, arbitration courts heard 102 cases.[15]

Why was the process slow under the old bankruptcy law? To declare an enterprise bankrupt, the courts had to audit its balance sheet and calculate its ratio of assets to liabilities. Many enterprises that were nonviable in terms of their Soviet-era book values looked solid on paper when their assets were revalued at market prices. Moreover, many resourceful managers of moribund enterprises sold off valuable assets and disposed of the proceeds in the interval between the filing of a bankruptcy claim and the hearing of the case, leaving the creditors with no incentive to file bankruptcy proceedings. The creditors took recourse to other devices, including criminal acts.

**The Bankruptcy Law of 1998**

A new Law on Insolvency, which differed conceptually from its predecessor, became effective on March 1, 1998. More comprehensive in coverage, the new law included provisions on personal bankruptcy and the bankruptcies of individual entrepreneurs, private farms, and other units not covered by the earlier law. The provisions for personal bankruptcies were to become effective after amendments were made in the Civil Code.

Bankruptcies under the new law could be initiated against any enterprise that had defaulted on wage payment exceeding 500 times the minimum monthly wage for a period of more than three months, irrespective of debts owed to the potentially bankrupt enterprise itself. In other words, a supplier could not escape court proceedings as under the old law by arguing that his inability to pay was caused by a client who had not paid his bills. In principle, a citizen who had not received his wages could be evicted from his apartment for unpaid electricity bills.

Thus the new law improved on the earlier version that limited bankruptcy proceedings to businesses whose debts exceeded their total assets. Under the old definition, an enterprise could be solvent even though it withheld wages from workers or operated fitfully. By contrast, the new law introduced the principle of cash bankruptcy. Bankruptcy proceedings could be instituted in a court of arbitration against an enterprise that failed to pay its obligations to the budget at all levels, to off-budget funds, and to its employees or creditors for three months or more.

Again, the old law prescribed a moratorium of eighteen months on the debt of an enterprise under receivership. But the moratorium did not include fines and penalties that multiplied from claimants if the enterprise recovered during the period of receivership. The new version was accommodating to the debtor: Interest on the debt that was frozen was to be charged at the central bank discount rate, allowing the debtor to start without exaggerated claims by creditors.[16] Finally, the new law avoided lengthy proceedings by declaring a debtor bankrupt if he had failed to pay off a creditor for three months. A temporary manager would ensure that assets were kept intact while recommendations were worked up for the next steps.

Even with improved provisions, the law by itself could not handle complex decisions of enterprise liquidation or reorganization without the necessary infrastructure of bankruptcy referees and receivers, qualified judges, and independent auditors. Russia not only needed explicit and fair rules but also the mechanism for implementing them so that companies got the opportunity to start afresh after collapsing.

**Inadequate Infrastructure**

As a first step for effective enforcement of the laws, funds had to be found in the budget for supporting the reorganization of insolvent enterprises; and more personnel of arbitration courts and regional offices of the bankruptcy administration needed to be trained for implementing the law. Regional bankruptcy agencies operated in eighty-two regions of Russia, with more than 700 specialists checking company accounts and declaring 100 enterprises insolvent by early August 1994. The number of insolvent enterprises ranged from 40 to 70 percent of the total. In other words, half the Russian enterprises were potentially bankrupt.[17]

Supported by a firm legal basis and a network of regional agencies capable of enforcing the auditor's ruling, the bankruptcy administration expected to start the process in September, 1994. But bankruptcies did not appear rapidly. Creditors viewed defaulters as valued customers and irreplaceable partners in the production chain. Local arbitration courts lacked experience in issuing rulings on financial overhaul of insolvent companies. New entrepreneurs could not be found to replace old managers who had mismanaged company finances. The bankruptcy administration, in charge of deciding a debtor's solvency, could handle a limited number of cases. As a result, the agency, its regional branches, and creditors initiated only 400 insolvency cases in 1994.[18]

Haphazard bankruptcies also resulted from lack of strict auditing norms and weak enforcement of audits by the Certification and Licensing Commission. Russian companies and tax services operated according to Russian laws that did not require international auditing standards, although the six international auditing companies operating in Russia insisted on them. A company could borrow from a neighborhood bank and get its accounts audited by an unlicensed "Marya Petrovna" rather then spend $200,000 on a quality audit. In any case, a careful audit could be rejected by the Certification and Licensing Commission on appeal from the company director.[19]

The problems arising from lax auditing standards were compounded by the socialist leanings of bankruptcy court judges, who worried about the social consequences of bankruptcy enforcement and persuaded creditors to settle their disputes with debtors by soft-pedaling their demands. Creditors failed to take to court the majority of 1,500 enterprises declared bankrupt by the bankruptcy administration in February 1995. Bankruptcies could not make headway unless judges implemented bankruptcy procedures for reorganizing enterprises rather than for sorting out debt disputes.[20]

## Breakdown of Authority

The failure of the central authorities to prevent the provincial and local administrations from manipulating the bankruptcy laws to their advantage also hobbled progress on their implementation. Instances of such manipulation abounded. At ZIL, the Moscow Likhachov Automative Plant, annual truck production had slumped from 210,000 to 34,000 units, a daily loss of 2 billion rubles adding to its massive debt of 300 billion rubles. Instead of agreeing to lease their excess capacity and idle equipment to potential takers, ZIL managers survived under a rescue plan of mandatory purchases of ZIL vehicles by the defense and agriculture ministries and clients from the CIS states.

In 1994, the bankruptcy administration wanted to initiate bankruptcy proceedings against the company, but the attempt was countered by the president's staff and Moscow city administration, which protected the plant—a leading giant of socialist industry—from the trauma of a demonstration bankruptcy.[21]

When the bankruptcy administration filed a lawsuit in mid-November 1996 that declared the Moskvich automobile joint stock company bankrupt, the Moscow city government, ready to serve as the plant's trustee and restore its solvency within four months, intervened with a promise to begin paying its arrears to the budget in five months. The Moscow Court of Arbitration rejected the bankruptcy administration's lawsuit, arguing that the book value of Moskvich's assets, calculated according to Russian accounting procedures, exceeded its debts several times over.[22]

The government managed, however, to discipline two tax dodgers, the Gorky Automobile Plant (GAZ) and the Volga Automobile Plant (VAZ), by suspending the general director of the former and initiating bankruptcy procedures against the latter in the face of vehement opposition by both.

Agencies implementing bankruptcy laws normally rely on signals emerging from several market economy watchdogs for assessing business solvency. Commercial banks that lend to companies, shareholders who own them, and the stock market that tracks their economic health screen managerial decision making and its impact on company balance sheets. In Russia, however, banks, shareholders, and the stock market failed to fill the vacuum created by the elimination of administrative controls over enterprise management.

Enterprises had in fact founded several banks. The state and former state enterprises held about a 50 percent stake in the equity of the former Soviet-era specialized banks and 20 percent in the new commercial banks. Banks distributed credits from the budget to enterprises without monitoring their performance because the credits were guaranteed by the state. Many small and medium-sized banks had no resources for monitoring enterprise activities.

A significant fraction of enterprise stock was owned by labor collective insiders, giving management control over enterprise fortunes. (The stock market did not influence enterprise performance because few enterprises had their shares traded on the stock market.) Half the enterprises lacked outside shareholders and two-thirds were without outside shareholders on their boards of directors. Enterprise boards of directors had few outside members. Such representation of supplier or customer enterprises was 25 percent; of investment funds 9 percent; and of banks a miniscule 7 percent in enterprise boards.[23]

At the same time, while the state planners had withdrawn from their Soviet-era role of specifying output targets, undertaking investments, and setting prices, and the ministries had stepped back from automatically bailing out bankrupt units, a variety of credit instruments and surrogate money (noted in chapter 2) rescued enterprises from financial collapse.

### The Role of Surrogate Money

Surrogate money prevented bankruptcy enforcement. Treasury tax credit (TTC) instruments issued by the federal government starting in 1995 in payment to enterprises for state orders traveled briskly as means of payment in enterprises linked by production activity as means of payment, ultimately returning as sharply discounted paper to the treasury for redemption. Enterprises similarly used IOUs issued by regional administrations for settling accounts with them for paying bills among one another.

The issue of these credit instruments by the federal and regional governments effectively sabotaged financial discipline all around by deliberately promoting huge debt liabilities that could not be cleared on time. It not only weakened the enforcement of bankruptcy as a viable threat but excluded it as a feasible option. Most debtors, including central and regional governmental agencies, managed to survive without going into default. As a result, the payments crisis persisted and debts owed by governments to suppliers and by enterprises to banks, suppliers, and the workforce accumulated.

Although the cash-flow problems in the government sector and in privatized enterprises were merely postponed by widespread recourse to surrogate money, they arose and persisted from the unwillingness of both groups to streamline their activities and cut back their workforce. The relative price shifts following price liberalization in early 1992, however, had varying impact on the financial viability of different industries and sectors and of the government. At the same time, exchange rate–based inflation control required prolonged real appreciation of the ruble, damaging the competitiveness of Russian industries, among them the consumer goods sector. How could workable bankruptcy criteria involving enterprise solvency be devised if correct relative prices fail to provide equilibrating signals as in a functioning market economy?

### Bankruptcies and Unstable Relative Prices

Several factors contributed to relative prices imbalance. First, the price structure was out of balance because prices of monopoly items were to be gradually raised to world levels—unlike those of consumer goods, which were freed more readily in 1992, enabling them to settle close to world prices (translated into rubles plus import duties). By 1995, all prices were freed except those for natural gas and petroleum products, electric power, pipeline use, freight and passenger charges, plane fares and postal services, defense items, precious metals, and gems.

Second, households were heavily subsidized via ridiculously low utility and passenger charges, and industrial users were penalized. In August 1993, Russian households paid 1 percent of the world price for electricity and 10 percent for gasoline.[24] The average charge for a kilowatt-hour of electric power was 220 rubles in April 1997, but households paid 89 rubles.[25] In August 1995, households paid token prices for natural gas of about $1.50 for 1,000 cubic meters, compared to $51 for industrial users.[26]

Third, the monopoly suppliers of natural gas, electric power, and railways bailed out the subsidized sectors by overcharging targeted sectors for their items. Gazprom more than made up for the low rates in the domestic market from phenomenal revenues earned from exports. The company intended paying 7 trillion rubles to the federal budget by June 1, 1997 to partially clear its outstanding debt of

15 trillion rubles, although it failed to receive payment for 55 percent of natural gas shipments to customers, its cash receipts amounting to only 5 percent of actual receipts.[27] The railroads overpriced freight traffic for industrial users in order to cover losses from underpriced passenger traffic on long-distance and suburban routes. Higher rates for electric power to industrial users subsidized low household rates.

Fourth, the price structure could not be rationalized without prying open the cost components of prices charged by the monopolists. The cost breakdown on a unit of natural gas between production and transportation were tightly concealed in Gazprom's integrated balance sheet. Again the hidden relative costs reflected production and distribution structures that were not only integrated but unbalanced. A handful of nineteen regional railroads carried more than 70 percent of Russia's freight traffic. The Unified Power System originally had a grid that covered the entire country, except the Far East and parts of Siberia that were separated from the structure after the dissolution of the Soviet Union. In 1992, energy users were effectively tied to local monopoly power companies when Russia's electric power industry got a feudal imprimatur: High-voltage grids and major power plants remained properties of the Unified Power System, whereas low-voltage grids and local power plants, converted into joint stock companies, became local energy barons by effectively tying local customers to their domain.[28]

The physical breakup of the natural gas, power, and railroad monopolies raised an array of problems. The enormous resources of each gave them exceptional lobbying clout. When regulators in the federal commission sought balance sheet details of the power and gas industries, the commission was converted into an autonomous agency with a dummy chairman who was a protégé of the Ministry of Fuel and Power. The operation of a federal wholesale electricity market that could bring down electricity rates by generating competitive pressures was opposed by governors who feared that solvent energy producers in their regions would hook up with the wholesale outlet, cutting back supplies for local needs of households and enterprises.

Occasionally arguments against restructuring the monopolies took nationalist and xenophobic overtones. Anatoly Dyakov, former chairman of Unified Power System, characterized the demands of the "home-grown hotheads" to dismember the company as emanating from IMF pressure.[29] Rem Vyakhirev, chairman of Gazprom, drew loud applause from members of the Duma when he suggested that the initiative to break up Gazprom originated from U.S. oil and gas companies supported by the IMF.[30]

Ultimately, the reformers in the government settled for extracting taxes from the monopolies rather than insisting on their cost-price transparency and demanding their physical restructuring. Gazprom, the Unified Power System, and the railways had abundant cash and the government needed it to clear wage arrears.[31] Monopoly pricing continued, contributing to a lopsided price structure.

Finally, the appreciating real exchange rate undermined the profitability of exports and import substitutes. Some exporters were not only hit by the overvalued exchange rate but also by the high prices of raw materials and monopoly charges for fuel, energy, and power that outstripped the inflation rate in 1995, slashing their profit margin. Thus, in the small town of Solikamsk in the Urals, managers of three plants that exported most of their magnesium, paper, and pulp products complained of 1995 price rises of 200 percent for raw materials, 50 percent for electricity, 30 percent for freight, and 180 percent for leasing a railroad car.[32]

The unbalanced price structure shifted radically when the ruble slumped from 6 rubles to a dollar to 26–30 rubles beginning in mid-August 1998. In figure 3.1, the ranking of producer price indexes in eleven sectors of Russian industry (with January 1995 = 100) had switched dramatically in the postdevaluation phase of September 1998 to March 1999, compared to the earlier phase of January 1995 to August 1998. Thus the price indexes of electrical power, construction materials, and fuel industries—ranking in that order from highest to lowest at the top of all indexes—in the first phase had moved in the middle, with the fuel price index close to the bottom of the entire set in the second phase. By contrast, the non-ferrous metallurgy index, at the bottom from January 1995 to August 1998, was at the top from September 1998 to March 1999. Food and light industry indexes of concern to consumers had moved up to the second- and third-highest positions in the second period from their close-to-bottom rankings in the first phase. Domestic prices of these items matched the higher prices of imported goods in the postdevaluation phase. The ferrous metallurgy index, in the middle from January 1995 to August 1998, had slumped to the bottom from September 1998 to March 1999. Machinery and equipment, chemical and petrochemical industries, logging and woodworking, and pulp and paper industries had remained in the middle.

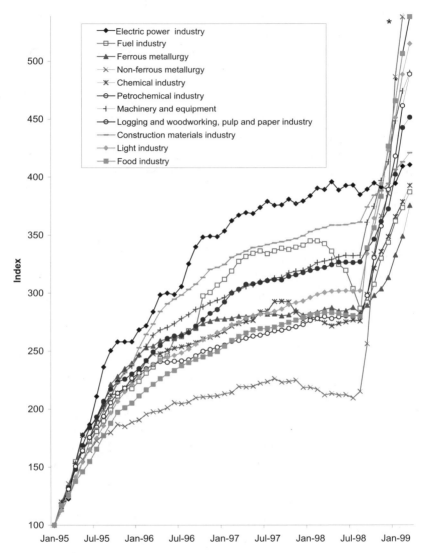

**Figure 3.1**
Producer price indexes by industry
January 1995 = 100.
*Source*: Goskomstat.
* Value for nonferrous metallurgy for March 1999 is 566.

The across-the-board relative price shifts revived several domestic industries. The competitive advantage to domestic producers depended on a variety of factors, among them the extent of excess capacity, the domestic sourcing of inputs, product quality, and management innovativeness. The conversion of the faint pulse of recovery into full-blown growth relied on successful inflation control and new investment-based restructuring of production capacities in response to demand.

In any case, the widely divergent relative price structures in the pre– and post–ruble meltdown phases illustrate the difficulties of identifying bankrupt units in the two situations. An insolvent cigarette manufacturer of 1998, for example, escaped being classified as bankrupt in 1999.

Russia's bankruptcy administrators were perhaps influenced in their decision making (or the lack of it) by factors other than relative prices. But a near-stable relative price structure is generally essential for assessing business profitability and solvency and identifying bankrupt units. The incomplete price decontrol combined with the overvalued exchange rate contributed to relative price outcomes that penalized some industries and enterprises and favored others, complicating bankruptcy decisions.

### Banking Sector Reorganization

The August ruble meltdown shifted relative prices in favor of Russia's consumer goods industries. It also led to the adoption by the duma, in June 1999, of the law "On Restructuring of Credit Organizations," resulting in the creation of the Agency for Restructuring Credit Organizations (ARCO), which was entrusted with the task of restructuring the large Moscow banks and spreading banking facilities in the regions. Banking sector supervisory and monitoring functions, formerly exercised by the Central Bank of Russia, were assigned to ARCO.

Not surprisingly, the process of bank cleanup has been slow. the number of banks fell from nearly 2,100 in early 1996 to around 1,400 at the start of 2000, marking a consolidation of banks: The share of banks with capital in excess of 30 million (new) rubles rose from 11 percent in January 1998 to 25 percent. ARCO, endowed with 10 billion (new) rubles, required five times as much funding for extensive banking sector overhaul, stretching beyond a spotty recapitalization of troubled banks. Despite limited resources, it had launched eight new banks in the regions. It is not clear if the choice was driven by transparent, efficient criteria.

**Conclusions**

The next-to-nothing record of bankruptcies in Russia involving effective closure or efficient revival of insolvent enterprises reflected a variety of factors, including an inflexible industrial structure dominated by the defense sector (discussed in the appendix), changing bankruptcy laws, inadequate infrastructure, the go-slow approach of enforcers, and meddlesome practices of state operatives who sabotaged the bankruptcy administration's procedures. Enterprise balance sheets, profitability calculations, and insolvency ratings were also distorted by unstable relative prices. The relative price structure, dominated by monopoly enterprises in the energy sector and the railroads and affected by an overvalued exchange rate in the pre-August 1998 period, differed radically from the post–ruble meltdown phase.

Enterprise managers adopted survival strategies of nonpayment to the budget and to workers combined with barter transactions instead of bankruptcy procedures involving plant closures and worker layoffs. The escalating wage arrears resulting from these strategies, and our methods of estimating them across demographic groups, regions, occupations, and industries, are presented in the next chapter.

**Appendix: Restructuring Dilemmas**

Specific features of inherited structures interacting with the policy decisions that were made from early 1992 complicated the restructuring of Soviet-era industry and the defense sector. For one thing, Russian industry was highly monopolistic from the start. Emerging imbalances in the fuel and energy branch that fed industrial and defense complexes aggravated the restructuring challenge.

*Industrial Monopolies*

Among the many indicators of monopoly prevalence in Peck and richardson (1991, pp. 63–67), we cite the following: In several product groups, a single manufacturer accounted for more than half the market share in the Soviet Union in 1988. Thus, in the electric power machinery group, such domination in the market prevailed in 90 percent of product groups (out of a total of 34); in railroad machinery, 69 percent (out of 13); in construction and road machinery, 75 percent (out of 12); in ferrous metallurgy, 82 percent (out of 33 product categories). A single Soviet-era manufacturer controlled more than half the market share in almost 66 percent of product groups (out of a total of 344); by contrast, in the United States, "in less than one-third of the U.S. 4-digit industries do the *top four* companies account for a comparable percentage of output [in 1982]."[33]

According to the *Shatalin Report*, "96 percent of all diesel locomotives, 100 percent of all air conditioners, 100 percent of all deep water pumps, and 66 percent of all batteries are supplied by a single enterprise clearly suggest[ing] genuine monopoly.[34]

In manufacturing activity, however, comparison with the United States is misleading. Given their tendency toward gigantomania, Stalin's planners created artificial monopolies, even setting up a single plant in Lithuania that supplied ice cream cones over vast areas. Again, machine building in the capitalist West is scattered: Manufacturers undertake subcontracting and buy rolled steel from outside. by contrast, russia's Soviet-era enterprises have not only been major and occasionally single suppliers of products but also highly integrated, especially in machine building and raw-material processing. Again, located in company towns, these were miniature welfare states that provided housing and other entitlements to workers, restricting free labor mobility. Such features are alien to corporate businesses in market economies.

### Absence of a Labor Market

In Soviet times, workers moved across different sections of the enterprise in search of better jobs without terminating their contract with management, but labor movement beyond current job location was slow. Moscow and St. Petersburg still require worker registration, limiting entry of new job seekers. Rapid restructuring via bankruptcy enforcement in the absence of a labor market—which can emerge only as a result of freely available affordable housing—is therefore impractical.

Managers of these lumbering units, used to fulfilling planners' output quotas without concern for labor and material saving, were not geared for the decision making necessary to combat the price liberalization that began in early 1992. first, the manufacturing sector as a whole faced unfavorable prices from the suppliers of fuel, energy, and railway freight. Next, the swift opening of the economy in 1992, accompanied by an appreciating real ruble in the interest of rapid-fire, unsustainable inflation control, brought in consumer goods' imports that by 1995 met 60 percent of domestic consumption. The faint pulse of recovery in the consumer goods and processed food sectors following the sharp decline of the ruble and the favorable relative price shifts (demonstrated in figure 3.1) can turn into sustained growth if, as demand picks up, current capacities are refurbished and extended with new investment.

### The Defense Sector

The Russian military-industrial sector, which belonged in large measure to the machine building and metal working (MBMW) branch, was massive.

The number of industrial enterprises belonging to russia's defense sector "ranged from 731 to 4,000 for industrial enterprises and 714 to more than 1,125 for research and development and design facilities." (Noren 1994, p. 498). There were, however, no doubts about the heavy concentration of defense manufacturing in a few enterprises in the MBMW branch and their location in select cities. Thus 317 MBMW enterprises, representing only 7 percent of the total in MBMW, turned out 34 percent of the branch production. Most of them were located in Moscow, St. Petersburg, and the closed cities of Arzamaz-16, Chelyabinsk-45, and Krasnoyarsk-70 in Siberia. It would be cost effective to demolish these plants rather than convert them to making civilian items, which could be made with less cost in new factories. However, this would imply abandoning a few townships in Siberia. Skilled engineers and technicians in the military plants, which serviced nuclear warheads and made rockets, missiles, cannons, tanks, and ships in these company towns, had nowhere to go if they were laid off.

The rapid fire decision to cut back government procurement of armaments by 67–68 percent in early 1992 was imposed without an orderly long-term procurement schedule and contributed to a sharp output decline. The production of military goods was reported to have slumped as a result by 38 to 50 percent in 1992 alone (Noren 994, p. 407). The much slower cutback in the workforce resulted in wage nonpayment and accumulated arrears.

Some conversion did take place, albeit in a haphazard fashion. Occasionally factories received state orders (plus budgetary support) in preference to a potential foreign supplier for manufacturing items that could be turned out with the technology in place. Thus, Sevmashpredpriyatie, which manufactured multipurpose nuclear-powered submarines in the northern city of Severodvinsk, was assigned the state order for offshore gas- and oil-drilling platforms for Rosshelf, which planned to drill for gas on the Barents Sea shelf.[35] Before this order actually materialized, however, the factory started making barges and hulls for tugboats so that its workforce could remain employed. The submarine factory in Nizhny Novgorod produced irons, kettles, and home-heating systems for the domestic market. Defense industry managers explored export outlets to stem the decline in military exports from $10 billion in 1990 to $2.15 billion in 1993 (Noren 1994, pp. 513 and 514). Recently, purchases by Russia's traditional defense hardware clients, among them India and China, have revived substantially.

Beyond the restructuring burdens imposed by industrial monopolies and the defense sector, the Russian economy faces long-run adjustment problems arising from the impending depletion of oil and gas production in current locations, the unbalanced production capacities of the coal sector, and the uneven distribution of power from existing thermal plants to industry.

## The Long-Term Restructuring of the Fuel and Energy Sectors

Enormous fuel-guzzling industrial complexes, created near energy sources, face increasing shortages of these raw materials, requiring massive investments in new technologies that would not only boost current outputs of oil and gas but also cut back energy use by industrial consumers. The environmental degradation resulting from excessive use of thermal power generated with low-grade coal deposits also calls for a switch to alternative fuel use and cleaner technologies. These problems, accumulating during the Soviet days, have become worse for lack of new investment and infusion of modern technologies in the recent period.

For example, the fuel resources of the Urals[36] feed the region's ferrous and nonferrous metallurgy, chemical, and petrochemical industries. Steady decline in natural gas production, however, has transformed the region from a natural gas exporter into an importer from Tyumen' oblast in Western Siberia. However, gas production in Tyumen' oblast is threatened with a decline from its current levels because of lack of new investment and modern technologies.

Again, crude oil production in Tyumen' oblast, which feeds the chemical and petrochemical industries of the Urals, peaked in 1988 and has been declining as a result of the depletion of traditional richer fields, the increasing costs of development of smaller fields and poor access to new reserves. Oil flow from Western Siberia (where Tyumen' oblast is located) to European Russia witnessed a decline of 23 percent as early as 1992 compared to 1990.

The situation is no less demanding in the Western Siberian industrial complex, which is partly fed by thermal power. The huge complexes of coal engineering, ferrous metallurgy (at the giant Kuznetsk and West-Siberian combinates), aluminum (at the Novokuznetsk aluminum plant), and the Belovsk lead and zinc plants face a power shortage because coal production in the Kuznetsk coal basin, a major coal producer and supplier of thermal power to the complexes, has declined to 35 percent of total Russian output in 1993, from 52 percent in 1988. The emerging power shortage in the region requires new investments and technologies that use environmentally safe coal-burning methods.

The situation in Eastern Siberia and Far Eastern region requires a major shift away from decades of reliance on thermal power to hydraulic and nuclear power plants in energy-deficit areas to prevent further pollution. The Northern and North-Western region in the extreme north, the Central and Central Black-Earth, Volga-Vyatski, and Volga Basin regions in European Russia, and North Caucasus in the south have equally daunting problems. The Timan-Pechora fuel and energy complex in the Republic of Komi and Nenets autonomous okrug (AO) in the Northern region was developed on the basis of the oil, gas, and coal resources of the area. Its technology, outdated by international standards, requires massive financial commitments for its updating.

The electric power, machinery, chemical, and processed food industries in European Russia, fed by the oil and gas reserves of the Volga Basin region, face a similar depletion of gas reserves in the basin (except in Astrakhan' Province).

North Caucasus is a mixed agrarian-industrial economy with a concentration of coal, oil, and natural gas. According to the Petroleum Economist's assessment, however, the gas and oil reserves in the region are getting depleted and the coal sector, feeding the region's thermal power plants, is hobbled by outdated technology.

How do we rate the prospects of Russia's industrial restructuring based on these emerging economywide imbalances? Although a proper bankruptcy law is necessary, its effective application, depending as it does on the growth of new manufacturing and service activity away from the defense sector and traditional natural resouce–based industries, will necessarily be slow. The flow of new technologies financed by foreign investments in the oil, gas, and energy sector, the growth of small and medium-sized cost-efficient businesses in manufacturing, and labor mobility encouraged by housing availability are necessary ingredients in the process that will stretch over several years.

# 4   Patterns of Wage Nonpayment

Russian governments, federal and regional, and enterprises repeatedly failed to pay wages in full to large groups of their employees in the course of the economy's transition to a market system. The wage non-payment problem worsened over time, leading to public outcry, orga-nized demonstrations, and trade union militancy, which posed serious problems for Russia's market economy reforms. According to official estimates, outstanding wage arrears increased substantially through-out 1996, rising from 22,114 billion rubles at the end of the first quarter (constituting 71 percent of the monthly wage bill) to 38,712 billion rubles at the end of the fourth quarter (at 114 percent of the monthly wage bill).[1] Averaged over employees who were actually owed wages, outstanding unpaid wages amounted to approximately 275 percent of monthly wages (*Russian Economic Trends*, 1997.1).[2]

The rising trend in these arrears from 1992 to 1997 is seen in table 4.1, which focuses on three sectors of the economy for which Goskomstat has been releasing information since 1992. Comparison of total wage arrears in 1997 to earlier years is problematic because sectors for which wage arrears were reported were not comparable: Only medium-sized and large enterprises in industry, construction, and agriculture re-ported data on wage arrears from 1992 to 1994; the transportation sec-tor was added in 1995; in 1996, four noncommercial sectors were added (health care, education, culture, and science). That coverage continued into 1997.

The constant dollar value of outstanding wage arrears steadily in-creased between 1992 and 1997, by approximately twenty-six-fold in industry, fourteen-fold in construction, and twenty-fold in agriculture. As a fraction of the sector's monthly wage bill, the rise was nearly twenty-nine-fold in industry, fourteen-fold in construction, and thirty-six-fold in agriculture.

**Table 4.1**
Trends in sectoral wages arrears

(1) Outstanding wage arrears (billions of December 1995 rubles)

|      | Industry | Construction | Agriculture |
|------|----------|--------------|-------------|
| 1992 | 1,034    | 541          | 397         |
| 1993 | 2,653    | 840          | 2,092       |
| 1994 | 5,019    | 1,686        | 3,009       |
| 1995 | 7,734    | 1,941        | 2,571       |
| 1996 | 18,185   | 5,310        | 4,855       |
| 1997 | 27,565   | 7,441        | 7,742       |

(2) Ratio of outstanding wage arrears to the monthly wage bill (percent)

|      |     |     |     |
|------|-----|-----|-----|
| 1992 | 5   | 6   | 6   |
| 1993 | 13  | 10  | 36  |
| 1994 | 31  | 23  | 68  |
| 1995 | 61  | 40  | 102 |
| 1996 | 111 | 74  | 158 |
| 1997 | 145 | 83  | 213 |

*Source: Russian Economic Trends,* 1997.1 and 1997.3.
*Note:* 1997 data are cumulated for three quarters of the year. Comparable data for 1998 are not available.

While Goskomstat's aggregate numbers provide a graphic portrayal of the trend in arrears over the period, they tell us little about the distribution of wage arrears across the population. Among the questions that arise are: Which workers were most likely to face wage withholding? How did the amounts withheld vary across people with different attributes and different employment settings? In this chapter, we analyze patterns in wage arrears across demographic groups defined by gender, age, and education, and in various occupations, industries, and regions of Russia.

## The Russian Longitudinal Monitoring Survey

Our empirical analysis employs the Russian Longitudinal Monitoring Survey (hereafter RLMS), a nationally representative longitudinal survey of Russian households.[3] The RLMS has gone through two phases, each consisting of a different sample of households whose members were interviewed. Phase I had four rounds of interviews conducted during 1992 and 1993; Phase II involved four rounds, Rounds V–VIII, fielded in the fall of 1994, 1995, 1996, and 1998 respectively.

The survey contains detailed information on demographic and employment characteristics by occupation and job location of working men and women, which helps us analyze their labor-market experiences. Although the RLMS began in 1992, our analysis is restricted to the 1994–98 period because information on unpaid wages became available only in Phase II of the survey, during which respondents were asked a series of questions on wage nonpayment. The RLMS sample is based on dwelling units and does not attempt to follow individuals who have moved away. Attempts to estimate the possible attrition bias in the RLMS indicate relatively little attrition, most likely a result of the relative lack of population mobility across regions and housing units; as expected, the greatest attrition occured in the urban centers of Moscow and St. Petersburg.[4]

### Incidence, Cumulated Amount, and Relative Amount in Months of Wage Nonpayment

We adopt three measures of wage arrears in this book: the percentage of respondents who were denied wages (hereafter the *incidence* of nonpayment), the average cumulated ruble value of wages withheld at the time of interview (hereafter the *amount* of nonpayment), and finally, the cumulated value divided by average monthly wage (hereafter the *relative amount*).

We derive these measures from household member responses to a series of survey questions posed to all respondents irrespective of their employment status. We measure the *incidence of nonpayment* as an affirmative response to the question:

At the present time, does your place of work owe you any money, which for various reasons was not paid on time?

Household members who said that they were currently owed unpaid wages were then asked:

How much money in all have they not paid you?

We calculate the *amount of nonpayment* based on the responses to this question and convert it into constant December 1995 rubles. To calculate the *relative amount of nonpayment in months*, we estimate contracted monthly wages from responses to the question:

How much money in the last thirty days did you receive from your primary workplace after taxes?

**Table 4.2**
Trends in wage arrears

|  | 1994 | 1995 | 1996 | 1998 |
|---|---|---|---|---|
| Percentage of people owed wages |  |  |  |  |
| All | 41.23 | 42.75** | 60.43* | 63.61* |
|  | (4,329) | (4,005) | (3,791) | (3,589) |
| Currently employed | 30.30 | 29.58 | 44.86* | 54.29* |
|  | (3,261) | (2,826) | (2,307) | (2,378) |
| Amount of wage arrears |  |  |  |  |
| All | 940,073 | 853,063* | 1,377,519* | 1,238,550* |
|  | (1,517) | (1,398) | (1,882) | (1,978) |
| Currently employed | 933,694 | 783,028* | 1,299,172* | 1,141,795* |
|  | (846) | (719) | (904) | (1,158) |
| Months of outstanding wages (currently employed) | 1.083 | .969* | 1.600* | 3.667* |

*Source:* RLMS.
*Note:* All tables include women ranging in years of age from 18 to 55 and men from 18 to 60. The last three rows report averages (in December 1995 rubles) for people who were owed wages. Sample sizes are listed in parentheses. The last row is calculated as the amount of outstanding wage arrears divided by the monthly contracted wage. Sample sizes here are the same as those in the row directly above.
* Denotes a significant difference at 5 percent between adjacent columns denoting years.
** Denotes a significant difference at 10 percent.

Clearly the answers will understate contracted wages by the wage arrears incurred during the past thirty days. We therefore estimate contracted wages as actual wages paid plus estimates of the monthly outstanding wage obligations by the employers, the latter calculated as the cumulated nonpayments divided by the number of months for which these wages were owed.[5]

## Patterns of Wage Nonpayment

The estimates reported in table 4.2 indicate a deteriorating pattern of wage nonpayment in terms of our three measures. Rounding out the numbers, we notice that the fraction of people who were owed wages increased in row (1) from 41 percent in 1994 to 64 percent in 1998 for the entire sample, and from 30 percent to 54 percent in row (2) among household members who were employed at the time of the interviews. Not surprisingly, wage nonpayment, representing lack of earnings, was higher among people who were no longer employed, suggesting that nonpayment either led to unemployment or labor force withdrawal, issues we address more fully in later chapters.

Average (per person) outstanding enterprise debt to all workers (calculated for workers who were owed wages) similarly increased in row (3), in constant December 1995 rubles, from 940,073 rubles in 1994 to 1,238,550 rubles in 1998. Similar increases, and lower outstanding accumulated wage debt, are seen in row (4) among the currently employed.

How many months worth of wages were withheld by employers? Calculated as ratios of average contracted (real) monthly wages, outstanding enterprise obligations to their employees increased in row (5) from approximately one month's wages in 1994 to over three and one-half months of wages in 1998. Except for the incidence of wage withholding for those who were either unemployed or who withdrew from the labor force, our estimates in row (1) dip in 1995 in all categories. The interviews conducted in the late fall of 1995 reflected the partial clearance of arrears as the December 1995 Duma elections approached.

## Relative Severity of Wage Nonpayment

How might one expect wage nonpayment to vary by the demographic features of gender, age, and education, and by occupation and job location? Are there distinct patterns in the incidence and magnitude of wage arrears across different sectors of the economy and across individuals with different attributes? We expect the relative severity of wage nonpayment resulting from the impact of market forces to be nonrandom with distinct patterns.

The choices facing state-sector employers and enterprise managers were to retain a worker with full wage and benefits, remove him from the job, or deny him payment for some time while keeping him on the job. Given the cash-flow problems discussed in chapter 2, it was difficult for an employer to keep a worker on the job at the old wage. At the same time, managerial predisposition toward keeping workers on the job, workers' readiness to accept temporary wage loss in return for the entitlements of being officially on the payroll, and government hesitation to implement bankruptcy laws slowed the pace of involuntary job loss. The feasible option was to slow employee layoffs and enforce a flexible wage by withholding payments.

State-sector decision makers and enterprise managers were therefore likely to devise strategies of wage nonpayment that best helped them lower wage outlays and maintain or increase sales revenues. The managers of financially stressed companies, unlike those in charge of a few viable units, would focus on the short-term problem of juggling their finances rather than on the long-term goal of trimming the workforce with a view to promoting enterprise productivity and profitability.

Given the high labor turnover in Russian factories, employees with marketable skills could be expected to move to a better job in the enterprise or leave it altogether.[6] Holding back wages of the better-paid workers in the interest of containing the wage bill could therefore backfire: These workers, evidently the more productive, might actually be producing more per ruble than their lower-paid, less productive cohorts. Denying them wages might cut into the revenue flow more if they moved away than would be gained from retaining less productive workers. Of course, some better-paid workers might simply be reaping rents from higher seniority and networking abilities. The patterns of wage withholding would reflect managerial attempts to retain desirable employees in the face of growing market-oriented demand for their skills.

We begin with the differential impact of employer decision making on nonpayment to women.

## Gender and Wage Nonpayment

Russian women combined household chores with job responsibilities and failed to upgrade their skills through training. For lack of time and motivation, they also missed improving their clout through factory networking. Arguably treated as supplementary household wage earners by managers, they dominated in low-skill jobs with relatively weak market prospects. Women were unlikely to be concentrated in occupations and industrial sectors and in white-collar and service jobs that fared relatively better as the transition progressed. (These themes are developed from a historical perspective with supporting evidence in chapter 10.) We expect women workers to be subjected to more frequent and higher wage nonpayment than men.

In table 4.3, the (the statistically significant) estimates of nonpayment incidence in column (1) suggest similar frequencies for men and women in 1998, at 54 percent. The higher average amount withheld from men in 1994 and 1998 in column (2) resulted from higher average male wages. The amount withheld relative to average monthly wages

**Table 4.3**
Differences in wage arrears by gender, currently employed (1994–1998)

| Gender | Percentage | Amount | Months of wages |
|---|---|---|---|
| Males (1,533) | 30.46 | 864,562 | 1.057 |
| | 54.19[b] | 1,260,052[b] | 2.909[b] |
| Females (1,670) | 28.38 | 508,976[a] | 0.947 |
| | 53.85[b] | 776,067[a,b] | 2.513[b] |

*Source:* RLMS.
*Note:* For each gender, the first row is the 1994 value, the second row is the 1998 value. The 1994 sample sizes for each gender are listed in parentheses.
a. Denotes a significant difference at 5 percent between men and women.
b. Denotes a significant difference between 1994 and 1998.

in column (3), similar for both sexes at about one month of contracted wages in 1994, rose to about two and one-half to three months of wages in 1998. Finally, wage nonpayment increased in terms of all three measures for men and women between 1994 and 1998.

### Age and Wage Nonpayment

The youngest workers, eighteen to twenty-four years old, were new entrants in the workforce with less skill and shorter work experience. On the other hand, they had more recent education and were potentially more mobile than older workers. By contrast, older, more tenured workers possessed more experience and perhaps better skills acquired on the job, but were less mobile. They presented less threat of losses to the firm from quitting as a result of wage withholding. Again, seniority-based wage profiles, coupled with relatively lower levels of on-the-job training, generally provided higher rents to older than younger workers, giving them an incentive to remain in old jobs. Managers could withhold their wages and capture some of their rents without fear of net losses resulting from their quits.

Were older, more settled employees subjected to higher incidence and larger wage withholdings than younger workers? Focusing on 1998 estimates that are statistically significant in table 4.4, we notice that the incidence of withholding in column (1) exhibits a weak relationship to age. The amounts withheld, absolute and relative in months, in columns (2) and (3), tell a different story. As the nonpayment crisis deepened in 1998, managers increasingly shifted a higher burden to older workers, perhaps for retaining a portion of rents that

**Table 4.4**
Differences in wage arrears by age, currently employed (1994–1998)

| Age groups | Percentage | Amount | Months of wages |
|---|---|---|---|
| 18–24 years (363) | 22.59 | 486,637 | 0.924 |
| | 50.34[b] | 721,876[b] | 2.068[b] |
| 25–34 years (902) | 30.27[a] | 707,000[a] | 1.025 |
| | 54.26[b] | 892,468[a,b] | 2.608[b] |
| 35–44 years (1,059) | 32.96[a] | 693,041[a] | 1.003 |
| | 55.27[b] | 1,026,455[a,b] | 2.810[a,b] |
| 45–60 years (879) | 26.96 | 683,783[a] | 0.989 |
| | 53.83[b] | 1,160,732[a,b] | 2.874[a,b] |

*Source:* RLMS.
*Note:* For each gender, the first row is the 1994 value, the second row is the 1998 value.
The 1994 sample sizes for each gender are listed in parentheses.
a. Denotes a significant difference at 5 percent between men and women.
b. Denotes a significant difference between 1994 and 1998.

would have otherwise been received by older workers, and perhaps for holding on to younger workers with more current skills and training as market pressures intensified. While the burden of wage arrears seems to have shifted over time to older workers, we notice that the incidence as well as absolute and relative amounts of nonpayment increased between 1994 and 1998 for all age groups.

## Education and Wage Nonpayment

What might one expect of the connection between education and wage nonpayment? Skills and marketability improve with higher education. Therefore the more educated should experience a lower incidence and amount of wage withholding than the less educated. Within the skill spectrum, the acquisition of vocational and professional skills tends to increase the worker's marketability.

In 1998, with the exception of holders of general secondary school education,[7] who recorded wage nonpayment incidence of 66 percent in column (1) of table 4.5, workers with specific market-oriented skills such as vocational and professional courses and university training experienced lower wage nonpayment, at 50 to 56 percent. The amounts withheld, absolute and relative in months, in columns (2) and (3) suggest minor differences by education level in 1998. All groups, with the exception of the resident graduates (at one and one-half months)

**Table 4.5**
Differences in wage arrears by education, currently employed (1994–1998)

| Education | Percentage | Amount | Months of wages |
|---|---|---|---|
| General  secondary (439) | 30.98 | 579,003 | 0.893 |
|  | 65.63[b] | 757,892[b] | 2.701[b] |
| Professional courses (856) | 33.64 | 749,630[a] | 1.044 |
|  | 50.10[a,b] | 1,190,540[a,b] | 2.647[b] |
| Ordinary vocational (310) | 35.16 | 757,950[a] | 0.945 |
|  | 55.81[a,b] | 1,065,481[a,b] | 2.553[b] |
| Secondary vocational (570) | 27.54 | 697,427 | 1.135[a] |
|  | 51.39[a,b] | 986,644[a,b] | 2.427[b] |
| Specialized secondary (967) | 28.96 | 632,663 | 0.942 |
|  | 54.83[a,b] | 1,014,871[a,b] | 2.873[b] |
| University (776) | 27.06 | 696,271[a] | 0.928 |
|  | 51.41[a,b] | 1,132,636[a,b] | 2.527[b] |
| Graduate, residency (44) | 9.09[a] | 625,930 | 0.484 |
|  | 55.56[b] | 1,032,914 | 1.471[a,b] |

*Source:* RLMS.
*Note:* See the notes to tables 4.3 and 4.4. The "general secondary" education category is used as the base group for comparisons.

experienced between two and one-half to three months of wage nonpayment.

The absence of a clear educational pattern in the incidence and amounts of nonpayment suggests that the practice of wage withholding prevailed among all educational classes, in industries and occupations employing workers with different levels of education, and across regions characterized by more and less developed educational systems. Formal educational attainment per se was not associated with the market power of workers and their corresponding ability to extract payments from their employers.

In assessing managerial decisions on wage nonpayment allocation decisions across workers with different attributes, we need information on wage withholding and worker characteristics *within* establishments. For example, we would like to know if managers in a given firm were more likely to withhold wages from their less-educated, less-skilled employees. The RLMS data for household rather than firm respondents do not allow us to empirically assess firm-level nonpayment patterns that would enable us to uncover wage withholding features across demographic groups within enterprises.

**Table 4.6**
Differences in wage arrears by regions, currently employed (1994–1998)

| Regions | Percentage | Amount | Months of wages |
|---|---|---|---|
| Moscow and St. Petersburg (409) | 21.27 | 1,081,327 | 1.044 |
|  | 24.40 | 860,927 | 1.074 |
| Northern and North Western (228) | 37.28[a] | 1,413,795[a] | 1.144 |
|  | 70.35[a,b] | 1,820,821[a] | 3.680[a,b] |
| Central and Central Black-Earth (604) | 26.32[a] | 769,859 | 1.092 |
|  | 47.62[a,b] | 814,474 | 3.004[a,b] |
| Volga-Vyatski and Volga Basin (550) | 30.91[a] | 526,160[a] | 1.050 |
|  | 63.13[a,b] | 846,245[b] | 3.069[a,b] |
| North Caucasus (359) | 25.91[a] | 492,651[a] | 0.959 |
|  | 49.33[a,b] | 767,667[b] | 2.204[a,b] |
| Urals (518) | 33.78[a] | 776,973 | 0.984 |
|  | 59.38[a,b] | 1,081,649[b] | 2.912[a,b] |
| Western Siberia (301) | 30.23[a] | 1,402,509[a] | 1.588[a] |
|  | 59.81[a,b] | 1,862,664[a] | 4.756[a,b] |
| Eastern Siberia and Far Eastern (292) | 43.84[a] | 1,488,691 | 0.967 |
|  | 57.66[a,b] | 1,488,061[a] | 4.434[a,b] |

*Source:* RLMS.
*Note:* See the notes to tables 4.3 and 4.4. Moscow and St. Petersburg are used as the base group for comparisons.

We now turn to the geographic distribution of wage arrears. Did wage withholding affect workers equally across Russia or were there distinct geographic patterns?

### Geographic Variations in Wage Nonpayment

We expect wage withholding to vary with a region's general economic viability; the commitment of local administrations to continue paying wages to state employees from federally transferred funds; the prevalence in a region of defense and heavy industries located in company towns with limited employment alternatives outside their peripheries; and above all, the domination in the region of the natural resource sector with high wages. Moscow, a bustling financial center with a construction and restructuring boom, differed sharply from other regions.

In table 4.6, the incidence in column (1) and the relative amount of withholding in column (3) were significantly lower in Moscow and St. Petersburg than in all other regions in 1994 and 1998. Problems of converting the military plants in Western Siberian company towns, among them Arzamus-16 and Krasnoyarsk-70, aggravated the economic plight of their highly paid technicians with few alternative job opportunities, leading to the highest amounts withheld relative to contracted wages in column (3) at over four and one-half months in 1998. Wage arrears in the Premorye region of the Far East amounting to over four and one-half months of withholding in 1998, second highest among the regions, was aggravated by a prolonged power struggle between the regional governor, Yevgenii Nazdratenko, and the federal government, which accused the governor of misusing federal funds.

We also find that in all regions, with the exception of Moscow and St. Petersburg, the incidence and absolute and relative amounts of nonpayment significantly increased between 1994 and 1998. Apparently the economies of the two metropolises not only produced lower levels of nonpayment than in other regions, but also insulated local workers from the general deterioration in pay compliance over the 1994–98 period. (The role of the regional factor in wage nonpayment is analyzed in greater depth in chapter 5.)

## Occupational Patterns of Wage Nonpayment

We expect nonpayment incidence by occupation to be determined by the ranking of occupations in relation to demand for their skills. Highly skilled workers, among them technicians and professional cadres, machine operators, and assemblers, would bear a heavy impact of nonpayment if the demand for a wide assortment of locally manufactured goods including machines were to decline. At the other end of the spectrum, the most unskilled workers would again be subjected to severe nonpayment burden because of the nonsaleability of their services in alternative occupations.

In table 4.7, we see that service and market workers experienced the lowest incidence of nonpayment in column (1) at 18 percent in 1994 and 34 percent in 1998, and the shortest duration of nonpayment in column (3) at about three quarters of a month in 1994 and two months in 1998. These workers, who could remain or move into the expanding service, marketing, and tertiary sector activities, were least affected in terms of these measures. Legislators, senior managers, and officials suffered less incidence of wage withholding because of their political and managerial clout; so did clerks, the inevitable fixtures of Russia's bustling bureaucracy. All occupation groups, regardless of their relative

**Table 4.7**
Differences in wage arrears by occupations, currently employed (1994–1998)

| Occupations | Percentage | Amount | Months of wages |
|---|---|---|---|
| Legislator, manager, official (45) | 17.78 | 791,997 | 1.137 |
|  | 44.90[b] | 1,531,043[a,b] | 2.581[b] |
| Professional (682) | 29.62[a] | 659,984[a] | 0.862 |
|  | 53.55[a,b] | 1,026,095[a,b] | 2.469[b] |
| Technician/associate professional (506) | 26.88[a] | 495,323 | 0.885 |
|  | 61.50[a,b] | 850,900[b] | 2.727[b] |
| Clerk (212) | 26.89[a] | 578,806 | 1.012 |
|  | 44.79[a,b] | 779,750 | 3.022[b] |
| Service (market) worker (233) | 17.60 | 465,555 | 0.792 |
|  | 33.70[b] | 772,919[b] | 2.034[b] |
| Craft or related trades (600) | 31.33[a] | 809,226[a] | 1.060 |
|  | 56.25[a,b] | 1,211,502[a,b] | 3.054[a,b] |
| Machine operator or assembler (581) | 35.97[a] | 862,508[a] | 1.085[a] |
|  | 57.21[a,b] | 1,166,730[a,b] | 2.952[a,b] |
| Unskilled (302) | 30.46[a] | 447,229 | 1.275[a] |
|  | 53.23[a,b] | 648,019[b] | 2.029[b] |

*Source:* RLMS.
*Note:* See the notes to tables 4.3 and 4.4. The service (market) worker occupation is used as the base group for comparisons.

burden from withholding, experienced increases in arrears over the period.

### Industrial Pattern of Wage Nonpayment

Finally, industrial patterns of wage withholding are shown in table 4.8 for select industries. The incidence and duration of withholding varied significantly across industries, the incidence in column (1) reaching 75 percent in mining from a low of 18 percent in trade in 1998. The amount withheld similarly varied greatly across industries in 1998, ranging from less than a month's worth of wages in communications in column (3) to over half a year in mining. Although a number of industries did experience an increase in 1998 in the incidence and relative amounts of nonpayment, about half the industries experienced no change in withholding.

Our estimates also reveal that low incidence (at less than 50 percent) is associated with low relative amounts (less than two months) in

**Table 4.8**
Differences in wage arrears by industry, currently employed (1994–1998)

| Industries | Percentage | Amount | Months of wages |
|---|---|---|---|
| Manufacturing (749) | 32.71[a] | 693,332[a] | 0.986[a] |
|  | 56.50[a,b] | 1,004,795[a,b] | 3.011[a,b] |
| Agriculture (191) | 58.12[a] | 592,988 | 1.733[a] |
|  | 61.94[a] | 934,376[a,b] | 4.452[a,b] |
| Construction (237) | 40.08[a] | 983,477[a] | 0.958 |
|  | 65.74[a,b] | 1,704,538[a,b] | 4.153[a,b] |
| Transportation (255) | 25.49[a] | 766,004[a] | 0.937 |
|  | 49.43[a,b] | 1,067,737[a,b] | 2.102[b] |
| Trade (281) | 16.73 | 477,940 | 0.764 |
|  | 18.26 | 552,961 | 1.612 |
| Communications (29) | 17.24 | 556,947 | 0.693 |
|  | 38.64[a,b] | 502,590 | 0.760[a] |
| Housing/utilities (148) | 20.95 | 937,778[a] | 0.975 |
|  | 66.91[a,b] | 1,226,467[a] | 3.617[a,b] |
| Health (207) | 20.29 | 331,747 | 0.623 |
|  | 77.66[a,b] | 723,361[a,b] | 2.140[b] |
| Education (365) | 31.78[a] | 450,073 | 0.796 |
|  | 67.70[a,b] | 655,449[b] | 1.978[b] |
| Public administration (184) | 19.57 | 590,890 | 0.672 |
|  | 65.81[a,b] | 1,050,108[a,b] | 2.132[b] |
| Personal services (44) | 15.91 | 368,107 | 1.285 |
|  | 30.00 | 1,096,798 | 1.586 |
| Mining (10) | 80.00[a] | 1,199,494[a] | 0.823 |
|  | 75.00[a] | 3,164,385[a,b] | 6.500 |
| finance/insurance/real estate (43) | 16.28 | 754,821 | 0.479 |
|  | 22.22 | 691,686 | 1.900 |
| Forestry services (12) | 16.67 | 556,198 | 1.417 |
|  | 41.67 | 353,468 | 1.008 |
| Professional services (52) | 23.08 | 424,745 | 0.623 |
|  | 45.36[a,b] | 808,195[a,b] | 1.963[b] |
| Entertainment and recreation (35) | 31.43[a] | 266,480[a] | 0.881 |
|  | 57.14[a,b] | 977,603[a,b] | 3.074[a,b] |
| Science (47) | 38.30[a] | 483,614 | 0.645 |
|  | 42.22[a] | 1,025,802[a,b] | 1.807 |
| Business and repairs services (57) | 33.33[a] | 859,115[a] | 1.611 |
|  | 40.54[a] | 1,379,397[a,b] | 2.257 |
| Oil and gas (88) | 22.73 | 1,388,183[a] | 1.187 |
|  | 37.50[a,b] | 1,902,217[a,b] | 3.143 |

*Source:* RLMS.
*Note:* See the notes to tables 4.3 and 4.4. Manufacturing industry is used as the base group for comparisons.

trading, personal services, finance, insurance and real estate, and professional services, to name a few; and high incidence (at more than 50 percent) is associated with more than two months' of wage nonpayment in agriculture and construction (both depressed activities), housing and utilities, health, education, public administration (in the budget sector), and mining (a volatile industry).

## The Single-Variable versus Multivariable Estimates

Tables 4.3–4.8 provided a graphic portrayal of the distribution of wage nonpayments across different segments of the Russian population. These patterns do not, however, signal associations between wage nonpayment and the potential bargaining capability of a worker arising from his higher education or better location (providing him with an alternative job opportunity), his lower age (endowing him with recent education and greater mobility), or his occupational choice (he is a marketing expert instead of a coal miner) that put him ahead in the struggle for receiving the wages that were his due.

The chief shortcoming of these statistics is that they describe nonpayment in terms of a single characteristic, such as gender, without netting out the effects on withholding of other factors such as women's occupation, the industry in which they work, their education and age. For example, the gender-related ratios of table 4.3 do not address the question of the differential incidence of wage nonpayment between men and women in the same occupation and industry who had an employment contract specifying the same monthly wage rate. Were women, for example, with a contract to receive the same wage as men more likely to experience wage nonpayment, or were average differences by gender in nonpayment incidence attributable to the influence of lower average female wages on the wage nonpayment likelihood?

To resolve these questions—that is, to isolate the impact of a given factor on wage withholding—we formulate a multivariate specification in which the incidence and amount of nonpayment are regressed on gender, age, education, region, occupation, industry, and a number explanatory variables. The resulting multivariate estimates, reported in table 4.9, indicate the impact of a given factor on wage nonpayment net of the influence of the remaining variables in the regression.

## The Estimation Procedure

A probit procedure is used when the dependent variable is a measure of the individual experiencing *some* wage withholding during the year, that is, the dependent variable is assigned a value of 1 if the individual experienced wage arrears, and a value of zero if he or she was paid in full. We employ multivariate maximum likelihood probit estimation for assessing the partial impact of individual attributes, region of residence, and other factors affecting the probability that an individual experienced wage withholding. As is well known, ordinary least squares (OLS) estimation is inappropriate in the case of a 0–1 dependent variable because, among other reasons, the error term in the regression would be heteroskedastic, leading to inefficient estimates, and the predicted probability of occurrence could lie outside the 0–1 range. Probit estimation would steer clear of these problems.[8]

The resulting coefficients give the effects of the explanatory variables on the probability that the dependent variable was 1, that is, on the probability that an individual experienced wage arrears. For example, a positive estimated coefficient of the female dummy variable implies that, controlling for the other variables in the regression, females were more likely than men to face wage arrears. For continuous explanatory variables, such as the monthly contracted wage and tenure with the firm, the coefficients measure the effect of a small change in the explanatory variable on the likelihood of wage nonpayment.

The remaining variables in table 4.9 are dummies; the estimated coefficients give discrete changes in the probability of respondents with a particular attribute experiencing wage arrears relative to people in a base group. The base or comparison group is the omitted category for each group of dummies, which define a set of attributes such as age, occupation, and education. Although it is strictly correct to assess all coefficients relative to the overall base group, defined as 18- to 24-year-old men with the lowest level of general secondary school education living in Moscow or St. Petersburg who are in the service worker occupation and the manufacturing industry, we follow the common practice of interpreting the dummy coefficients of the attribute in question relative to the omitted category for that attribute. For example, the nonpayment incidence coefficient with respect to location is interpreted in relation to the base, omitted category of Moscow and St. Petersburg. The nonpayment incidence coefficient with respect to education is

**Table 4.9**
Multivariate estimates of the incidence and amount of wage arrears

| Explanatory variables | Incidence (8,035) | ln(amount) (2,824) |
|---|---|---|
| *Years* | | |
| *d*1995 | 0.032* (.014) | −0.169* (.055) |
| *d*1996 | 0.180* (.016) | 0.387* (.041) |
| *d*1998 | 0.328* (.017) | 0.573* (.044) |
| *Gender* (female) | 0.059* (.016) | −0.216* (.044) |
| *Age Groups* (17.12*, 1.83) | | |
| 25–34 | 0.062* (.023) | 0.174* (.075) |
| 35–44 | 0.026 (.023) | 0.133* (.076) |
| 45–60 | −0.010 (.024) | 0.134 (.089) |
| *Education* (14.39*, 5.41*) | | |
| Professional courses | 0.035* (.015) | −0.002 (.047) |
| Ordinary vocational | 0.006 (.023) | −0.122* (.059) |
| Secondary vocational | −0.011 (.018) | −0.112* (.062) |
| Specialized secondary | 0.013 (.016) | 0.145* (.042) |
| University | −0.028 (.020) | 0.168* (.061) |
| Graduate, residency | −0.105* (.052) | −0.565 (.426) |
| *Regions* (111.79*, 8.12*) | | |
| Northern and North Western | 0.259* (.034) | 0.597* (.132) |
| Central and Central Black–Earth | 0.132* (.028) | 0.267* (.118) |
| alphaVolga–Vyatski and Volga Basin | 0.259* (.029) | 0.304* (.116) |
| North Caucasus | 0.176* (.032) | 0.291* (.128) |
| Urals | 0.200* (.029) | 0.423* (.120) |
| Western Siberia | 0.166* (.034) | 0.606* (.130) |
| Eastern Siberia and Far Eastern | 0.243* (.033) | 0.609* (.128) |
| *Occupations* (14.90*, 1.72) | | |
| Legislator, manager, official | −0.114* (.042) | −0.073 (.134) |
| Professional | −0.022 (.033) | −0.130 (.116) |
| Technician/associate professional | −0.001 (.032) | −0.169* (.088) |
| Clerk | −0.014 (.035) | −0.108 (.097) |
| Craft or related trades | −0.007 (.033) | −0.133 (.091) |
| Machine operator or assembler | 0.029 (.034) | −0.114 (.092) |
| Unskilled | 0.039 (.034) | −0.262* (.089) |

**Table 4.9**
(continued)

| Explanatory variables | Incidence | ln(amount) |
|---|---|---|
| *Industries* (302.28*, 9.58*) | | |
| Agriculture | 0.198* (0.036) | 0.240* (0.087) |
| Construction | 0.015 (0.026) | 0.270* (0.068) |
| Transportation | −0.144* (0.021) | −0.058 (0.065) |
| Trade | −0.219* (0.020) | −0.452* (0.147) |
| Communications | −0.190* (0.039) | −0.658* (0.137) |
| Housing/utilities | −0.065* (0.028) | 0.253* (0.082) |
| Health | 0.002 (0.029) | −0.195* (0.068) |
| Education | 0.063* (0.026) | −0.326* (0.067) |
| Public administration | −0.084* (0.026) | −0.112 (0.088) |
| Personal services | −0.198* (0.035) | −0.097 (0.186) |
| Mining | 0.184* (0.095) | 0.639* (0.166) |
| Finance/insurance/real estate | −0.278* (0.019) | −0.509* (0.234) |
| Forestry services | −0.078 (0.083) | −0.208 (0.291) |
| Professional services | −0.101* (0.037) | −0.391* (0.124) |
| Entertainment and recreation | 0.044 (0.055) | −0.540 (0.322) |
| Science | −0.026 (0.052) | −0.051 (0.181) |
| Business and repair services | −0.106* (0.036) | 0.259* (0.125) |
| Oil and gas | −0.227* (0.023) | 0.336* (0.105) |
| *Other variables* | | |
| ln(monthly wages) | 0.128* (0.009) | 0.518* (.036) |
| Months with current employer | 0.0004 (0.0001) | 0.0007* (0.0002) |
| $R^2$ | 0.1337 | 0.3750 |

*Source:* RLMS
*Note:* Parameter estimates are reported with robust standard errors in parentheses. *F*-statistics from joint significance tests for each group of explanatory factors are listed in parentheses, first for the incidence and second for the amount regressions at the head of each group. We report slope estimates of the incidence regression estimated by maximum likelihood probit. The amount regression is estimated by ordinary least squares. Sample sizes are listed in parentheses below the heading of each regression.
* Denotes significance at 5 percent.

interpreted with respect to the base, omitted category of general secondary school education, and so on.

Finally, the estimated coefficients in table 4.9 represent the average effect of an attribute for the entire 1994–98 period. But how do we measure changes over time in the impact of a given attribute, say educational attainment, on wage withholding? We can repeat the analysis of table 4.9 based on data for each of the four years (excluding the year dummies) and compare the estimated coefficients across the years. Alternatively, we can add in the specification a series of interactions of the three-year dummies (1995, 1996 and 1998) with each variable already in the regression of table 4.9: The coefficients of these interactions would indicate the changes in the effect of the attribute on wage withholding between a given year and 1994.[9] Such an exercise would be similar in spirit to our comparisons in table 4.3–4.8 of the patterns in wage arrears across a given attribute, say educational attainment, in 1995 over 1994 and the remaining yearly pairs. However, given the plethora of numbers that such an analysis would generate, we have opted to report only the average attribute effects for 1994–98 in table 4.9, leaving our detailed analysis of changes in regional and gender patterns of wage nonpayment in chapters 5 and 10.

### Incidence of Wage Nonpayment

According to the estimated coefficients of the year dummies in column (1) of table 4.9, the likelihood of a worker experiencing wage arrears increased monotonically between 1994 and 1998: The probability of wage nonpayment was 3 percent higher in 1995 than in 1994, 18 percent higher in 1996 relative to 1994, and 33 percent higher in 1998 than in 1994. These estimates are net of the impact of other factors in the regression. The year dummy coefficients exclude the effect on the incidence of wage nonpayment of our sample respondents having moved to a new occupation, industry, or region because these have been controlled for via the inclusion of the relevant dummies in our multivariate specification.

Women were 6 percent more likely in column (1) to experience arrears than men. This estimate contradicts the univariate results reported in table 4.3, which failed to find any difference in incidence by gender. By contrast, the multivariate estimate accounts for the fact that lower-wage workers were less likely to face wage withholding regardless of their gender: The estimated coefficient of the impact of the wage variable on nonpayment incidence in column (1) is 0.128. When we control for the influence of the generally lower wages of women, we find that women were more likely to face wage withholding than men.

People who were twenty-five to thirty-four were more likely by 6 percent to experience arrears than those who were eighteen to twenty-four, the base comparison group. Workers thirty-five years or older, however, were no more likely than the young comparison group to be subjected to wage withholding: The coefficients are statistically not significant.

The relatively weak educational patterns in arrears of table 4.5 are borne out by the estimates: People who took relatively unskilled "professional courses" were somewhat more likely to face arrears, while those with postgraduate credentials were about 11 percent less likely to face arrears than those with the lowest education levels.

Significant regional differences in wage nonpayment persist with people in Moscow and St. Petersburg (our base group) generally facing a lower probability of experiencing wage arrears than people in any other region. Again, these results suggest that regional variations in the incidence of arrears do not reflect the regional distribution of industries that were more or less prone to partially pay their workers, because we control for the effect on nonpayment incidence of industrial affiliation.

There is relatively little occupational variation in the incidence of arrears, although legislators and officials faced 11 percent lower probability than our comparison group of service-sector workers; once again, this is an average result over 1994–98.

Finally, there was substantial industrial variation in the incidence of wage arrears. Workers in agriculture and mining were subjected to 20 and 18 percent higher nonpayment incidence than in manufacturing, our base comparison industry; by contrast, communications (at 19 percent lower), personal services (at 20 percent lower), finance, insurance, and real estate (at 28 percent lower), and business and repair services (at 11 percent lower) fared better. Oil and gas industry workers faced a 23 percent lower chance of nonpayment. These estimates do not reflect the impact of regional location of industries or workers' education level, because we account for the impact of these factors on wage nonpayment incidence.

We now turn to an analysis of the extent to which personal attributes such as gender, age, and educational attainment, plus region of residence and industry of employment, influenced the value of outstanding wage debt as opposed to the likelihood of experiencing arrears per se.

### Amounts of Wage Debt

We report OLS estimates of the real ruble amount of outstanding wage debt owed to workers in column (2) of table 4.9. These regressions include only people who faced a nonzero value of outstanding arrears. Specifying the dependent variable as a logarithm allows us to interpret the coefficients as measures of the percentage effect of an attribute on the amount of outstanding arrears.[10] Again, we include the contracted monthly wage as an independent variable to control for the effect of different wage levels on absolute amounts owed. An alternative approach would have been to use the cumulated amounts owed divided by the contracted monthly wage (our "months of wages" variable in the final columns of tables 4.3–4.8) as the dependent variable. We opted instead for the monthly wage as a regressor because it offers a less restrictive functional form while allowing us to interpret the attribute effects on amounts withheld in the same way as with the inclusion of relative amounts owed (i.e., cumulated amounts owed divided by the contracted monthly wage) as the dependent variable.

Cumulated wage debt rose by 57 percent in 1998 over 1994 levels after having dipped by 17 percent in 1995 (the result of arrears clearance on the eve of the December 1995 parliamentary elections). Conditional on facing nonpayment, women were owed 22 percent less than men of similar age, education, tenure, monthly wages, region of residence, occupation, and industry of employment. Amounts owed with respect to age followed an inverted U-shaped pattern, peaking in the twenty-five to thirty-four age group at 17 percent higher than the comparison group of eighteen to twenty-four years.

Contrary to our expectation of arrears decreasing with education level and greater marketability as they did from professional to vocational schooling, people with specialized secondary and university education faced outstanding arrears at 17 percent higher than for the lowest group with secondary education. Regional patterns of wage debts were similar to the incidence patterns, with higher levels of outstanding debt in all regions relative to those in the major urban centers of Moscow and St. Petersburg.

Outstanding debt across occupations (controlling, once again, for differences in age, education level, monthly wage, and so forth) did not differ significantly from the base service workers group with the exception of technicians, associate professionals, and unskilled workers, who exhibited significantly lower amounts owed. Even though there were significant differences in amounts owed and for the noted occupation groups, the joint test of significance of the vector of occupation dummies (of 1.72 in parenthesis) failed to confirm an association between occupational affiliation per se and cumulated wage arrears.

Finally, we see that there were substantial differences across industries in the value of outstanding arrears. The mining sector registered a whopping 64 percent higher level in accumulated debts to miners than workers in the manufacturing sector. Among the industries marking a wage debt that was at least 50 percent less than in manufacturing were finance, insurance and real estate, entertainment and recreation, and communications.

Turning to the other variables of importance in our analysis, we note that higher-wage workers were more likely to experience wage non-payment incidence and in higher amounts. However, the implied tax from wage withholding was regressive: With a positive estimated intercept (noted in footnote 11) wage arrears were a regressive tax on the workforce, falling more heavily on workers who were less able to pay the implicit tax.[11] We address this issue of the regressivity of the implicit wage tax in some detail in chapter 8, and argue that rather than acting as an implicit equalizing redistributive mechanism, wage arrears actually hit the lower-paid workers more severely than the better-paid workers.

Finally, the more senior workers with longer tenure faced a slightly higher incidence and amount of withholding than less senior workers. Perhaps managers, less concerned about retaining senior workers with relatively high pay and lack of up-to-date skills, used wage denial to successfully extract rents from them despite their clout.

## Conclusions

We analyze wage arrears in terms of three measures defined as the percentage of respondents in our data who were denied wages (giving us the incidence of nonpayment); the average cumulated ruble value of wages withheld at the time of the interview (giving us the amount of nonpayment); and the cumulated arrears divided by average monthly contracted wage (giving us the relative amount withheld).

We regress incidence and amount of nonpayment in multivariate specifications on a number of demographic variables such as gender, age, and education, and employment variables such as region, occupation, and industry to isolate the impact of a given factor—for example, gender—on wage nonpayment net of the influence of the remaining explanatory variables in the regressions.

Based on this procedure, the following are among our note-worthy results with regard to the pattern of wage nonpayment in Russia during 1994–1998. First, with regard to the incidence of nonpayment:

• The likelihood of a worker being subjected to nonpayment was 33 percent higher in 1998 than in 1994.

• Women were 6 percent more likely to experience arrears than men.

• Moscow and St. Petersburg respondents faced a lower probability of expereincing wage arrears than people in any other region.

• The incidence of arrears varied widely among industries. Workers in agriculture and mining experienced 20 and 18 percent higher nonpayment than in manufacturing. By contrast, Russia's "growth industries"—communications, personal services, finance, insurance and real estate, business and repair services, and the oil and gas industry—fared much better.

Next, with regard to the amounts of nonpayment in December 1995 rubles:

• Cumulated wage arrears rose by 57 percent in 1998 over 1994 levels.

• Conditional on facing nonpayment, women were owed 22 percent less than men with similar demographic and employment features, reflecting the lower average wages of women.

• Regional patterns of wage debts were similar to the incidence patterns, with higher levels of outstanding debt in all regions relative to those in Moscow and St. Petersburg.

• There were substantial differences in outstanding wage debt among industries. The mining sector had a whopping 64 percent higher arrears than manufacturing. By contrast, finance, insurance and real estate, entertainment and recreation, and communications had at least 50 percent less arrears than manufacturing.

Wage nonpayment and accumulated arrears, displaying a varying pattern across Russia's regions as noted above, and the factors contributing to the regional variations form the substance of our next chapter.

# Center versus Periphery: Regions and Arrears

Wage arrears affected regions of Russia's vast territory (represented in figure 5.1) at varying rates. Tables 5.1, 5.2 and 5.3[1] show a distinct regional pattern in the incidence and amounts of wage nonpayment. In table 5.1, 1998 per capita wage arrears in Eastern Siberia and the Far Eastern region were ten times their lowest level of 33,619 rubles in the urban centers of Moscow and St. Petersburg. In 1998, working men and women in table 5.2 had the lowest incidence of arrears, again in Moscow and St. Petersburg at approximately 24 percent; by contrast, 70 percent in the Northern and North-Western region suffered nonpayment. Cumulated outstanding arrears in 1998 varied from a low of 767,667 (constant 1995) rubles in North Caucasus to a high of 1,862,664 rubles in Western Siberia, more than twice the amount. As a fraction of monthly wages, outstanding debt in 1998 similarly varied in table 5.3 from a low of a little more than a month's worth of wages in Moscow and St. Petersburg to nearly five months of pay in Western Siberia.

Uneven regional wage withholding undoubtedly resulted from the varying impact of the seismic economic measures launched in 1992. We focus on three features of the process relevant for our analysis of the wage nonpayment issue. First, most prices were liberalized in early 1992 from their administered levels; wages had been freed at managerial initiative at varying speed even earlier. The relative wage/price shifts combined with macroeconomic belt tightening had strikingly different impacts on enterprises that over time were deprived of automatic, Soviet-style budget bailouts.

Second, various expenditures were transferred from the federal budget to the regions without matching funds. The regions, responsible for collecting taxes for the federal treasury, retaliated by arbitrarily withholding tax payments to the center, weakening the center's budgetary

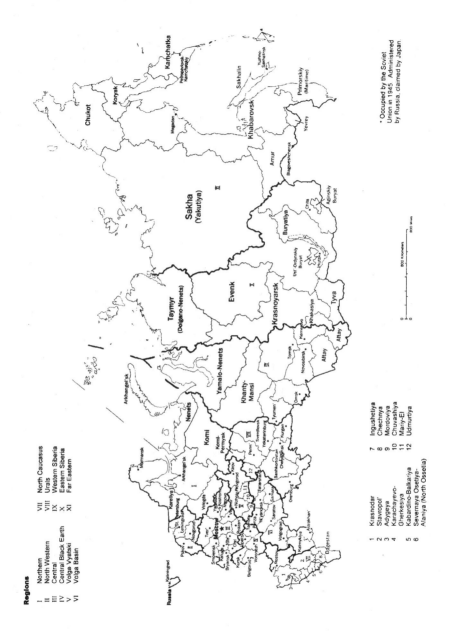

**Regions**

| | | | |
|---|---|---|---|
| I | Northern | VII | North Caucasus |
| II | North Western | VIII | Urals |
| III | Central | IX | Western Siberia |
| IV | Central Black Earth | X | Eastern Siberia |
| V | Volga Vyatski | XI | Far Eastern |
| VI | Volga Basin | | |

| | | | |
|---|---|---|---|
| 1 | Krasnodar | 7 | Ingushetiya |
| 2 | Stavropol' | 8 | Chechnya |
| 3 | Adygeya | 9 | Mordoviya |
| 4 | Karachayevo-Cherkesiya | 10 | Chuvashiya |
| 5 | Kabardino-Balkariya | 11 | Mariy-El |
| 6 | Severnaya Osetiya-Alaniya (North Ossetia) | 12 | Udmurtiya |

* Occupied by the Soviet Union in 1945. Administered by Russia, claimed by Japan.

capability of transferring cash to the deficit regions. The regional administrations spent the available resources for meeting obligations of their choice rather than paying budget-sector employees, occasionally diverting federal funds for illegitimate purposes. As we note later, the nonpayment to budget-sector employees was essentially a regional issue.

Finally, regional governors exercised local autonomy vis-á-vis the center, testing Moscow's authority and bargaining muscle. The prolonged political tug-of-war between Governor Nazdratenko of the Premorye Region in the Far East and the Kremlin, an extreme case of center-periphery dissonance, had implications for wage arrears in the region.

**Figure 5.1**
Regions of Russia
*Source*: The figure is based on the U.S. government map.
*Notes*: We locate the eighty-nine oblasts (provinces), republics, krais (territories), and autonomous okrugs (regions in Soviet definition) of Russia in eleven regions of the figure and then convert them into seven regions (excluding Moscow and St. Petersburg) for the wage nonpayment analysis of the chapter. The initial eleven regions are marked in dark outlines and indicated by roman numerals in the figure. The industrial features of these regions are sketched in the appendix to chapter 3.

The Northern region includes Arkhangel'sk, Vologda, and Murmansk oblasts; Nenets autonomous okrug (AO); and the Republics of Kareliya and Komi.

The North-Western region consists of St. Petersburg city, and Leningrad, Novgorod, Pskov, and Kaliningrad oblasts.

The Central region includes Moscow city and twelve oblasts of Moscow, Bryansk, Vladimir, Ivanovo, Tver', Kaluga, Kostroma, Orël, Ryazan', Smolensk, Tula, and Yaroslavl'.

The Central Black-Earth region consists of Belgorod, Voronezh, Kursk, Lipetsk, and Tambov oblasts.

The Volga-Vyatski region includes Nizhni Novgorod and Kirov oblasts, and the republics of Mari-El, Mordoviya, and Chuvashiya.

The Volga Basin region consists of Astrakhan', Volgograd, Samara, Penza, Saratov, and Ul'yanovsk oblasts, and the republics of Kalmykiya and Tatarstan.

North Caucasus region covers Krasnodar and Stavropol' krais, Rostov oblast, and the republics of Adygeya, Karachayevo-Cherkesiya, Dagestan, Kabardino-Balkariya, North Ossetia, and Ingushetiya.

The Urals region consists of Kurgan, Orenburg, Perm', Sverdlovsk, and Chelyabinsk oblasts, Komi-Permiyak AO, and the republics of Bashkortostan and Udmurtiya.

Western Siberia encompasses Kemerovo, Novosibirsk, Omsk, Tomsk, and Tyumen' oblasts, Altai krai, the republic of Altai, and Yamalo-Nenets and Khanty-Mansi AOs.

Eastern Siberia includes Krasnoyarskii krai, Irkutsk and Chita oblasts, and the republics of Khakasiya, Buryatiya, and Tyva.

**Table 5.1**
Regional patterns in per capita wage arrears (Goskomstat)

|  | 1994 | 1995 | 1996 | 1997 | 1998 |
|---|---|---|---|---|---|
| Entire Russian Federation | 62,125 | 54,490 | 152,442 | 271,739 | 289,253 |
| Moscow and St. Petersburg | 6,585 | 5,902 | 8,528 | 37,673 | 33,619 |
| Northern and North Western | 66,294 | 37,818 | 57,629 | 229,109 | 206,299 |
| Central and Central Black-Earth | 39,658 | 22,800 | 34,662 | 109,584 | 99,156 |
| Volga-Vyatski and Volga Basin | 54,336 | 30,393 | 46,263 | 138,289 | 125,472 |
| North Caucasus | 27,513 | 17,070 | 24,721 | 77,540 | 69,932 |
| Urals | 65,286 | 37,632 | 58,366 | 175,938 | 158,705 |
| Western Siberia | 118,454 | 74,377 | 115,996 | 332,229 | 299,247 |
| Eastern Siberia and Far Eastern | 145,987 | 79,834 | 120,823 | 386,695 | 349,705 |

*Sources:* Regional population is from *Regioni Rossii,* Moscow: Goskomstata Rossii, vols. 1, 2, 1997; overdue wages (monthly) are from *Sotsial'no-ekonomicheskoye polozheniye Rossii,* published by Goskomstat.
*Note:* The figures are total overdue wages per region, average for the months of January and July of each year, divided by regional population as of January of each year. The last column gives total overdue wages as of December 1, 1998, divided by population as of January 1, 1998.

We discuss the regional impact of wage-price decontrol, fiscal disarray, and political power play that affected wage withholding in the regions, before proceeding to the formulation and estimation of empirical models that help us explain the pattern of the incidence and amount of wage nonpayment shown in tables 5.1, 5.2, and 5.3.

## Regional Impact of Wage-Price Decontrol and Budget Slashing

The freeing of wages at managerial initiative created occupational wage disparities within and between regions. As early as November 1992, the average monthly wage in Krasnoyarsk Territory varied from 3,200 rubles in the glass industry to 83,000 rubles in the natural gas industry. Price decontrol added to the differentiating impact. Retail prices of basic food products, regulated at the start of 1992, were freed by two-thirds of the regions by the third quarter. Production decline and severed ties among enterprises again varied from region to region, depending on the inherited production structure and managerial response to financial pressures and relative price shifts.[2]

Russia's cotton textile industry, located in Ivanovo Province, provided an extreme example of the economic distress brought on by price

**Table 5.2**
Regional patterns in the incidence and amount of wage arrears

| Major regional groups | 1994 | 1996 | 1998 |
|---|---|---|---|
| Moscow and St. Petersburg | 21.27 | 24.39 | 24.40 |
| | 1,081,327 | 1,612,039 | 860,927[a] |
| Northern and North Western | 37.28[b] | 60.11[a,b] | 70.35[a,b] |
| | 1,413,795 | 2,378,272[a,b] | 1,820,821[a,b] |
| Central and Central Black-Earth | 26.32[b] | 36.27[a,b] | 47.62[a,b] |
| | 769,859[b] | 856,307 | 814,474 |
| Volga-Vyatski and Volga Basin | 30.91[b] | 47.90[a,b] | 63.13[a,b] |
| | 526,160[b] | 780,021[a,b] | 846,245 |
| North Caucasus | 25.91[b] | 44.70[a,b] | 49.33[b] |
| | 492,651[b] | 884,428[a] | 767,667 |
| Urals | 33.78[b] | 52.81[a,b] | 59.38[a,b] |
| | 776,973[b] | 1,182,860[a] | 1,081,649[b] |
| Western Siberia | 30.23[b] | 49.77[a,b] | 59.81[a,b] |
| | 1,402,509 | 1,428,306 | 1,862,664[a,b] |
| Eastern Siberia and Far Eastern | 43.84[b] | 54.59[a,b] | 57.66[b] |
| | 1,488,691 | 2,067,279[a] | 1,488,061[a,b] |
| Standard deviation (across 8 regions) | 7.119 | 11.336 | 13.966 |
| | 407,609 | 590,516 | 462,411 |
| Standard deviation (across 38 regions) | 15.525 | 18.872 | 18.797 |
| | 595,868 | 656,550 | 584,434 |

*Source:* RLMS.
*Note:* Two numbers are listed in each cell: the first row reports the percentage of people in the region who faced outstanding wage debts at the time of the survey; the second row lists the (real) ruble value of outstanding wage debts for people who faced positive outstanding wage arrears. The 1994 sample sizes for each region are listed in table 4.6.
a. Significant differences (at 10 percent or better) within regions between 1994 and 1996, and between 1996 and 1998.
b. Significant differences (at 10 percent or better) between each region and the Moscow/St. Petersburg comparison group.

decontrol and severed inter-republic ties. By 1993, the production of cotton fabrics and apparel plummeted by 70 percent and of knitwear by 50 percent because of inadequate supplies of raw cotton from Uzbek suppliers, who preferred to export it in hard currency markets. The traditional swapping of Russian oil for Uzbek cotton worked erratically.

As a result, 250,000 workers were thrown out of work in January through March, 1993 in the province, where the textile industry dominated and provided nearly 100 percent of its budget. Schools and cultural centers were closed and heat and water supplies to housing became increasingly irregular.[3]

**Table 5.3**
Regional patterns in wages and number of months of outstanding wage debt

| Major regional groups | 1994 | 1996 | 1998 |
|---|---|---|---|
| Moscow and St. Petersburg | 963,047<br>1.044 | 1,108,078[a]<br>1.233 | 642,741[a]<br>1.074 |
| Northern and North Western | 1,022,096<br>1.144 | 1,292,655[a,b]<br>1.984[a,b] | 743,294[a,b]<br>3.680[a,b] |
| Central and Central Black-Earth | 594,760[b]<br>1.002 | 682,647[a,b]<br>1.516[a] | 462,150[a,b]<br>3.004[a,b] |
| Volga-Vyatski and Volga Basin | 484,973[b]<br>0.965 | 540,670[a,b]<br>1.650[a,b] | 419,950[a,b]<br>3.069[a,b] |
| North Caucasus | 490,835[b]<br>0.959 | 695,729[a,b]<br>1.309[a] | 409,150[a,b]<br>2.204[a,b] |
| Urals | 696,808[b]<br>0.984 | 793,767[a,b]<br>1.367[a] | 503,562[a,b]<br>2.912[a,b] |
| Western Siberia | 1,124,568[b]<br>1.588[b] | 1,448,235[a,b]<br>1.514 | 842,789[a,b]<br>4.756[a,b] |
| Eastern Siberia and Far Eastern | 1,159,070[b]<br>0.967 | 1,017,119<br>2.310[a,b] | 677,452[a]<br>4.434[a,b] |
| Standard deviation (across 8 regions) | 281,695<br>0.382 | 321,421<br>0.721 | 161,788<br>1.967 |
| Standard deviation (across 38 regions) | 351,801<br>0.214 | 431,990<br>0.367 | 294,930<br>1.183 |

*Source:* RLMS.
*Note:* See note to table 5.2. Two numbers are listed in each cell: the first row reports the average (real, December 1995) monthly wage; the second row lists the ratio of the (real) ruble value of outstanding wage debts to the (real) monthly wage, calculated for those people who faced positive outstanding wage arrears.

The regional impact of the liberalization measures was striking in 1992. As a result of the population's income shift from the European to the eastern regions including the Urals, the differential between the average per capita income of the recent "rich" east of Russia including the Urals and the "poor" west increased from 3.2 times at the start of 1992 to 4.9 times at the end. Fifty-six of eighty-nine Russian regions in figure 5.1 had per capita incomes below the average for Russia in November 1992. The republics of Chechnya, Ingushetiya, Mari-El, Dagestan, North Ossetia, Kabardino-Balkariya, and Mordoviya, and Moscow and Penza provinces, with the lowest per capita incomes, differed sharply from Sakha-Yakutiya and Komi Republics, Kamchtka, Magadan, Murmansk, Sakhalin, and Tyumen' Provinces, and the city of Moscow with the highest per capita incomes. Thirty percent more pensioners and 33 percent fewer employed lived in the poor areas. Rural residents relatively concentrated in the poor areas and subsisting on private auxiliary farming carried produce to Moscow and the provincial centers.[4]

Regional administrations began routinely supporting "strapped" enterprises by giving them easy credits and allowing them deferred payments and tax breaks into local budgets, in the process receiving fewer taxes and inflating regional budget deficits. Local deficits exceeded 30 percent of revenues in twenty-seven regions, among them the North Caucasus republics, the Mari-El and Mordoviya Republics, and Pskov province, and a number of regions in Southern Siberia and the Far North. Money-losing enterprises in Southern Siberia defaulted on tax payments to the local budgets that continued supporting them by slashing outlays on social support to the population. The tax police used strong-arm tactics in the North Caucasus regions to improve their tax collection. The Mari-El and Mordoviya Republics, and Pskov Province, economically depressed because of high shares of declining defense industries, had double the unemployment rate of the Russian average.[5]

### The Northern Territories: Special Status in Decline

Russia's Northern Territories, traditionally a planned deficit area, were a drain on the federal budget. In the Soviet days, caravans of ships delivered them essential items, from needles and flour to gasoline and building materials, on command from the Communist Party. Beginning in 1992, a crash campaign replaced the Ministry of Trade and the State Supply Committee with commercialized trading organizations, who swiftly switched to the rules of the market: People earning paltry wages could not afford the market prices including traders' profits and high transport costs.[6]

Shortage of funds contributed to lower fuel deliveries to the 11 million northerners, especially in parts of Yakutiya and northern Sakhalin, in the late summer of 1994. Northern rivers in twenty-eight regions, navigable only from late spring to midsummer, required, at the minimum, a month for delivery of goods in some parts. Pensioners and the disabled could not be moved to central regions because of limited resources. The funding was adequate for constructing only 400 apartments for the tens of thousands who awaited relocation. Funds for medical care for children were slashed. The North, which produced 20 percent of Russia's GDP and 90 percent of its foreign exchange, became a massive burden for the country.[7]

For our empirical work, we need to select appropriate variables representing the impact of the liberalization measures on the economic viability and wage payment potential of Russian regions. Were wages withheld more frequently and in larger amounts in economically more depressed regions with redundant labor, allowing managers to get away with partial wage payment because workers, lacking alternative employment options, tacitly accepted nonpayment in order to remain employed? We employ regional per capita incomes and unemployment rates in our model (of table 5.6) as proxies for assessing the impact of the liberalization policies on accumulated wage arrears in sixty-three of eighty-nine Russia's regions in 1995, the latest year and regional breakdown for which the necessary information is currently available.

## The Regions and Fiscal Disarray

As a result of the unplanned 1992 fiscal rearrangement, the regions became responsible for financing education, health care, culture, physical education, housing, road construction, and federal programs, including capital investments in rural areas, subsidies for livestock products, and passenger transportation. But their budgetary revenues were not raised correspondingly. Within this constraint, the regions became responsible for paying an array of state-sector employees.

Following Soviet practice, Russia's eighty-nine regions automatically retained varying fractions of taxes collected by them. The continuation of the single-track taxation system of the Soviet era contributed to lagging revenue flows in the federal treasury. The tax service and the tax police watched helplessly as regional tax collection declined and transfers to the federal treasury plummeted.

Three features of the traditional arrangement aggravated the fiscal disarray. First, the tax retention norms penalized the economically better-off regions that were also heavily populated. Thus in the 1993 budget, the regions were allowed to keep between 5 and 50 percent of the value-added tax collected by them; substantial tax contributors with large tax bases such as Moscow and Moscow Province; Krasnoyarsk Territory; St. Petersburg; Samara, Sverdlovsk, Nizhny Novgorod, Vladimir, and Volgograd Provinces kept 5 percent of taxes

which was inadequate to finance the social needs of these densely populated areas.[8] Among the next set targeted for large contributions to the
federal budget were Komi Republic; Tambov, Tver', Kostroma, Perm'
and Chelyabinsk Provinces; the Northwest, Central, and Central Black-
Earth regions (except Leningrad Province); and the Khanty-Mansi Autonomous Region.[9] These twenty contributors out of eighty-nine com-
prised 40 percent of Russian population and 45 percent of its GDP in
1998.

Second, the tax retention norms by region, originally legislated by
the Duma, became arbitrary and unstable over time. For example, the
shares of value-added tax that the regions were allowed to keep by law
varied from 20 to 60 percent, the average being 24.4 percent in 1992.
The ratios noted above were different in 1993.

The retentions were calculated to prevent regional differences and
social instability from snowballing. Tuva, Buryatiya, Dagestan, Mari-
El, and Kabardino-Balkariya—the truly poor recipients of transfers
from the center—had half the per capita budget expenditure of Russia,
inclusive of subsidies. Again, Sakhalin, Kamchatka, and Chita Provinces in the far north received budgetary support on the basis of inhospitable climate and geographic location. However, only 10 percent of
the total giveaway arose from legitimate claims based on severe climate and extreme poverty. Having given up one-fourth of its revenues,
Ul'yanovsk Province was left with per capita budget outlays amounting to two-thirds of neighboring (transfer-exempt) Tatarstan.
Chelyabinsk Province, a net donor, kept half as much money per capita
in its till as neighboring Bashkortostan.[10]

Third, the redistribution practices of the center, devoid of rational
and transparent rules of fiscal federalism, were subject to pressures
from local administrators. As already noted, the norms were continuously violated. In early September, 1993, Yaroslav'l Province Administration cut the federal share of value-added tax from 80 percent to 50
percent; Voronezh Province slashed the share to 2 percent in retaliation
for Finance Minister Boris Fyodorov's cutback of funding to Voronezh
farms. In the first half of 1993, Tatarstan, Bashkiriya, and Sakha-
Yakutiya diverted 250 billion rubles due to the center for their use. The
Maritime Territory Administration suspended tax contribution to the
federal budget on August 14 because of a territory-wide strike. Samara
Province threatened to halt the transfer of taxes to the center in early
August. The number of regions taking tax matters into their own hands
had multiplied, destabilizing the federal budget.[11]

The consequences of local heavy-handedness were compounded by offers of populist, budget-busting gifts to regional applicants from top officials, including the Russian president. In a zero-sum situation, the largesse could be financed only by redistributing budgetary allocations or increasing the deficit. In 1993, First Deputy Prime Ministers Oleg Soskovets and Aleksandr Zaveryukha (during their tour of the Far East) and Oleg Lobov (traveling in four central Russian cities) signaled budgetary support to local industries that countered the anti-inflationary priorities of the government. The exchange between Deputy Prime Ministers Fyodorov (in charge of finance) and Zaveryukha (in charge of agriculture) illuminated the policy tensions in the government. When the Minister of Finance accused the Minister of Agriculture of wrecking government finances through excessive subsidization, the latter invoked his firm stand of support for Russian agriculture. The contradictions within the government damaged the center's fiscal health.[12]

The finance minister's cheery optimism with regard to the situation flew in the face of the mounting fiscal chaos. Deliberately underplaying the regional tendency to slash or halt tax payments to the federal budget, he claimed that the unruly defaulters were few despite their noisy statements. In his view, regional officials preferred complying with the tax law to prosecution by the local prosecutor. The center could alternatively use the carrot or the stick by granting or denying credits and subsidies for republic programs, supplying cash to the provinces, or excluding them from the unified banking network. The prodigals could be brought back to their senses, he declared.[13]

Empirically, the connection between high revenue retention by the regions (ostensibly enabling them to pay budget-sector employees) and the wage nonpayment crisis is difficult to establish and explore. As noted above, arrears in the budget sector were predominantly a regional issue. In July 1997, First Deputy Finance Minister Alexei Kudrin noted that regional governments owed the bulk of government sector wage arrears: Regional budget-sector debt stood at 25.6 trillion rubles (or $4.4 billion), compared with federal government wage debts amounting to 7.7 trillion rubles (including wage arrears to the military).[14] In fact, the importance of the regional distribution of arrears to the Russian electorate was clearly brought out in the voting patterns of the parliamentary elections of 1993 and 1995 and the 1996 presidential election. In a careful analysis of regional voting patterns, Daniel Treisman (1999) found that the extent of wage arrears in a region was the only measure of economic performance that had a significant impact on regional voting decisions—higher back payments owed to workers were associated with more frequent voting against progovernment blocs and against Boris Yeltsin.[15]

But did higher tax retention by regions result in better regional performance of wage payment to budget-sector employees? Higher revenue retention, implying more regional resources, is necessary but not sufficient for assessing a region's wage payment potential. The funds were often diverted to other urgent uses such as a local administration's need to finance subsidized home heating for local residents; occasionally the cash was siphoned off by local officials and converted into hard currency. In any case, while we have scattered information on the net donors and recipients of the implicit federal transfers noted above, we lack detailed data on regional tax retention ratios.

More to the point, budget-sector nonpayment was a relatively small fraction, fluctuating around 20 percent of wage arrears in the economy; privatized industry carried the dominant share of back wages. The regional distribution of industries, with the natural resource regions marching ahead of the declining defense and heavy industries, affected wage payment potential from industry to industry. Acute problems of converting military plants in the Eastern Siberian company towns, among them Armaz-16 and Krasnoyarsk-70, aggravated the economic plight of their highly paid technicians, who had few alternative job opportunities. By contrast Moscow, a bustling financial center with a construction and restructuring boom, stood apart from other regions in its wage payment potential. We therefore include in our models (of tables 5.5 and 5.6) a vector of industry variables, in addition to the per capita income and unemployment noted above, as explicit variables affecting regional wage arrears.

Finally, political conflicts influenced regional distribution of wage arrears. For example, the wage nonpayment problem in the Premorye region of the Far East was worsened by a prolonged power struggle between the regional governor, Nazdratenko, and the federal government, which accused the governor of misusing federal funds.

## Political Muscle Flexing: Moscow versus Premorye

The breakdown of the web of relations between the center, the regional electric power companies, and the suppliers of coal and fuel to the power companies erupted into threats, counterthreats, and intense negotiations between First Deputy Prime Minister Chubais and Governor Nazdratenko of the Far East Maritime Territory in September 1996.

Defense industry enterprises, military establishments, and other service units under federal jurisdiction, including the prosecutor's office and prisons, owed massive debts to Dalenergo, the maritime power supplier. As a result, Dalenergo owed payments to coal and oil suppliers who stopped shipping fuel to the company, threatening a power shutdown in the territory. The center charged that the governor's administration had diverted part of the federal funds allotted for payment to the local mineworkers to the power industry. It also objected to Dalenergo's policy, tolerated by the local authorities, of charging inordinately high energy rates, which averaged 390 rubles per kilowatt-hour as against the prevailing average rate for Russia of 189 rubles. As the 1997 winter approached, local industry groups sought support from Prime Minister Chernomyrdin for the territory's power and fuel complex while supporting the governor, who in turn organized a territory-wide referendum seeking public support. President Yeltsin ordered the governor to settle the crisis by September 15. The governor fired his deputy, released centrally allocated funds to pay the coal miners, and instructed the power companies to open bank accounts in which payments by their clients could be directly deposited. The middlemen were done away with. He then rushed to Moscow, seeking more cash from the center just as Dalenergo workers went on strike, allowing just the minimum flow of energy to debtor enterprises in the military-industry complex and social service agencies. There was chaos everywhere.[16]

Moscow's response to the deteriorating center-periphery fiscal balance—a result of continuing noncooperation by the regions spilling into outright confrontation, as in the Premorye region—varied from accommodation to sanctions. The former involved arrangements involving provision of financial substitutes in lieu of cash resources; the latter verged on punitive measures via a string of presidential decrees commanding the regional authorities to behave as law-abiding taxpayers and revenue spenders. Neither resulted in easing the fiscal and nonpayment crisis.

**Moscow Acts**

With a view to imposing sanctions on regional tax defaulters, the Russian president signed a decree authorizing the Russian government, from November 1, 1993 through January 31, 1994 , to suspend financial support of local enterprises and institutions, to withhold from the regions lucrative export quotas, to deny them deliveries of centrally financed items including essential imports, and to regulate the allocation of central credits to them. The decree empowered the Central Bank of Russia to deduct the amounts of regional debts from the regions' accounts with the bank.[17]

A presidential decree of April 1996 offered the regions federally owned blocks of shares to settle the center's debt to them. The regions objected because federal indebtedness to certain regions exceeded the total value of federally owned shares in local enterprises. Even if they managed to sell the shares according to the guidelines of the privatization plan, they were required to remit 70 percent of the proceeds to "higher authorities." The implementation of the presidential decree faced hurdles raised by the regions.[18]

According to the presidential decree of July 15, 1997, "On Measures to Pay Off Wage and Salary Arrears to Employees of Budget-Financed Organizations in the Members of the Russian Federation," the federal budget provided resources for half of the local budgets' debts to employees of schools and medical institutions. The Ministry of Finance reached agreements with eighty-six federation members on the proposed cash transfer, to be repaid by them out of their 1998 tax contributions, enabling them to clear their wage arrears. The regions were also required to disclose to the center their local revenue potential. Thus Dagestan was to cover 20 percent and Voronezh Province 50 percent of their payment obligations. St. Petersburg and Moscow, Samara and Perm' Provinces, Krasnodar Territory, and Yamal-Nenets Autonomous Region were expected to clear their arrears on their own. The regions would take the initiative for clearing the debts, and the center would monitor the use of the money for its intended purpose. The federal government intended raising the cash promised to the regions from the sale of its shares in the Tyumen' Petroleum Company and the Svyazinvest communications joint stock company, The treasury also expected to raise substantial revenue from taxing the sale of securities and foreign currency transactions.[19]

The impact of the joint scheme on clearing back payments to employees in the budget-funded organizations varied from region to region. Moscow and St. Petersburg oblasts, Yamal-Nenets Autonomous Region, and the Jewish Autonomous Province cleared their back pay to employees in the budget sector during the interval. Others, however, owed back wages ranging from two to four months. Eleven federation members, among them Irkutsk, Krasnoyarsk, Kemerovo and Sverdlovsk Provinces, the Republics of Sakha and Tatarstan, and Altai Territory owing almost half the debt, added 700 billion rubles to their obligations. The campaign to pay off debts was hampered because regions diverted funds to housing subsidies or to home heating in preparation for the winter months.[20]

These sporadic life-support measures at their best kept the comatose regional budgets alive without restoring them to a balanced routine marked by well-defined tax revenue norms, their sustained implementation, and the use of assigned cash from the center for easing the nonpayment problem in the budget sector. However, the back-and-forth bargaining ploys, which occasionally degenerated into hardball tactics that nevertheless failed to ease wage nonpayment, are difficult to track down precisely and incorporate in our empirical models. Therefore our models based on the RLMS data (of tables 5.4 and 5.5) incorporate time dummy variables, which help us analyze if the incidence and (constant ruble) amounts of wage arrears increased over time in relation to 1994 and diverged sharply from those in Moscow and St. Petersburg when the impact of other demographic and job characteristics of the respondents are controlled in the multivariate specifications.

**Empirical Patterns**

We begin with simple, descriptive measures of regional wage nonpayment in tables 5.1, 5.2, and 5.3, proceeding next to an analysis of their trend and divergence in relation to Moscow and St. Petersburg in table 5.4. We analyze the impact of the regional distribution of industries on regional wage nonpayment in table 5.5. Finally, we investigate in table 5.6 if regions "in distress" (measured by their per capita GDP, labor force unemployment, and industrial sector distribution) were liable to have higher wage arrears. The specifications in tables 5.2–5.5 use the RLMS individual respondent data from the 1994–98 rounds, whereas the model in table 5.6 employs aggregate Goskomstat data for 1995.

*Descriptive Patterns of Regional Wage Nonpayment*

In table 5.1, we report the real (1995 values) of outstanding wage debts per capita calculated as ratios of total overdue wages in each region divided by the region's population. Per capita wage arrears were lower in all years in the major urban centers of Moscow and St. Petersburg than in any other region, with Western Siberia and the Far East consistently exhibiting the highest levels of per capita wage nonpayment. Again, the accumulated outstanding real wage nonpayment had increased over time in each region, indicating that the growth in wage arrears occurred throughout the Russian Federation rather than in specific regions.

In tables 5.2 and 5.3, we use RLMS individual response data in contrast to the Goskomstat aggregate measures of per capita wage arrears across regions for assessing regional patterns of the percentage of the working population that faced some wage withholding; the average (per person) accumulated ruble value of outstanding wages calculated for respondents who faced some wage nonpayment; and the average number of months of outstanding wage debt derived by dividing the total outstanding ruble value of wage arrears by the contracted monthly wage.

Consistent with the per capita accumulated wage debt of table 5.1, we notice in table 5.2 that Moscow and St. Petersburg residents experienced lower levels of nonpayment in the three years in terms of all three measures. Again, the incidence of nonpayment in rows (1) of table 5.2 increased in all regions between 1994 and 1998, for example, from 37 percent of the working people in the Northern and North-Western region in 1994 to more than 70 percent in 1998. Moscow and St. Petersburg, relatively insulated from the crisis, were notable exceptions to this upward trend between 1994 and 1998.

Although the ruble value of outstanding (real) debt in rows (2) of table 5.2 increased for some regions between 1994 and 1996, it remained unchanged or declined for some between 1996 and 1998. This pattern, however, is misleading because real monthly wages reported in rows (1) of table 5.3 generally dropped between 1996 and 1998. Outstanding debt as a fraction of contracted monthly wages in rows (2) of table 5.3 increased significantly in all regions between 1996 and 1998.

Did these upward trends in incidence and nonpayment as a percentage of contracted monthly wages in the periphery imply increased inequality in contrast to the corresponding robust patterns of Moscow and St. Petersburg? Did regional inequality in wage nonpayment increase over time?

## Rising Regional Inequality in Patterns of Wage Nonpayment

In tables 5.2 and 5.3, the standard deviation across regions in the incidence, amounts, and accumulated debt as percentage of monthly contracted wages increased between 1994 and 1998, indicating growing regional inequality in the crisis.

Thus the standard deviation of nonpayment incidence in eight regions increased to 14 percent (to 19 percent for thirty-eight regions) from 7 percent (from 15 percent for thirty-eight regions) in the final rows of table 5.2. The spread in interregional distribution of accumulated amounts was up slightly when measured for eight regions, but had dipped when measured for thirty-eight regions in the final rows of table 5.2. The most dramatic increase in the spread of interregional distribution between 1994 and 1998 in the final rows of table 5.3 in accumulated wage debt as fraction of monthly contracted wages was fivefold (from 0.382 months to 1.967 months) using eight regional groups and more than fivefold (from 0.214 months to 1.183 months) using thirty-eight regions.

But how disparate did wage nonpayment in terms of the three measures become when we assess the dispersion in relation to the least affected Moscow-St. Petersburg urban centers? Did the initial 1994 differences in arrears between the twin cities, economically the most energetic focal points in the transition, and the rest of the country increase over time?[21]

### Dispersion in Patterns of Wage Arrears in Relation to Moscow and St. Petersburg

The estimates of table 5.4 measure the differences in 1998 over 1994 in the incidence, amounts, and months of wage arrears between these leading urban centers and the rest of the country. The eight regions are represented by dummy or indicator variables, with Moscow and St. Petersburg serving as the reference or comparison region. The parameter estimates in each row indicate the experience with arrears in a given region relative to Moscow and St. Petersburg in 1994, while the numbers in each succeeding row (reporting the interaction of the region dummy and a dummy for 1998) show the change between 1994 and 1998 in this effect; that is, the effect in 1998 is the sum of the region dummy and the corresponding interaction term. For example, based on the incidence regression,[22] the likelihood of experiencing wage arrears, 14.9 percent

**Table 5.4**
Growth in differences in arrears between center and periphery

|  | Incidence (5,639) | Amount (2,004) | Months of wages (2,004) |
|---|---|---|---|
| $d$1998 | 0.040 | −0.107 | 0.030 |
|  | (0.045) | (0.222) | (0.234) |
| Northern and North Western | 0.187* | 0.459* | 0.100 |
|  | (0.043) | (0.189) | (0.197) |
| Northern and North Western × $d$1998 | 0.293* | 0.258 | 7.101* |
|  | (0.060) | (0.271) | (2.648) |
| Central and Central Black-Earth | 0.064* | −0.256 | 0.048 |
|  | (0.035) | (0.170) | (0.200) |
| Central and Central Black-Earth × $d$1998 | 0.185* | 0.318 | 2.541* |
|  | (0.055) | (0.249) | (0.672) |
| Volga-Vyatski and Volga Basin | 0.117* | −0.429* | 0.006* |
|  | (0.035) | (0.160) | (0.193) |
| Volga-Vyatski and Volga Basin × $d$1998 | 0.285* | 0.614* | 1.989* |
|  | (0.052) | (0.241) | (0.482) |
| North Caucasus | 0.059 | −0.430* | −0.085 |
|  | (0.039) | (0.174) | (0.171) |
| North Caucasus × $d$1998 | 0.207* | 0.423 | 2.001* |
|  | (0.061) | (0.262) | (0.881) |
| Urals | 0.149* | 0.006* | −0.060* |
|  | (0.036) | (0.160) | (0.181) |
| Urals × $d$1998 | 0.217* | 0.331 | 2.747* |
|  | (0.055) | (0.243) | (0.765) |
| Western Siberia | 0.110* | 0.406* | 0.544* |
|  | (0.041) | (0.188) | (0.247) |
| Western Siberia × $d$1998 | 0.259* | 0.334 | 11.976 |
|  | (0.059) | (0.282) | (7.727) |
| Eastern Siberia and Far Eastern | 0.252* | 0.399* | −0.077 |
|  | (0.038) | (0.178) | (0.174) |
| Eastern Siberia and Far Eastern × $d$1998 | 0.096 | 0.149 | 3.437* |
|  | (0.063) | (0.270) | (0.804) |
| $R^2$ | 0.068 | 0.085 | 0.022 |

*Source:* RLMS.
*Note:* Parameter estimates are reported with robust standard errors in parentheses. Maximum likelihood probit estimates are reported for the incidence regressions in the first column; regressions in the last two column are estimated by OLS for the sample of people who are owed wages. The analysis in this table is restricted to the years 1994 and 1998. Sample sizes are listed in parentheses under column headings.
\* Indicates that the estimate is significant at 10 percent or better. Each region is represented by a dummy variable (the reference category is the Moscow and St. Petersburg region). The variable $d$1998 is a dummy equal to 0 for 1994 and equal to 1 for 1998.

higher in the Urals than in Moscow and St. Petersburg in 1994, shot up to 36.6 percent (.149 + .217) by 1998. The significantly positive interaction effects in the incidence regression for the regions indicate that the incidence of arrears increased relative to those in Moscow and St. Petersburg between 1994 and 1998 in all regions. In other words, not only did the prevalence of wage arrears increase in all regions (as seen in table 5.2), but the experience of wage nonpayment became more widespread among the working population in other regions of the country relative to Moscow and St. Petersburg.

By contrast, the insignificance of the interaction effects in column (2) of the regression estimates of table 5.4 suggests that average (per person) outstanding wage debt in each region was unchanged relative to that in Moscow and St. Petersburg between 1994 and 1998. This outcome may be the result of regional differences in average wage rates.

Finally, the positive coefficient estimates of the majority of interaction terms in column (3) of the regression results suggest that the amount of withheld wages, calculated as a percentage of the monthly wage, increased in the regions (with the exception of Western Siberia) relative to Moscow and St. Petersburg between 1994 and 1998.[23]

How did the distribution of industries in the regions account for regional differences in arrears?

## Wage Arrears and Regional Distribution of Industries

We approximate the regional importance of industries in the regions on the basis of the employment pattern of the RLMS sample in each region. In other words, we locate the fraction of respondents in a region employed in a given industry from the RLMS regional sample.

Keeping in mind the limitation that the regional employment pattern by industry can only partially represent the importance of an industry in a region, we assess the link between regional distribution of industry and wage arrears in two steps. We regress incidence of nonpayment and amounts of wage debt by turn, initially on the region and year dummies in regressions (1) in panel (a) of table 5.5. Next, we introduce a vector of twenty industry dummies in regressions (2) and assess the effect of these industry employment variables on the size and significance of the regional effects on nonpayment. The inclusion of the industry of employment in regression (2) generally reduces the size of the regional coefficients in the incidence and in the amount regressions.

**Table 5.5**
Effect of industry of employment on regional differences in wage arrears

| | Panel (a) | | | |
|---|---|---|---|---|
| | Incidence (9,862) | | Amount (3,360) | |
| | (1) | (2) | (1) | (2) |
| Northern and North Western | 0.310* | 0.293* | 0.731* | 0.558* |
| | (0.027) | (0.029) | (0.134) | (0.132) |
| Central and Central Black-Earth | 0.125* | 0.094* | 0.007* | −0.038 |
| | (0.024) | (0.025) | (0.120) | (0.117) |
| Volga-Vyatski and Volga Basin | 0.230* | 0.203* | 0.014* | 0.0001* |
| | (0.024) | (0.025) | (0.120) | (0.118) |
| North Caucasus | 0.151* | 0.119* | −0.062 | −0.050 |
| | (0.028) | (0.028) | (0.132) | (0.129) |
| Urals | 0.227* | 0.196* | 0.276* | 0.229* |
| | (0.024) | (0.025) | (0.119) | (0.117) |
| Western Siberia | 0.214* | 0.193* | 0.561* | 0.524* |
| | (0.028) | (0.029) | (0.129) | (0.129) |
| Eastern Siberia and Far Eastern | 0.286* | 0.263* | 0.614* | 0.543* |
| | (0.027) | (0.028) | (0.134) | (0.130) |
| Joint test | 188.67* | 166.36* | 23.02* | 19.86* |

| | Panel (b) | | | |
|---|---|---|---|---|
| | Without control variables | | With control variables | |
| | (1) | (2) | (1) | (2) |
| Incidence | 0.2750 | 0.5010 | 0.5626 | 0.6004 |
| Amount | 0.5010 | 0.5326 | 0.5128 | 0.5809 |

*Source:* RLMS.
*Note:* See note to table 5.4. In panel (a), for each of the two dependent variables, regression (1) only includes three-year dummies and the listed region dummies; regression (2) additionally includes twenty industry dummies. The row "joint test" reports the test statistic for a test of the joint significance of the region dummies. Sample sizes are listed in parentheses under column headings. Panel (b) lists adjusted $R^2$ values: The entry in column (1) does not control for industry; the entry in (2) includes industry variables. The "without control variables" column only includes year dummies, while the "with control variables" column additionally includes wages, education, age, gender, and occupation.

In other words, differences in the incidence and magnitude of wage arrears between Moscow and St. Petersburg and the other regions of the country were partly due to regional patterns of employment by industry. The fact that the Urals, Western Siberia, and Eastern Siberia and the Far Eastern Region employed workers in natural resource industries rather than in agriculture or textiles contributed to a slight easing in their wage nonpayment incidence and amounts. We note, however, that the reductions in the coefficients are not large, so that the regional distribution of industry does not go very far in accounting for the regional distribution of arrears.[24]

As a further check for assessing the impact of the regional distribution of industry on regional variation in the incidence and amounts of nonpayment across regions, we sequentially measure the value of $R$-square by separately regressing the average incidence of wage nonpayment and the amount of arrears across thirty-eight regions initially on the three-year dummies and then add a series of twenty region-specific industry employment pattern variables—that is, each industry variable gives the percentage of wage earners in the region who are employed in that particular industry. We next perform the same exercise, but add our control variables of regional age, regional wages, regional education level, the percentage of working women in the region, and regional employment by occupation. These control variables are averaged from RLMS data across thirty-eight regions.

In panel (b) of table 5.5, the simple regression of nonpayment incidence (the dependent variable is the percentage of wage earners in each region who are owed wages) on the three-year dummies in the first row of column (1) yields an $R$-square of 0.2750, suggesting that about 28 percent of the variation in the incidence across regions is accounted for by simple year effects. When we add the series of twenty employment by industry measures in the regression, the $R$-square increases to 0.5010: Regional industry employment patterns explain an additional 22 percent of the total variation in interregional incidence of wage nonpayment. With regard to the interregional differences in the amount of wage debt, the simple regression with the three-year dummies accounts for 50 percent of the interregional variation (reported in the last row of panel (b)), increasing to 53 percent when industry variables are included.

The industry employment patterns in columns (2), however, may include the influence of many factors, such as occupation of employment, education level, the age and contracted wage of respondents, and the percentage of working women, which may be correlated with industry of employment. When we include these control variables in the estimation but exclude the regional industry employment shares, the regressions in the right panel column (1) explain 56 percent of the interregional variation in the incidence of arrears and 51 percent of the interregional variation in the amounts of nonpayment When we throw in these excluded employment shares by industry in the regression in the right panel column (2), the $R$-squares rise from 56 to 60 percent in the incidence exercise and from 51 percent to 58 percent in the outstanding arrears exercise.

These summary $R$-square measures in the full-blown multivariate specifications of the right panel column (2) in panel (b) suggest that regional distribution of industry, approximated by industry of employment of our sampled RLMS respondents, did not substantially influence regional wage withholding patterns of incidence and amounts withheld.

We extend the above analysis in two directions: We employ Goskomstat data on arrears in sixty-three regions in 1995 (the latest year available), covering the employed workers. Second, we introduce regional per capita income and unemployment rate (representing its economic health), regional industrial sector of importance, and average regional wage as explanatory variables. Did regional differences in wage arrears depend on variations in the regions' economic well-being, in industrial sector importance, and in average wage level?

## Interregional Differences in Wage Arrears and Regional Economic Health

In table 5.6, we use Russia's sixty-three regions as units of our analysis for identifying the factors that contributed to interregional wage non-payment differences. We regress the ruble value of outstanding wage arrears per capita[25] in each region on regional per capita income and unemployment rate, regional presence of industry measured as the percentage of industrial output produced by each of the nine industrial sectors in the region, and the median wage in each region. Outstanding arrears, ceteris paribus, will tend to be higher in regions with higher wages.[26]

The results suggest that arrears tended to be higher in regions with weaker economic performance. The positive estimates of row (1), linking higher average arrears per employed person with a higher unemployment rate, are consistent with the notion that arrears tended to be higher when workers had weaker employment options with other

**Table 5.6**
Explaining inter-regional wage arrears (Goskomstat 1995)

|                          | (1)       | (2)       |
| ------------------------ | --------- | --------- |
| Unemployment rate        | 6.2985    | 7.0485    |
|                          | (2.176)   | (2.1053)  |
| GDP per capita × 1,000   | −0.1285   | −0.1444   |
|                          | (0.043)   | (0.049)   |
| ln (median wage)         | 2.3595    | 1.4893    |
|                          | (0.3631)  | (0.5253)  |
| Industry variables (9)   | No        | Yes       |
| Adjusted $R^2$           | 0.6078    | 0.6849    |

*Sources:* Regional per capita GDP, employment, and population are from *Regioni Rossii*, Moscow: Goskomstat Rossii, vols. 1, 2, 1997. Overdue wages (monthly) are from *Sotsial'no-ekonomicheskoye polozheniye Rossii*, published by Goskomstat. Unpaid wages per employed worker for selected regions are calculated from:1995 employed population by region, published in *Trud i Zanyatost' v Rossii*, 1996, Goskomstat, Moscow 1997. Average wages (including social payments) by region, December 1996, and total wage indebtedness of enterprises and organizations by region, January 1997, are published in *Sotsial'no-ekonomicheskoye polozheniye Rossii*, 1, 1997, Goskomstat, Moscow.
*Note:* Parameter estimates are reported with standard errors in parentheses. The regressions are estimated by OLS. The analysis is based on 63 regions ($n = 63$). All estimates are significant at 1 percent. The vector of nine industry variables in specification (2) is jointly significant at 2 percent.

potential employers.[27] In other words, managers were more likely to withhold wages when the likelihood of workers leaving for other firms was reduced.[28] In row (2), regions with stronger general economic performance (controlling for tightness in the labor market), measured by GDP per capita, tended to have lower average outstanding arrears. Finally, we include a vector of nine industry variables in specification (2), each measuring the weight of an industrial sector in the region, to net out the impact on regional wage arrears arising from the presence and importance of specific industrial sectors. We find that the positive effect of the regional unemployment rate and the negative effect of regional GDP per capita on wage arrears remain significant. At the same time, the inclusion of the vector of industry dummies increases the explanatory power of the regression from 61 percent to 69 percent. In other words, 69 percent of the regional distribution of arrears can be accounted for by regional differences in unemployment rates, GDP per capita, average regional wages, and regional variations in industrial sector importance.[29]

## Conclusions

Failing to include critical qualitative features relevant to the issue of regional diversity of wage arrears, among them the wide variations in the ability and willingness of regional authorities and industry managers to ease the nonpayment crisis, we employ economic variables for explaining the varying regional pattern of wage arrears. Despite the limitation, our empirical results suggest important conclusions.

• Wage nonpayment afflicted all regions of the Russian Federation and, with the exception of the bustling urban centers of Moscow and St. Petersburg, the crisis had grown worse over the years of the transition, leading up to 1998.

• Between 1994 and 1998, regional dispersion in the incidence of wage withholding and in the outstanding amounts withheld as fractions of contracted monthly wages had increased.

• Regional variation in the importance of industries, measured in terms of the regional share of industry of employment, contributed only marginally to the interregional variations in the incidence and amounts of wage nonpayment.

• Finally, the economic viability of a region measured in terms of its per capita GDP, unemployment rate, and the median wage influenced variations in per capita regional wage arrears. Lower per capita GDP resulted in higher per capita wage arrears; higher unemployment rate implied higher amounts withheld. Higher median wage rate (again ceteris paribus) signaled higher nonpayment. Overall, workers in the "distressed" regions were more likely to experience wage nonpayment.

We turn now from the regional patterns of wage arrears to an analysis of the critical situation afflicting three strategic groups of the economy, military personnel, pensioners, and coalminers, beginning with a discussion of the sharp budget cutbacks that contributed to the disintegration of the Russian army.

# The Military: Budget Cutbacks and Disintegration

Beginning in early 1992, the Russian military faced sharp and sustained cutbacks from the federal budget that affected state orders of military hardware, deprived the military-industrial complex of traditional budgetary support, reduced the armed forces to a state of penury, and forced a drastic review of Russia's defense priorities. Thus wage nonpayment to servicemen and -women was only part of a bigger problem that devastated the military. We deal with these wide-ranging issues from the perspective of their impact on the financial deprivation that afflicted the livelihood and living conditions of military employees.

Monthly information on nonpayment to Russian service personnel, a politically volatile issue, is not available. During the six years beginning 1992, the Russian military was subjected to sweeping policy changes and restructuring not witnessed in any other sector including manufacturing and agriculture. In terms of manpower cutbacks, the chaotic process in the military outstripped the downsizing in the coal industry (analyzed in chapter 8). This chapter focuses on the factors leading to the military's unparalleled economic and social impoverishment, of which wage nonpayment was a significant but by no means a dominating part.

Nineteen ninety-two marked a sharp departure from four perspectives relevant for our analysis in the traditional decision making that had shaped the unique position of the military in Soviet days.

## Policy Changes

### Loss of Status

First, the military lost its special status of the Soviet days.

The Soviet military took orders from the Communist Party of the Soviet Union, but it was the party's favorite candidate for hefty budgetary appropriations for purchases of hardware (via defense orders from the military industry complex), salaries, and maintenance of military installations followed by their guaranteed and timely allocations from the budget.

Beginning in 1992, the Ministry of Defense was increasingly reduced to the status of a client of the Ministries of Finance and Economics, which actively participated in working up the overall military budget and its components. At the same time, the industrial enterprises, research institutes, and design bureaus became increasingly autonomous. Gone were the state orders to be automatically fulfilled by the military-industrial complex at the command of the Ministry of Defense. Instead, the relations between the ministry and the defense enterprises were put on a contractual basis even as budget capping operated.

### New Tensions amid Financial Cutbacks

Second, budget slashing created tensions at various levels of the military and the defense industry complex. Cutbacks in the overall military budget required a shift from equipment purchases and maintenance of military installations on the one hand to paying the officers and soldiers and meeting their social needs on the other. By 1993, the 1980s' ratio of 3:2 between these two components had turned to 1:3, substantially favoring fulfilling the military's social needs.[1]

Another source of tension was budgetary allocations for the overall military budget (as defined above) and support for the defense industry complex. In principle, the conversion of Soviet-era military industry to civilian production and exports was to take place increasingly without budgetary support. In practice, the defense industry, along with coal and agriculture, not only remained a drain on the budget but also maintained its mobilization capacity, resisting conversion at least untilthe end of 1993. The complex managed to stay afloat by extracting loans and subsidies from the government without any restructuring and by exporting part of its gigantic stockpiles of metals and raw materials.

### Lagging Political Support

Third, political support for a substantial military budget and defense industry upkeep via budgetary allocation was eroding. Civilian control was calculated to rein in military spending as military reform proceeded and defense industry enterprises were restructured. Again, the military, unlike the agrarians, lacked clout in the government and the Duma. In the 1994 budget debates, a large chunk of the left opposition and the centrists, among them the Agrarians, Women of Russia, the Party of Russian Unity and Accord, and the Democratic Party of Russia voted against higher outlays for the military budget and defense industry support. The generals, who stood by the president and the prime minister during the bloody dissolution of the parliament in October 1993, lost out to the agricultural lobby led by Deputy Prime Minister Zaveryukha.[2]

Aggregate military disbursements had declined from 7.6 percent of GDP in 1990 (for the Soviet Union) to 3.5 percent in 1998, to a planned 2.4 percent in 1999.[3] The steady cutbacks reflected the success of the finance ministry in staving off pressures from the defense ministry. However, the planned allocations were expected to be raised to 3.5 percent in the 2000 federal budget, Prime Minister Sergei Stepashin having asked Finance Minister Mikhail Kasyanov to be "patriotic" in working up the numbers.[4] The war in Kosovo had evidently raised concerns about Russia's national security and lifted the mood of the military establishment. The substantial budget outlays for financing the Chechen war operation in the final quarter of 1999 not only outstripped the initial budget allocations for the military but also led to a postponement of the second installment of IMF credits of $4.5 billion, adding to financial hardships.

The relative decline of military spending also resulted from a substantial disparity between planned and actual disbursements, the latter trailing behind the former by a substantial margin. According to a defense ministry complaint, it had been underpaid by 90 billion (new) rubles in 1998 prices.[5] The annual defense budget around that time was close to 70 billion rubles.[6] Finally, the downsizing of the Soviet army of 4 million was a fait accompli, the result of a consensus to convert it into a lean, professional fighting force.

### Downsizing the Army

Contractual military service started functioning in 1993. Soon thereafter the army faced a shortage of manpower: 70,000 professional recruits served in the army as of May 7, fewer than the projected 110,000; however, the army was set to releasing 580,000 men, who had served from eighteen months to two years, into reserves, creating a shortage of men to guard weapons and ammunitions stockpiles, military equipment, arms depots, and air defense missile sites. At the same time, 79,000 servicemen quit the army in 1992 and more than 270,000 planned to leave in 1993, half of them without pensions. Understandably, officers did not wish to replace soldiers as guards and boiler stokers. In view of the impending shortage, the Ministry of Defense requested a cancellation of draft deferment for youngsters at vocational schools with high school diplomas.[7]

During 1993 and 1994, the armed forces were cut back by 700,000, bringing the army's size to 2,002,000 men. It had 2,070 generals. In early 1999, it was down to 1.2 million men.[8] The army preferred transferring an officer to the reserve force rather than discharging him because, on being discharged, an officer had to be provided with housing and severance pay. Hasty decision making and massive cash shortage reduced the process of downsizing and professionalizing the army to chaos.

### The Consequences of Budget Cutbacks

Budget slashing to military personnel aggravated nonpayment, which rose precipitously. Year after year the military was hit with arbitrary budget cutbacks, with actual funding falling short of appropriations. Increasingly they failed to cover the cost of housing for families of servicemen discharged from the military, wage arrears of servicemen and employees of the defense enterprises, and the mounting bills for payment of electricity, fuel, materials, and components. As much as 40 percent of the annual defense appropriations were in the form of government indebtedness to the Ministry of Defense that was carried over from one year to the next. With such funding practices, the ministry was headed toward digging into food and clothing allocations for personnel and soldiers that were also depleted. If an emergency were to arise, the first-line reserves would be called upon to march in defense of the fatherland in bedroom slippers. As for the defense industry, it was in appalling shape, battling arrears for payments of military hardware, weapons, and R&D supplied by military enterprises.

The fighting men were also deprived of essential food rations. The military needed 8.2 billion rubles (new) for food, but 6 billion were allocated in the 1998 budget. The army and navy had stopped receiving food supplies July 1998 because the defense ministry had failed to pay for earlier shipments. Accumulated arrears to officers for their allowances stretched over twenty months.[9]

Actual outlays did not reach their destination because of misappropriation. Funds transferred from the federal budget to military districts (*voennye okrugi*) for salaries and maintenance of servicemen began charting mysterious trajectories from mid-1992.

## Misuse of Funds

Federal funds targeted for servicemen's pay and provisions could not be located for periods varying from five to eighteen months after they had been transferred from Moscow. The generals, responsible for timely payments to the districts, blamed the serpentine network of the Central Bank of Russia for the delay. The central bank, with its numerous subdivisions, was indeed a clumsy organization. But military intelligence officers, who were usually able to locate lost shipments in ten to twelve days, stood aside as the money was misused en route. In late December 1992, an officer from the Central Military Inspectorate evidently investigated a case in which the temporarily "lost" cash transfer amounted to a monthly wage fund for an entire district (Baranets, 1998, p. 334). The situation deteriorated quickly: Cash transfers turned out to be so irregular in 1994–96, that even officers based in Moscow headquarters encountered delays in wage payments. Such delays became a part of everyday life in faraway military districts.

Misappropriation of funds had reached other areas of the military as well. In the aftermath of the breakup of the Soviet Union in 1991, senior officers became shopkeepers, selling army property for their enrichment. Army and navy assets, marked for sale at the start of 1993 in the amount of 200 trillion rubles, were almost four times Russia's annual military budget. By the end of 1995, almost 60 trillion rubles had disappeared (Baranets 1998, p. 313). The endemic corruption of the Soviet army of the 1970s and 1980s paled in comparison with such staggering embezzlement.

Particularly detrimental to the officers' morale was the widespread misappropriation of housing construction funds. According to presidential decrees and government resolutions, proceeds from the sale of assets belonging to the Soviet army in the (former) German Democratic Republic were to be used for housing construction to settle families of returning officers. Asset sales sizzled but the coffers of the housing fund remained meager. Among the most publicized cases of misappropriated cash was the purchase of two Mercedes-500s, one of which found its way into the garage of a former defense minister, Pavel Grachev, nicknamed "Mercedes Pasha" by Russia's vibrant press. The two luxury automobiles were worth a new block of apartments for some of Russia's 100,000 homeless officers. Following the court's decision in a legal case that ensued over the issue, the Ministry of Defense reimbursed the housing fund by wiring the cash from its regular budget (Baranets, 1998, p. 314). Yet the Russian army's housing problem went beyond this particular episode, and indeed overshadowed the wage nonpayment issue.

## The Army's Housing Problem

The Soviet military attracted highly qualified young men to its officer cadres because it offered them higher wages and better pensions than they would find in the civilian sector. It also promised them housing. But serious problems accumulated. City apartments did not coordinate with the assignment of an officer-recruit to a distant garrison. Temporary barracks were abysmal: Nearly a fourth of military school graduates, having failed to endure the hardships of homelessness, terminated their contracts. The army not only lost personnel but also failed to retrieve the cost of its training. In mid-1999, the rate of departure was one–third of able-bodied servicemen.[10] At the same time, new officer-recruits needed housing. The number of homeless officers in the army and navy totaled 93,000 in 1999.[11]

The government resorted to two devices for combating the housing shortage: It issued housing certificates to officers who were released from duty that could be converted into living quarters; and it sought help from Russia's far-flung provinces to aid the center in easing the severity of living accommodations.

### Housing Certificates

These certificates met the same fate as similar schemes of converting paper promises into tangible assets. The issue of certificates needed to be backed by budgetary appropriations that the finance ministry was unwilling to guarantee. Roman Popkovich, chairman of the Duma Defense Committee, commented on the evasiveness of the finance ministry in the proposed 1999 budget by noting the absence of the president's housing certificate program in the ministry budget proposals: "There was a brief sentence to the effect that housing certificate was a way of addressing the housing problem of retired servicemen." The Duma committee proposed setting aside 4.5 billion (new) rubles for financing the housing certificate program out of a proposed defense budget of 107 billion rubles.[12]

The military's record of delivering promised housing to retired army officers based on certificates was bleak, leaving little hope for its fulfillment in the future. Stavropol' territory was promised 612 certificates in 1998, of which the Ministry of Finance distributed 45. But only 14 officers with these certificates managed to get accommodation. Ninety-seven certificates out of the 137 handed out by the Ministry of Defense were exchanged for apartments. Over 100,000 retired officers of the Russian armed forces spent 70 percent of their paltry pensions on accommodation, awaiting their turn for government allocation. The law specified a waiting period of three months. In fact, it was no less than six years.[13]

## Regional Role

The concrete support from the regions was insignificant. Defense Minister Sergeyev mentioned receipt of 700 apartments from the Orenberg municipality in Trans-Volga Military District. Housing for officers was allocated by regional authorities in Samara, Bashkortostan, Tatarstan, Chuvashia, and Mordoviya regions. These agreements involved offsetting their tax liabilities to the federal budget in exchange for housing.

## The Fait Accompli and Its Acceptance

Nobody protested the swift economic blow to the army and to the defense industry that began in 1992, or at least not enough to reverse or slow the process. Analysts in the Academy of Sciences, who kept quiet, were soon forced to accept budget cutbacks. The trade unions were also silent. Perhaps the military's traditional submission to decisions from above stifled dissent. Wages in the military-industrial complex declined relative to those in industry. Engineers, scientists, and technicians, men and women, were put on forced leave. Soldiers were denied wages. Nurseries, clinics, hospitals, and schools were dumped from the budgets of defense enterprises.[14]

The unrest among the defense industry workers in the closed cities of Arzamas-16, Chelyabinsk-45, Krasnoyarsk-80, and others where nuclear warheads were serviced and rockets, cannons, tanks, and ships were made did not explode although their wages (half the average in machine building) were withheld and the equipment they produced and the services they provided were acquired at old rates despite substantial cost increases.[15]

## Scattered Protests

In mid-1993, scientists, design engineers, and technicians at the nuclear weapons facilities at Arzamas-16 protested against their low pay and inadequate safety. Surviving on the potato patches provided by the company, they worried about the government's economizing on nuclear reactor safety, which could in their view lead to another Chernobyl. On June 9, 1994, 374,000 defense industry workers of 206 enterprises in thirty-seven regions of Russia suspended civilian goods production, turned on the plants' sirens, and organized street rallies.[16] Military construction workers of the Northern Fleet in the northern city of Murmansk went on strike around the same time because they had not been paid fully since the beginning of the year. The All-Russia Officers' Assembly, a collection of low-ranking officers of the army, was banned by the Ministry of Defense, preventing it from becoming a political force in the army.

### Futile Resettlement Plans

Schemes devised by the Ministry of Defense to help resettle servicemen by providing them with housing and plots of land were largely ignored by local administrations. Former Defense Minister Grachev's plan to settle discharged servicemen as private farmers on land bought from the agriculture ministry in exchange for surplus army property was of little avail. Funds allocated from the federal budget for constructing servicemen's housing was diverted by local administrations to other uses. The Ministry of Defense sold off military facilities or turned them over to local administrations instead of handing them over to army personnel for starting small-scale enterprises.

In 1997, the defense ministry received just enough cash (55.6 percent of the budget appropriations) to cover civilian employees' salaries and servicemen's pay. The budget did not provide for training exercises, new equipment purchases, military hardware upgrading, and R&D. Only a third of officers subjected to forced retirement via personnel cutback were to receive housing.[17] By the fall of 1997, pay arrears to servicemen were largely cleared, with cash received from the sale of state stock in the communications conglomerate, Svyazinvest. Soon thereafter they started accumulating once again. The state's indebtedness to the armed forces stood at a whopping 70 billion (new) rubles on November 30, 1998, equaling the annual defense budget. Arrears to the servicemen, three months behind schedule, totaled 14 billion rubles.[18]

## Conclusions

In this chapter, we addressed the issue of wage arrears to the defense industry workforce and army personnel in the context of the near collapse of a formidable military industry and a fighting force denied financial resources and lacking active political support. The Russian military, effectively brought under civilian (from Communist Party) control, subjected to severe financial and personnel cutbacks, lacking leadership and political clout, devoid of organizational muscle, and demoralized and disintegrating, could not mount a counteroffensive. Wage denial to army personnel was part of a much bigger problem of the swift cutback in the armed forces within a half-decade, imposing severe hardships of homelessness, joblessness, and pension denial to the vast majority of the nearly 2 million laid off.

In contrast to the armed forces, Russia's 37 million pensioners exercised political clout. Plans to reform the pay-as-you-go pension arrangements, which were burdened by repeated pension hikes by the president and the parliamentarians, were postponed in 1998. The factors influencing the denial of pension benefits to retirees and the resulting consequences on their welfare form the subject matter of the next chapter.

# Pension Arrears, Poverty, and Populist Politics

Russia's pension system, inherited from the Soviet days, guaranteed pensions to retirees from a pension fund to which they contributed very little. Over time, the fund became increasingly short of cash as enterprises cut back their contributions and the government diverted it for other uses. A multilayered structure, the system tended to be misused at various collection and distribution points.

At the same time, Russia's 37 million pensioners, one-third of its electorate—a group of committed and united pro-Communist voters—constituted a powerful lobby out-competing the defense and coal industries and the military in political clout. The president and the Duma raced each other in giving retirees minimum pension hikes and cost-of-living indexation without providing for the necessary cash.

Despite the populist thrusts, pensioners were an impoverished lot: Average monthly pensions kept ahead of the minimum wage, but they trailed behind the official subsistence level. Again, pension nonpayment pushed pensioners further below the poverty line. Government proposals to convert the current arrangements to an individual-saving-based system faced strong opposition from the lawmakers and the public, and was shelved in 1998.

Clearly, although wage arrears resulted from employers (including the state) reneging on contracts for current pay, pension arrears arose from the state reneging on contracts for deferred (retirement) pay. Both were forms of "work without pay": wage arrears were imposed on the currently employed, whereas pension arrears were forced (mostly) on the formerly employed, implying "work without deferred pay."

In this chapter, we analyze the factors contributing to the escalating demands on the Russian Pension Fund's depleting resources; the aborted plan to convert the pay-as-you-go system to a saving-based arrangement; the deterioration of the material condition of pensioners in relation to the official subsistence level (assuming that pensions were paid); and finally, the impoverishment of retirees who were denied pensions, the withholding pushing them into poverty according to the results we derive from the RLMS data set.

## Current Arrangements

The Russian Pension Fund, created in 1992, required each enterprise (and organization) to contribute to the fund, the contribution being 28 percent of the recorded payroll (wages and salaries) for the enterprises and 1 percent for the employees from their earnings. The system, which entitled retirees to an array of pension benefits without their paying a premium, was based on a "money-is-no-problem" approach. One million citizens joined the ranks of pensioners annually in the 1990s. The retirement ages for men at sixty years and for women at fifty-five years were set by a federal law in 1990, a change in the law requiring the consent of the Duma. In principle, the Pension Fund was a nonbudget fund of about 140 trillion rubles annually—approximately one-third of the budgetary revenues—of which enterprise contributions formed the lion's share, the remaining 3 to 5 percent flowing from the federal treasury.

Russia did not have a law on pensions until members of the Stability Group of the Duma deputies proposed a draft law in the summer of 1995 requiring the creation of an integrated federal pension system independent of the government and having the same status as the Central Bank of Russia. It stipulated that the entire process, from the collection of cash to payment to pensioners, be vested in a single authority, the Pension Fund. It proposed shifting the jurisdiction of the fund to the Duma. The government, however, did not want to lose management of an annual flow of 137 trillion rubles, which equaled the size of the federal budget deficit. The battles over controlling the fund were vigorous.[1]

## Falling Inflows and Rising Claims

The inflows into the fund steadily declined and the claims on its dwindling resources escalated over time. We analyze the reasons for the declining inflows into the fund, turning next to the question of galloping claims.

*Declining Contributions*

According to the law, enterprise pension contributions to the Pension Fund were based on wages paid out to employees. The contributions declined over time because the number of wage earners, 75.8 million in 1991, dropped to 68.5 million in 1995. Wages and salaries, 80 to 90 percent of income in 1992, were down to 47 percent by 1994. The fund was short of cash because employers evaded wage-linked contributions to the fund by rewarding their employees indirectly via food subsidies, travel money, valuable gifts, and bonuses (all unrecorded) in lieu of wages. Finally, few enterprises kept their wage fund in bank accounts, from which pension fund contributions would flow, preferring to pay workers in off-the-books cash.[2]

The Orenburg Construction Machinery Plant, for example, had recorded no wage payments to its workforce in 1995, thus completely avoiding pension contributions. The major defaulters to the fund were the fuel and power sector (owing 1.6 trillion rubles), the defense and coal industries (each owing more than 1 trillion rubles), machine building (with a debt of 900 billion rubles), and agriculture (owing nearly 1 trillion rubles).[3]

Thus the allotment-type pension system carried over from the socialist days encouraged enterprise directors to manipulate their wage payment and accounting practices. Pension arrears therefore resulted partly from wage arrears, because nonpayment of wages resulted in lower pension fund allocations by enterprises. The tying of pension payment obligations to the recorded wage bill provided an unintended incentive to managers to withhold wages, thereby justifying reduced pension contributions. Although the resolution of the wage arrears crisis would ease pension payment to retirees, pension arrears arose also from the diversion of the funding to other uses by the federal and regional governments and from a highly defective system riddled with shortcomings.

*Government Poaching of the Fund*

The government dipped into the fund to finance nonpension commitments such as support to veterans of the Great Patriotic War, to people disabled from childhood, and to victims of Chernobyl. One-fourth of all pensions went to military retirees, the disabled, and others in the "nonproductive" sphere. The government was supposed to reimburse the Pension Fund from the budget for these outlays, an obligation it did not fulfill on schedule in the brief history of the fund. It owed the Pension Fund 7.5 trillion rubles for 1996 alone, its total debt since 1992 standing at 12.5 trillion rubles.[4]

### Pension Hikes and Populist Politics

While the declining resources of the Pension Fund were diverted by the government to nonpension payments, the repeated hikes of pension benefits to retirees strained the fund as well. The Duma's quarterly indexation of pensions to cost of living, although backed by law, damaged the fund's solvency. Pension payment arrears accumulated as a result of repeated hikes awarded, in particular, on the eve of the (December 1995) parliamentary and the (June 1996) presidential elections. The president, the government, and the legislators, prisoners of their populist urges, granted pension hikes that busted the Pension Fund without ensuring the source of the funding.

The Duma doubled pensions to disabled veterans of the Great Patriotic War in 1995 without appropriating the required cash. It raised pension rates in May and June 1995, by 27 and 20 percents, followed by a raise in August, and a 10 percent hike on November 1. Thus, violating a law that allowed quarterly increases, it raised pensions four times in six months without the cash provision. Lawmakers were joined in the populist race by several department and ministry heads.[5]

Yet another pension hike from the Duma came in December 1996: Although the deputies knew that the federal budget owed the Pension Fund 14.2 trillion rubles, they increased pensions by 10 percent as of December 1, 1996. The president's decisions on the 50th anniversary of victory in World War II and during the presidential campaign of spring 1996 further sapped the fund's finances. The repeated hikes went into force because no one was ready to argue that pension benefits should be held back. By the end of 1996, pensions consumed 6 percent of the shriveled GDP.

### Multilayer Arrangement Leading to Leakage and Misuse

The Russian pension system, being a multilevel arrangement, was prone to leakage and misuse at various collection and distribution points, leading to dwindling resources and pension nonpayment. The fund, with an annual flow of 140 trillion rubles, was substantial, and the temptation to divert and misuse the cash was immense because the collection and distribution involved layers of agencies. Also, the Ministry of Finance had stopped monitoring the fund's activities in 1990.

Initially the center contributed 86 percent of the targeted amounts in the fund. But regions collected less and less: In 1994, subsidized regions received a transfer of 13 percent of their targeted payment to retirees from the center; by September 1995, the share of subsidies had swelled to 23 percent.[6]

Again, the cash allocated from the fund to its regional divisions, occasionally on the basis of inflated claims, traveled across half a dozen departments from the initial agency to the retiree. Regional social security departments padded their claims. A 1995 audit revealed that they milked the system of 103 billion rubles in 1994. The post offices, the next link in the chain, used the pension funds allocated to them to pay wages to their staff and buy furniture. These abuses increased over time.[7] Not to be left out of the opportunity for robbing the fund, pensioners demanded higher pensions on the basis of fictitious documents claiming higher retirement wages and longer job tenure.[8]

A significant burden on the fund's limited resources arose from the legitimate claims of working pensioners.

## The Problem of Working Pensioners

At a press conference on January 31, 1997, Vasily Barchuk, the chairman of the Pension Fund, called for a trimming of the pension benefits of 8 million *working* pensioners (out of a total of 37 million), who retired from jobs with a pension age of forty or forty-five. His suggestion evoked a storm of protests and a public dressing down by Boris Yeltsin. The beneficiaries—servicemen, miners, steelworkers, and oilmen, who retired before the normal retirement age of fifty-five for women and sixty for men—cost the Pension Fund more than 30 trillion rubles, almost a fifth of its annual budget.[9]

After a public reprimand by the president, the Ministry of Labor postponed pension reform until the end of 1997, the government entrusted pension policy adjustment to the Duma's Committee on Labor and Social Policy, and Yury Lyublin, the Deputy Minister of Labor and Social Development, announced that Barchuk's suggestion was his personal opinion.

He nevertheless warned that the Pension Fund was doomed to get less than the required inflows because 80 percent of payments in the economy had reverted to barter and mutual offsetting. The railways earned cash from passenger purchases of tickets, but paid their employees without contributing to the Pension Fund. The government granted disability awards and benefits for families with children from the fund rather than pay pensions to retirees. He hoped that the new arrangement of deducting 1 percent of an employee's wage as a contribution to his personal retirement fund would guarantee him automatic pension benefits upon retirement. As for the current arrangements, workers, in his view, were short-sighted in accepting higher earnings in the form of bonuses, certificates of deposits, and cash under the table; these arrangements allowed employers to avoid Pension Fund contributions linked to wage outlays. While a complete overhaul of the system would require at least twenty years, the deputy minister expected the situation to stabilize in 1997. He put nonworking pensioners at the top of the list of pension recipients.[10]

**Pension Reform**

The failing pay-as-you-go pension arrangement called for an overhaul. Changes in the pension system were considered at a conference of officials of local administrations and social security agencies in early 1994. The proposed measures, often revised, suggested a shift to a pension system based on the retirement annuity principle, with individual accounting of premiums and abandonment of benefit ceilings.

In 1996, pensioners constituted 16 to 17 percent of the Russian population, in contrast to about 30 percent in developed countries. But with a steady increase in the number of retirees, the country was calculated to catch up with the developed world by 2007. Therefore it needed to shift to a saving-based pension system in which each worker contributed 10 to 15 percent of his or her earnings. This would raise savings in the economy, whereas the prevailing distributive system in which pensions were financed from compulsory contributions imposed as a tax on employers pushed up labor costs, discouraged investment, and led to nonpayment finagling by employers.[11]

Mandatory contributions by wage earners to the state pension system in the latest 1997 proposals were calculated to guarantee each person 45 to 50 percent of the minimum living standard on retirement. An additional annual contribution of 1 percent during the working life of the individual would provide him or her with 50 to 70 percent of the minimum living standard. The third tier consisting of voluntary contributions by wage earners in their work places would involve agreements with employers concerning the rates of payment. A fourth level allowed beneficiaries the option of signing voluntary contracts with nonstate pension funds.[12]

The prevailing arrangements of collecting and distributing pensions also called for reform.

### Reform Issues

Debates, in the context of the overhaul of the system, swirled around the issue of who should collect pensions and proposals to merge the Pension Fund with the budget. The Minister of Social Protection argued that the Pension Fund, with a staff of 26,000, was stretched beyond limits in its task of distributing pensions. Some employees, in his view, could be transferred to the State Tax Service with the responsibility of collecting pension contributions. By contrast, the chairman of the fund, evidently desiring to retain control over vast sums of pension contributions (more than one-third of federal budget revenues) disagreed. The question of merging the Pension Fund with the budget aroused concern as well. In view of the finance ministry's habitual raiding of the fund to boost lagging tax collection and make up for cash shortage, the fund's chairman opposed the merger.

The issues of setting a floor to the monthly pension benefit and lifting its ceiling on the basis of objective criteria, such as monthly pay at the time of retirement and length of service, also surfaced from time to time. Following the time-honored bureaucratic tradition, the fund apparatchiks worked up ratios. Thus the minimum monthly pension (plus supplements) was reported at 92 percent of the minimum living standard in early May 1996, the highest since 1992 and way above the 47 percent of 1995. Formulas appeared bringing the maximum pension on par with the average wage. Concerned over the proliferating ratios, Pension Fund chairman Barchuk suggested that the solution lay in moving to a personalized accounting system, with substantial contributions by employees to their retirement benefits.[13]

The government approved a plan in December 1997 that would shift pension benefits to a saving-based system, probably from January 1, 1998. According to the plan, every citizen would set aside money for his or her old age by making contributions to an individual pension account. State pensions would be reduced to a minimum. Beginning in 2000, the arrangement was expected to shift from a "common pot" distributive system to a three-tiered mixed system consisting of a universally mandatory distributive pension that would provide benefits for all citizens in their retirement in accordance with their earnings; a mandatory saving-based component; and a supplementary voluntary saving-based component to be accumulated in nongovernmental pension funds. A nationwide system of individual pension accounts would be in place by 2000, enabling the government to start enforcing payments into the mandatory saving-based system without raising pension contribution rates for everyone except those citizens who retired before 2001. The traditional old-timers, who retired before 2001, would be exempted from the mandatory saving-based system, instead receiving pension benefits from the general pool. The contribution rates for mandatory saving-based pensions would rise smoothly and steadily up to 2010 at 1 percent of wages in 2000, 3 percent in 2003, 5 percent in 2006, and 7 percent in 2009.[14]

The new system, to operate with the existing system from February 1, 1998, proposed linking pensions with the length of service, other indices, and the average wage in the fourth quarter of 1997 that was set at 760,000 rubles a month in a government resolution of December 30, 1997, lower than the million rubles estimated by the State Statistics Committee. When the Duma sought an explanation from the prime minister regarding the difference between the two numbers, the lawmakers were assured that the monthly wage figure was trimmed, not out of "malice" but because of shortage of funds in the Pension Fund.[15]

Ultimately the effort came to nothing: The proposals were not put up for Duma approval. In the view of Labor Minister Oksana Dmitriyeva, the shift of the pension system to a saving-based arrangement required a stable and predictable financial market. In the meantime, reform efforts were better focused on closing the gap of 25 percent between the fund's outlays and receipts, slashing the overhead costs of distributing pensions, improving the arrangements of collecting pension contributions, and tracking individual citizens' earnings.[16]

Nevertheless, the battles between the government of Prime Minister Kiriyenko and the Duma over the existing arrangements continued. In his reform package presented to the Duma on June 23, 1998, the prime minister recommended abolishing the link between pension hikes and cost of living. In July 1998, the Duma turned down a bill lowering employers' pension fund contributions from 28 to 21 percent and raising citizens' contributions from 1 to 5 percent. On July 21, the prime minister signed a government resolution supplementing the prevailing 1 percent contribution of wage and salary earners to their pension benefits with an additional 2 percent to be collected from all forms of incomes.[17]

## Public Attitudes and Pension Reform

Resistance to reform came not only from the legislators but also from the citizenry. Russian citizens were not ready for radical reforms in the pension system, according to a survey conducted by the All-Russia Center for the Study of Public Opinion (ARCSPO) in fifty-one regions of Russia in October 1997. Eighty percent of the sampled interviewees declared that the state should support them in their old age. Seventy-five percent of respondents twenty-five to forty years of age wanted the state to take care of them in their retirement. In a three-way choice of old age support from the state, the workplace, or private saving, 28 percent responded that the enterprises where they worked before retiring should be responsible for looking after them in retirement. Only 6 percent were ready to be self-reliant in their declining years. Only 30 percent knew how the current pension system operated, and a bare 4.4 percent were aware of the merits and demerits of the state and private pension systems. The responses signaled the opposition of more than 80 percent of adults to a radical change in the pay-as-you-go system. The government could not count on popular support for changing the arrangements.

We finally address the issue of the material condition of Russian pensioners in the recent past. Assuming that pensions were fully paid, how did retirees fare compared to minimum-wage earners? Did pension hikes keep them above subsistence level? How badly off were they in relation to wage earners? More to the point, what was the trend in pension arrears during 1994–98?

### Pensions, Wages, and Subsistence Level

The data in figure 7.1 from January 1993 to December 1998 reveal the following picture. First, the minimum monthly pension was way ahead of the official minimum wage suggesting that pensioners were much better off than minimum-wage earners. The minimum pension, however, was barely 18 percent of average contracted wages in September

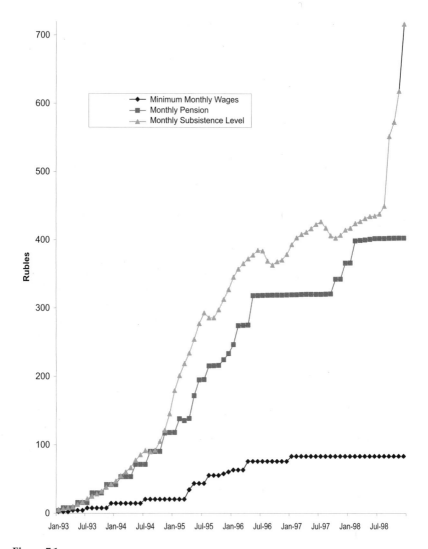

**Figure 7.1**
Official minimum monthly wages, average monthly pension, and official monthly subsistence level in (new) rubles
*Source*: *Russian Economic Trends,* various numbers.

1993. Second, the monthly pension lagged behind the official subsistence level and the gap increased over time. In other words, full payment of pension benefits would not have prevented retirees from being poor.

The above comparison of the well-being of an individual pension beneficiary with that of a wage earner does not throw light on the relative positioning of families on the poverty scale. Family well-being in Russia (as elsewhere) was highly linked with family size and the number of young children. In mid-1997, 7.3 percent of single pensioners were below the poverty line, the fraction being 0.3 percent for Moscow. By contrast, 14.7 percent of childless couples, 36.5 percent of families with one or two children, and 66 to 73 percent of families with three or four children were below the poverty line. The poorest Russian families with more than two children constituted 64 percent of the population nationwide and 30 percent in Moscow. Poverty increased in families with the cost of raising children as they grew older.[18]

Again, a major reason for increased poverty in Russia[19] was the failure of nominal wages and pensions to keep pace with inflation. Thus average real pensions in 1995 and early 1996 were approximately 50 percent of the late 1991 level, although they improved relative to real wages (Braithwaite 1997, table 2–8). However, poverty rates among pensioners did not show a clear trend of increased poverty (Braithwaite 1997, p. 58). Households with a younger household head and with children, as already noted, were most likely to face poverty (Foley 1997, table 3–8). A contributory factor favoring pensioners was that some of them continued working; 22 percent of retirees earned wage incomes in 1994 while still drawing benefits (Foley 1997, p. 84). While bypassing these complications, we analyze poverty among pensioners by focusing on its incidence attributable to nonpayment of pension benefits.

## Patterns of Pension Arrears

Monthly data of pension arrears, politically sensitive numbers, are not available from official sources. Instead, we represent pension contribution arrears to the Pension Fund at approximately 80 percent of accumulated arrears in off-budget contributions by enterprises in figure 7.2. Pensin contribution arrears, rising sharply from 27.2 billion (new) rubles in January 1996 to 237.9 billion rubles in December 1999, created the shortfall in the Pension Fund and the resulting pension benefits

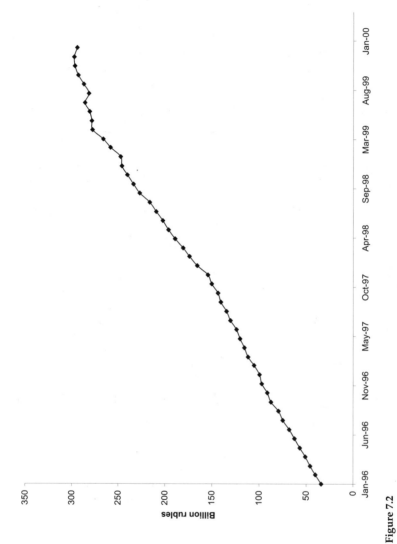

**Figure 7.2**
Arrears in enterprise off-budget contributions in billion (new) rubles
*Source:* Goskomstat.
*Note:* Arrears in pension contributions by enterprises, assumed at 80 percent of total enterprise arrears in off-budget contributions in the figure, rose from 27.2 billion rubles in January 1996 to 237.9 billion rubles in December 1999.

**Table 7.1**
Multivariate estimates of the incidence of pension arrears

| Explanatory variables | |
| --- | --- |
| *Years* | |
| $d$1995 | 0.1224* (0.0169) |
| $d$1996 | 0.4257* (0.0191) |
| $d$1998 | 0.2059* (0.0179) |
| Gender (female) | 0.0035 (0.0082) |
| Age | −0.0017* (0.0004) |
| *Education* (24.43*) | −0.0303* (0.0084) |
| Professional courses | |
| Ordinary vocational | −0.0202 (0.0134) |
| Secondary vocational | −0.0156 (0.0174) |
| Specialized secondary | −0.0107 (0.0100) |
| University, post-graduate | −0.0449* (0.0105) |
| *Regions* (138.67*) | |
| Northern and North Western | 0.0999* (0.0374) |
| Central and Central Black-Earth | 0.1315* (0.0306) |
| Volga-Vyatski and Volga Basin | 0.1189* (0.0308) |
| North Caucasus | 0.2559* (0.0410) |
| Urals | 0.0915* (0.0325) |
| Western Siberia | 0.2671* (0.0445) |
| Eastern Siberia and Far Eastern | 0.0682* (0.0341) |
| Pseudo $R^2$ | 0.1697 |

*Source:* RLMS.
*Note:* Maximum likelihood probit slope estimates are reported with robust standard errors in parentheses next to the estimates. The dependent variable is a dummy = 1 if the respondent had not received his or her pension benefits in the past thirty days. (Chi-squared statistics for joint significance tests are in parentheses at the head of the sections marked Education and Regions.) The sample size is 8,266.
* Denotes significance at 5 percent.

nonpayment. On July 1, 1997, however, the government cleared all outstanding pension debts. Arrears climbed again with lagging contributions to the Pension Fund and continuing structural problems in collecting and distributing pensions.

The RLMS also does not give data on actual amounts of pension nonpayment to the sampled individuals. However, the questionnaires and the responses provide information enabling us to estimate the incidence of pension arrears and their demographic distribution for 1994, 1995, 1996, and 1998, which we report in table 7.1 for retirees (excluding people who got pensions while continuing to work).[20] The retirees were asked if they currently received pension benefits; those who responded affirmatively were next asked if they "receive(d) a pension in the last thirty days." We use this question to measure the incidence of nonpayment of pension benefits by generating a dummy variable that equals 1 if the respondents indicated that they had *not* received their pensions in the thirty days prior to being interviewed for the survey.

### Pension Arrears Incidence

The estimated coefficients of the year dummies indicate that the incidence of pension arrears, net of the effects of the control variables,[21] increased in 1995 by 12 percent over 1994, and by as much as 43 percent in 1996 over 1994. The incidence had declined in 1998 from its 1996 level, but it was still higher by 21 percent in 1998 compared to 1994.

The gender distribution of pension nonpayment does not indicate a difference in nonpayment between men and women (the estimated coefficient of 0.0035 is statistically nonsignificant); older retirees were more likely to receive their pensions than younger retirees because the incidence of nonpayment declines slightly with age. Pension nonpayment was not associated with education level. Retirees with a university or post graduate education were 4 percent less likely than those with lowest secondary education (our reference category) to suffer nonpayment.

As with wage arrears, retirees in all regions were less likely to receive their pensions than Moscow and St. Petersburg retirees, although the percentage of retirees who experienced pension arrears varied from region to region, as evidenced by the large variation in the regional coefficients.

Did pension arrears contribute to poverty among pensioners? In tables 7.2 and 7.3, we extend our analysis of the impact of wage arrears on poverty by investigating the impact of pension arrears on poverty. A pensioner is classified as poor if his or her pension fell below the regional poverty threshold. Table 7.2 presents simple mean comparisons of poverty incidence in term of whether people experienced pension arrears. Poverty rates for pensioners who experienced pension arrears in row (1) were higher in all years in contrast to those who received their pensions in row (2). For example, in 1998, 69 percent of the

Table 7.2

Effect of pension arrears on the incidence of poverty

|  | 1994 | 1995 | 1996 | 1998 |
|---|---|---|---|---|
| Pension arrears | 44.90[*] | 71.76[*] | 69.42[*] | 69.26[*] |
|  | [49] | [170] | [677] | [283] |
| No pension arrears | 7.74 | 18.74 | 10.44 | 19.77 |
|  | [1,938] | [1,804] | [1,274] | [1,715] |

Source: RLMS.
Note: Each cell entry gives the percentage of respondents who live in families with incomes below the poverty level. The first row gives poverty percentages for respondents who reported that they faced pension arrears; the second row gives poverty percentages for people who did not report that they faced pension arrears. Sample sizes are listed in square brackets.
* Indicates a significant difference (at 5 percent) in poverty rates between respondents based on whether or not they faced pension arrears.

Table 7.3

Effect of pension arrears on the incidence poverty

| Explanatory variables |  |
|---|---|
| Pens30 | $0.4484^*$ (0.0688) |
| $d1995$ | $0.1616^*$ (0.0165) |
| $d1996$ | $0.0510^*$ (0.0181) |
| $d1998$ | $0.1813^*$ (0.0175) |
| Pens30 $\times$ $d1995$ | 0.0398 (0.0627) |
| Pens30 $\times$ $d1996$ | 0.1367* (0.0691) |
| Pens30 $\times$ $d1998$ | 0.0089 (0.0570) |
| Pseudo $R^2$ | 0.2104 |

Source: RLMS.
Notes: Maximum likelihood probit slope estimates are reported with robust standard errors in parentheses. The dependent variable is a dummy = 1 if the respondent lived in a family with income below the regional poverty thresholds. The variable Pens30 is a dummy = 1 if the respondent did not receive his or her pension benefits in the thirty days prior to the survey. The regression additionally includes a constant and variables for age, gender, education, and region of residence. The sample size is 7,910.
* Denotes significance at the 5 percent level.

sampled retirees who were denied pensions were also poor, whereas only 20 percent who received their benefits were poor.

Because poverty rates and pension arrears varied across the Russian population, we investigate the effect of pension arrears in table 7.3 on the likelihood of retirees experiencing poverty when their age, gender, education level, and region of residence are accounted for. The significantly positive coefficient of our indicator variable for the presence of pension nonpayment (*Pens30*) in row (1) indicates that pension arrears per se increased the likelihood of poverty by 45 percent. Again, the coefficients of the interaction terms indicate that pension arrears had a stronger (positive) effect on the likelihood of pushing a retiree into poverty in 1996 relative to the effect in 1994. Thus pension nonpayment increased the probability of a retiree being poor by 45 percent in 1994 but by 58 percent (0.4484 + 0.1367) in 1996. The effect of pension nonpayment on poverty declined to its 1994 level by 1998 (the interaction coefficient of 0.0089 is statistically nonsignificant). The RLMS unfortunately does not collect information on the magnitude of pension arrears; our estimated interaction effects imply that the ruble value of outstanding pension arrears increased between 1994 and 1996, but the fulfillment of government promises to clear outstanding pension obligations helped stabilize some of the adverse welfare consequences.

### Conclusions

Pension arrears in Russia resulted from repeated increases in pension rates that were not matched by adequate resources in the Pension Fund. The implicit lobbying pressure of Russia's 37 million pensioners, who represented a solidly united and committed electorate, contributed to frequent pension hikes instigated by the president and legislators. Since enterprise pension contributions were tied to recorded wage bills, accumulating wage nonpayment, barter transactions, and under-the-table rewards to employees curtailed cash flows into the fund. At the same time, government's attempt to launch a saving-based system with private contributions from workers was held back in 1998. Public opinion was also strongly opposed to reforming a system in which working men and women contributed almost nothing to future pension benefits.

As for the impact of pension nonpayment on poverty, we conclude on the basis of our multivariate model that pension denial increased the probability of a retiree being poor from 45 percent in 1994 to 58 percent in 1996, but it had moderated to its 1994 level by 1998 as a result of partial clearance of pension benefits to retirees.

Effective reorganization of Russia's massive coal sector, analyzed in the next chapter, was also held at bay by trade union activism and the intransigence of the soviet-era coal agency that managed the industry.

# 8         The Coal Industry: Wage Nonpayment amid Restructuring

The Russian coal industry, the largest in the world in 1992, offers a unique example of the crisis of wage nonpayment. The crisis was brought on by the release of coal prices on July 1, 1993, exacerbated by trade union militancy, and complicated by the overarching role of Rosugol, the Soviet-era Russian coal agency, which battled the World Bank and the reformist government—the former providing funds for miners' resettlement and the latter bent on efficiently downsizing the industry. The process brought out in the open the difficulties of resolving the problem of wage nonpayment via restructuring an industry that was marked by an oversized and militant workforce, burdened by a financially crippling infrastructure that included housing, and managed by an authoritarian agency intent on undermining the agenda of the World Bank and the federal government. Its scale and complexity provide important lessons for resolving wage nonpayment via rational downsizing, worker resettlement, and management switching in Russia's privatized industry.

We discuss below the main features of the interaction among the principal actors involved in the coal sector restructuring, beginning with a brief statement of its massive problems and ending with our analysis of wage arrears in the mining industries of Kemerovskaya oblast and Krasnoyarskii krai in the Kuznetsk Basin (hereafter Kuzbass), based on data assembled from coal industry sources.[1]

## The Russian Coal Industry

About 1,200 enterprises and organizations, 236 underground mines, and 65 open-cut mines, employing 1 million workers, operated in the Russian coal sector. The restructuring involved a staggering 15 million people in mining towns in twenty-one Russian regions. At the same time, 85 percent of the coal-mining machinery industry ended up out-side Russia after the breakup of the Soviet Union.

### Rosugol

Rosugol, controlled by its chairman Yuri Malyshev, managed the industry and ruled the coal-mining regions of Russia via a centralized, bureaucratic network of regional units. Rosugol representatives rather than local administrations sorted out decisions on allocating jobs, paying wages, and turning on heat in apartment buildings. It controlled sales revenues and budget funds, using them according to its own preferences. Its total lack of interest in dissolving itself set it at cross purposes with the World Bank, which suspected that Bank funds were being used by Rosugol insiders for consolidating their monopoly position rather than initiating market reforms.[2]

An outright confrontation with Rosugol, however, was counterproductive. During a threatened wintertime shutdown of thermal power stations in the Maritime territory (resulting from interrupted coal deliveries because of nonpayment to coal suppliers), only Chairman Malyshev could get coal delivered on time without prepayment by pulling the right strings and contacting the appropriate dispatchers.[3]

Rosugol used budgetary support from the Ministry of Finance—up to 15 to 20 percent of the enterprises' cash flow—for closing the difference between the cost of producing different types of coal and prices frozen at their low September 1992 levels, so that a ton of coal was valued at less than an imported Snickers bar. It allocated funds for tightening production schedules, improving miners' living conditions, fulfilling wage agreements, closing mines, compensating the unemployed, and adding to the reserve fund. Rosugol failed, however, to pay miners because of misallocation of funds among various uses.

### Reform and Restructuring

The industry began a slow transformation in 1993. Coal prices were freed on July 1, 1993 and the industry was exempted from the mandatory sale of foreign exchange earned from the export of coal and coal-based products. The decision was motivated by the need to abolish subsidies to the coal industry, wholesale coal prices accounting for only 15 percent of the cost of a ton of coal.

The six- to eightfold expected increase in coal prices threatened non-payment from the power and steel industries, already in debt to the coal suppliers in the amount of 100 billion rubles. (We test the hypothesis of higher coal prices relative to electric power and ferrous metallurgy prices contributing to higher wage arrears in the coal sector on the basis of recent data from two regions in Siberia.) On the other hand, reduced demand for coal could force the closure of unprofitable mines and reduce budgetary subsidization. The prospects for the industry's overhaul, however, were dim in view of the noncommissioning of a single new mine in Russia since 1988.[4]

In early November 1993, the Soskovets Commission on operational management decided to close forty-two mines by the year 2000 that employed 50,000 people and affected 3 percent of coal output. The colossal operation, requiring closure of unprofitable mining sites and re-settlement and retraining of the miners, marked a promising start. As a result of output cutbacks and mine closures, the coal industry workforce in 1994 was down by 243,000 from its level in 1993. However, miners who had put in the required number of years underground could retire at forty, qualifying for pension from the industry in addition to pension from the state. In 1992–1993, 41.8 percent of coal miners forty years and older had massive incentives to retire because wages in the industry, ranked second in 1990, had dropped to seventh place in 1996; besides, miners went unpaid for three to four months at a time.[5]

The decontrol of coal prices followed by step-wise freeing of railroad freight rates, energy, and coal machinery prices created havoc for coal industry cash flow. In four months of the liberalized price regime, non-payment for delivered coal increased from 100 billion to 480 billion rubles, an amount matching two months' delivery. On August 1, 1993, higher freight rates raised the coal industry's debt to the railways by more than 245 billion rubles. Over time, nonpayment by coal customers resulting from high freight charges and power rates, in excess of 20 trillion rubles by March 1997, contributed to escalating wage nonpayment to miners.

During a February 1994 meeting with mining industry executives and trade union leaders, Prime Minister Chernomyrdin suggested that the miners should resolve nonpayment problems by sorting out price and wage issues with coal users, industry managers, and other trade unions rather than forcing solutions on the government that could wreck the budget.

## Trade Union Militancy

In 1992, the Independent Trade Union of Miners (ITUM) actively supported the Gaidar government and economic reforms. Indeed, ITUM-supported strikes at the Vorkuta, Norilsk, and Chelyabinsk mines and at three mine-construction administrations in Severouralsk were called off as a result of a protocol signed by ITUM in December 1993 with Acting Prime Minister Gaidar, who promised alternative employment to the laid-off miners. However, miners' support for the reformist agenda involving the coal sector reorganization began to slacken. A one-day warning strike of miners of March 1, 1993, organized by the Federation of Independent Trade Unions of Russia (FiTUR) and supported by the directors of mines and the administrators of coal-mining regions, demanded budgetary subsidies for mines, replenishment of their working capital from the budget, and suspension of the presidential decree converting coal mines into joint-stock companies.[6]

The presidential decree of 1992 defining the procedures for converting Russian mines into joint-stock companies ended in December 1995. During the intervening period, the miners emerged as a politically powerful force, broadening their protests from concerns about the payment of wages to the management of the industry, demanding that Rosugol should continue distributing budgetary subsidies and managing state shares in the mining enterprises. The presidential decree of February 9, 1996 "On Measures to Further Improve the Structure of the Coal Industry in the Russian Federation," while declaring Rosugol to be an open-type joint-stock company with 100 percent state ownership, left substantial initiative with Rosugol for distributing state-funded subsidies. A Russian Federation Accounting Office audit of Rosugol uncovered diversion of tax rubles rather than its profits for housing construction, equipment purchases, and medical services, in violation of the Law on the Budget.[7]

The miners remained a powerful protest group, using a variety of means for extracting overdue wage payments and public sympathy. Neither the president nor the prime minister could tell the miners: "You're having problems getting paid? Go to the management of Rosugol and talk to them about reforming the way the industry is run."[8] No one could tell the miners to picket Rosugol sidewalks on Novyi Arbat rather than government headquarters at the White House.

The miners took to picketing railroads, testing public sympathy and police patience. In early August 1998, Kemerovo Province residents reacted positively to the peaceful resolution of the miners' blockade of the main transport lines by the regional internal affairs ministry police. However, an official of the Kuznetsk Basin Independent Miners' Union suggested that police professionalism on the rail tracks, limited to "words and bare hands," might push miners into adopting alternative strategies such as lynching mine directors, chief accountants, and cashiers who might have "money lying around."[9] The miners, however, lifted the blockade of the Trans-Siberian railroad on August 12, 1998 without an incident when the Chelyabinsk province governor Pyotr Sumin promised to clear their wage arrears.

*The Power Struggles*

Along with trade union activism, the mining sector was plagued by conflicting positions of Rosugol and the Ministry of Economics about its future direction. Rosugol and the Ministry of Economics differed widely on Rosugol's management ability. Rosugol wanted some state-owned shares of profitable mines to be sold to private investors, with the rest to be managed by itself. The Ministry of Economics wanted profitable coal mines to be completely privatized. The agency also wanted to turn around the fortunes of potentially profitable companies by claiming 25 percent of their shares as Rosugol's authorized capital. The economics ministry, disagreeing with such an optimistic assessment of Rosugol's management ability, wanted Rosugol to weed out unprofitable units by resettling miners with state subsidization—a task that Rosugol wanted to avoid. In 1995, Rosugol used only one-third of the 1 trillion rubles allocated by the finance ministry for liquidating unprofitable mines.[10]

A World Bank loan of $500 million, the first structural initiative for Russia, was designed to streamline the infrastructure facilities by transferring them to the accounts of city administrations, resettle the laid-off miners, and retrain the remaining workers in functioning mines. The first loan was linked with negotiations of a second funding of the same amount targeted for 1997.

Toward the end of 1996, the Bank required, as a precondition of renewing the second tranch of the loan, that Coopers and Lybrand audit six coal companies in the next three to four weeks and that the government set aside 1.8 trillion rubles in the budget for resettling miners by upgrading schools, hospitals, roads, and utilities in mining towns. (By December 1996, these outlays were 6.5 percent of the amounts agreed with the bank.) At the same time, the government had already included the second $500 million loan (approximately 3 trillion rubles), still to be negotiated, in the draft budget for 1997.[11]

The restructuring required formidable decisions, their firm implementation, and massive resources. The industry was in decline: Its output had fallen from 415 million metric tons at its peak to 250 million tons in 1995; fifty mines were closed and 180,000 people were laid off since 1993, saving 3 trillion to 4.5 trillion rubles in wage payments as against outlays of 1.8 trillion rubles incurred in closing the mines. By contrast, the miners' trade union (Rosugleprofsoyuz) accused the World Bank of ruining the "fatherland's coal kingdom," blamed the government rather than employers for the miners' predicament, and demanded that Rosugol, a joint-stock company, be reconverted into a ministry. In the meantime, the state Duma's accounting office reported that Rosugol and its subdivisions diverted cash, allocated for closing unprofitable mines, to other uses. The industry was a law unto itself as strikes became recurrent and nonpayments by coal customers escalated. The Ministry of Fuel and Power and Rosugol itself had stopped monitoring the lower-level subdivisions that received funds from the federal budget. Rostovugol (Rostov Coal Agency) turned up twice among the ten biggest violators of tax legislation in the first quarter of 1996, according to local auditors whose visits to Rosugol and Rostovugol offices were resented by both.[12]

*Middlemen and Corruption*

A network of middlemen firms, 230 in Kuzbass alone, headed by coal company directors or their relatives, diverted company funds to illegitimate uses. Rostovugol had ninety ruble and four hard-currency bank accounts in the near (CIS) and far abroad. Managers opened new accounts as soon as the tax authorities tracked down an old one. The directors of Berzovskpromstroi (Berezovsky Industrial Construction Company), who sold coal on behalf of Kuzbassrazrezugol (Kuznetsk Basin Opencast Coal Mine), transferred the cash to the Kuzbasskardi insurance company, bypassing the miners' accounts, and subsequently whisked it abroad to pay for the foreign schooling of their and the accountant's children. Company directors escaped assassination attempts by fourteen criminal groups that controlled about half the coal sales in Kuzbass. The directors of Intaugol in the North used budget funding for foreign travel, apartment purchases, and lavish salaries. Directors of meliye razrezy (small open-cut mines) in Maritime Territory used funds for paying hefty dividends to company executives and founders instead of using them for production improvement, tax payment, or wage clearance. Managers used funds earmarked for closing underground mines at Tulaugol (Tula Coal Company) for buying cars and financing trips abroad. The tax police tracked down 250 million extra rubles in mining companies' accounts in a two-week audit while miners picketed the White House in Moscow and the Trans-Siberian railroad in July 1998.[13]

Thus the restructuring of Russia's coal industry, the largest in the world, raised the complex issue of its successful modernization over the objection of Rosugol and its regional network, with continuing financial support from the World Bank. In mid-July 1997, the Bank postponed the second $500 million loan to the coal sector to April 1998 because, in the Bank's view, Rosugol, a commercial company, combined the dual role of managing the sector and distributing budget funds intended for mine closures, local development programs, and severance pay to laid-off miners. As a result, Rosugol fudged its accounts and misused funds. While Rosugol chairman Malyshev worked up schemes with the government to preserve the status quo, the Bank wanted the agency to be broken into two separate units, one focusing on the closure of unprofitable mines and the other on the financial reorganization of promising units. As originally constituted, Rosugol, in the Bank's judgment, was not an appropriate agency for handling World Bank funds.

## The Unfinished Restructuring

Amidst the continuing power struggle and postponement of bank support, First Deputy Prime Minister Chubais asked former fuel and power Minister Kiriyenko to propose measures for revamping the industry. Working in the Kuzbass (Kemerovskaya oblast in Western Siberia) for two weeks, the Kiriyenko Commission disclosed massive problems in the sector relating to its helter-skelter restructuring. The commission laid bare problems of the Kuzbass coal industry from the perspective of unprofitable, overstaffed mines carrying huge infrastructure burdens, its nonpayment problem (aggravated by misuse of funds by Rosugol), and by faulty energy pricing policies of the electric power company Kuzbassenergo (Kuznetsk Basin Power Company) that bought its coal. Restructuring led by the reformist government and supported by World Bank funding had barely gotten started.

### Unprofitable, Overstaffed Mines with Massive Social Infrastructure Burden

The country lost $3 billion a year from subsidizing 240 million tons of coal produced at a cost of $28 to $30 a ton instead of $12 to $15 a ton in the world's efficient coal enterprises. Kuzbass coal mines were unprofitable because they resisted restructuring: For example, advanced mining equipment in the Lenin Mine required laying off 1,500 workers. The basin could produce all the coal needed by the electric power and metallurgical industries in profitable mines, requiring closure and resettlement of entire populations of Prokop'evsk and Leninsk-Kuznetsky sector. Watchful managers could straighten out the marketing problems of unprofitable mines by depriving coal brokers of hefty kickbacks and coal deliveries on credit to customers who had no intention of paying.

A colossal parasitic infrastructure was attached to the mines that carried the burden of social support for the area's population. Kuzbassenergo received 3.5 billion rubles, far below the planned 66 billion rubles, for providing electric power to local users after allowing for subsidies to households and municipal middlemen's discounts. As a result of these losses, Kuzbassenergo could not pay its bills for the coal it bought.[14]

### Funding Misuse, Faulty Energy Pricing by User Industry and Political Interference

Budget funds were spent inefficiently at several points. For example, a mine bought a continuous cutter-loader from a middleman from budgetary funds for 4.5 to 5 billion rubles instead of 3 billion rubles from the manufacturer, and then sold it for 1.5 billion rubles to acquire badly needed cash. In the commission's view, such misuse of state funding needed to be stopped.[15]

Kuzbassenergo charged different rates to electric power users, setting higher charges for metallurgical plants than for household customers. Its failure to collect payments from both worsened the nonpayment problem of its coal supplier. It received only 3.5 billion rubles instead of 12 billion rubles a month from the subsidized household consumers because of low collection rates and a municipal broker's commission. The commission recommended power consumption ceilings based on payment performance for federal and regional customers.[16]

Arbitrary decisions by Kuzbass Province governor, Aman Tuleyev, added to the sector's problems. The governor mandated a daily coal shipment quota for mines irrespective of their ownership (by the state or in private hands) or of hardships encountered by them via nonpayment by customers. The penalty for quota nonfulfillment by the more profitable private units was higher tax charges; for loss-making state units, the penalty was withdrawal of subsidies. The commission called for an end of such heavy-handed arbitrariness.[17]

The commission's findings provided evidence of stalled restructuring of the Kuzbass coal sector, which was riddled with continuing operation of unprofitable mines, faulty pricing policies by the Kuzbassenergo energy supplier, and the imposition of arbitrary quotas on mines by the province governor. Proceeding from the commission's assessment of the Kuzbass coal mines, we investigate the coal sectors of Kemerovskaya oblast in the basin and Krasnoyarskii krai in Eastern siberia by analyzing trends in monthly wage arrears, real wages, and employment in the two regions over a two-year period from mid-1997 to mid-1999.

## Performance Record of the Coal Industry in Kemerovskaya Oblast and Krasnoyarskii Krai

We pose four questions in our analysis: Did monthly wage arrears decline? Did recorded real monthly wages trend upward, suggesting improved conditions for miners? Did employment decline, indicating ongoing restructuring? Finally, did relative price changes during the period, with coal prices rising at a faster pace than prices in user industries, contribute to arrears in the coal sector?

### Trends in Per Capita Wage Arrears, Monthly Wages, and Employment

In figure 8.1, average monthly arrears, relatively unchanged in Kemerovskaya oblast from mid-1997 to mid-1998, declined subsequently. They went up in the first period in Krasnoyarskii krai then

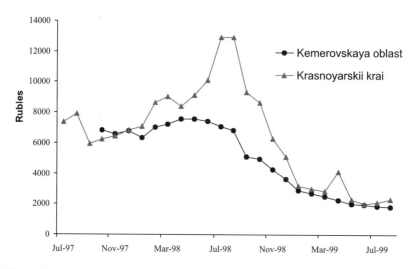

**Figure 8.1**
Arrears per employee
Arrears are in terms of December 1997 (new) rubles.
*Source*: Regional Coal Industry Sources.

turned steeply downward for the remainder of the period. Evidently attempts to reduce arrears in the coal sector were largely unsuccessful from mid-1977 through mid-1998, but significant progress in reducing per capita outstanding arrears was in evidence from mid-1998 to mid-1999.

In figure 8.2, real wages rose for the first few months of the period in 1997 in both areas, but declined thereafter. Clearing wage arrears in the latter period was evidently eased by declining wages.

Attempts to restructure the coal sector by closing inefficient mines, with accompanying reductions in employment, were effective in figure 8.3a in Kemerovskaya oblast during the entire period. In Krasnoyarskii krai, by contrast, employment declined in figure 8.3b during the first half of the period, but by May 1998 employment had rebounded, exceeding the July 1997 level by the end of the period.

### Impact of Relative Price Changes: Coal Prices versus User Industry Prices

Coal industry arrears were likely to be affected by changes in coal prices in relation to prices within sectors such as steel and electric power that use coal as input. A rise in the relative price of coal was

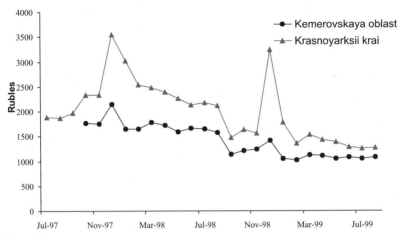

**Figure 8.2**
Monthly wages
Monthly contracted wages are in terms of December 1997 (new) rubles.
*Source*: Regional Coal Industry Sources.

likely to negatively affect the ability of the ferrous metallurgy and electric power industries to pay for the coal they used, leading to higher arrears in the coal sector.

We assess this possibility in table 8.1 by regressing the per capita real monthly arrears in the coal sector against the relative price of coal and electric power and, again, by regressing the arrears against the relative price of coal and the ferrous metallurgy industry.[18] All price variables are converted into indexes. We see that in both regions, and for both sets of relative prices, the predicted per capita values of wage arrears were positively associated with the relative price of coal.[19] In other words, a rise in the price of coal relative to prices in the electric power and ferrous metallurgy industries contributed to increased wage arrears in the coal sector. For example, in Kemerovskaya oblast, a 1 percent increase in the relative price of coal with respect to electric power (with respect to ferrous metallurgy) raised real per capita arrears by 3.82 (3.67) percent, while in Krasnoyarskii krai, there was a 8.61 (3.69) percent increase in real per capital arrears for each percentage increase in the relative price of coal with respect to electric power (with respect to ferrous metallurgy). The disappearance of high-cost mines and greater efficiency among viable units, resulting in lower coal prices, as suggested in the Kiriyenko Commission report, was necessary for curtailing wage arrears in the sector.

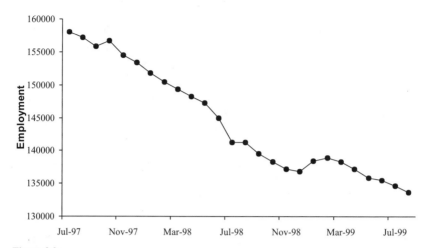

**Figure 8.3a**
Employment in Kemerovskaya oblast
*Source*: Regional Coal Industry Sources.

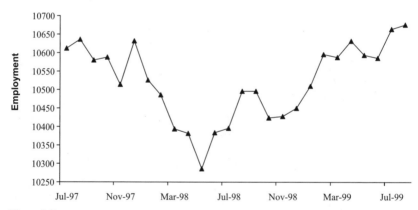

**Figure 8.3b**
Employment in Krasnoyarskii krai
*Source*: Regional Coal Industry Sources.

**Table 8.1**
Wage arrears and relative prices in the coal sector

|  | Kemerovskaya Oblast | | Krasnoyarskii Krai | |
| --- | --- | --- | --- | --- |
| $P_c/P_e$ | 3.82[b] | – | 8.61[a] | – |
|  | (1.82) |  | (1.05) |  |
| $P_c/P_{fm}$ | – | 3.67[a] | – | 3.69[a] |
|  |  | (0.42) |  | (0.40) |
| Adjusted $R^2$ | 0.2168 | 0.8260 | 0.7780 | 0.8209 |

*Source:* Regional coal industry sources.
*Note:* Ordinary least squares parameter estimates are reported with standard errors in parentheses. The dependent variable in the regressions is the real monthly value of wage arrears (December 1997 = 100) in rubles divided by the monthly employment level converted into an index with January 1995 = 100. Monthly observations range from July 1997 to August 1999 for the Kemerovskaya oblast ($n = 18$) and from October 1997 to August 1999 for the Krasnoyrskii krai ($n = 21$). The explanatory variables are $P_c/P_e$ = price index of coal divided by the price index of electrical power, and $P_c/P_{fm}$ = price index of coal divided by the price index of ferrous metallurgy, all converted into indexes with January 1995 = 100.
a. Denotes significance at 1 percent.
b. Denotes significance at 5 percent.

## Conclusions

Our analysis of Russia's coal sector provides evidence with regard to the halting progress of its restructuring. From July 1997 to July 1999, average arrears declined in Kemerovskaya oblast and Krasnoyarskii krai only in the second half, from mid-1998; employment declined steadily for the entire period only in Kemerovskaya oblast. Higher coal prices relative to prices in the user industries of electric power and ferrous metallurgy evidently contributed to wage arrears in the coal sector, requiring cost reduction via the sector's restructuring.

The sector's reorganization, aided by World Bank financing and pushed by the reformist government, was resisted by a militant trade union and by Rosugol, the stubborn Soviet-era management agency. The process was also hampered by its enormous scale and its colossal social infrastructure burden. It was further constrained by Rosugol's misuse of budget funds intended for mine closures and miner resettlement. The sector's scale and complexity defied quick results.

Restructuring in the rest of privatized industry, involving bankruptcies and factory closures, was also slow. Instead managers resorted to wage withholding and barter practices—issues that we address below, beginning with an analysis of managerial decisions on allocating wage nonpayment among different groups of the workforce.

# 9

## To Pay or Not to Pay: Managerial Decision Making

Despite mounting wage arrears and widespread concern over the issue, Russian managers' objectives in allocating arrears among workers have not been analyzed adequately. The soft budget constraints of the Soviet era and the periodic unanticipated surges in output targets encouraged enterprises to hoard labor. We argue in this chapter that rather than remove surplus workers from the payroll in response to unfolding market forces, managers effectively cut wages by resorting to partial wage nonpayment, tending to target these cuts toward workers with the weakest labor-market options.

Weak enforcement of bankruptcy laws, analyzed at length in chapter 3, provided few incentives to Russia's managers for releasing workers from the payroll. At the same time, they had economic incentives to retain rather than lay off redundant workers (Aukutsionek and Kapeliushnikov, 1997). Russian enterprises were required to pay three months' severance pay to workers who lost their jobs due to workforce cutbacks. Faced with the severance pay requirement, managers found it less costly to retain workers at the enterprises with reduced wages imposed via delayed wage payments and forced administrative leaves without pay. Moreover, if aggregate demand eventually recovered and growth picked up, the retained workers could provide a pool of trained labor, allowing the enterprise to readily expand production.

Workers also had incentives to retain their jobs in the face of pay delays. They were accustomed to receiving an array of benefits, including school, hospital, and day-care services as well as low-cost housing, all attached to large enterprises. Most workers therefore could be expected to settle for continuation of these entitlements with reduced pay in preference to losing their jobs and the associated benefits.[1]

Managers and workers thus opted for informal arrangements involving implicit payoffs for both sides rather than explicit contract renegotiations. The high economic (and political) costs of layoffs, combined with workers' readiness to accept temporary wage loss in return for the entitlements by being officially on the payroll and the hesitation by regional and federal governments to rigorously implement bankruptcy laws, contributed to managerial reliance on downward wage adjustments through partial wage withholding and forced administrative leaves without pay.

**Managerial Decisions**

We formalize the problem facing Russian employers as follows. Actual wage payments $w$ per worker are specified as a fraction $\beta$ of contracted wages $w^c$:

$$w = \beta w^c, \tag{9.1}$$

where $\beta$, the pay compliance rate, lies in the 0–1 range; $\beta = 0$ if wages are fully withheld, and $\beta = 1$ if wages are fully paid. Enterprise profits $\pi$ are given by:

$$\pi = \alpha L - \beta w^c L - q(\beta w^c - w^m)\lambda L \tag{9.2}$$

where, for simplicity, we assume a constant marginal productivity of labor $\alpha$.[2] The number of workers is denoted by $L$; output price is normalized to 1; $w^m$ is the expected wage opportunity outside the firm if the worker quits; and the quit rate $q = q(w - w^m)$, $q' < 0$, $q'' > 0$, is assumed to be a decreasing function of the wage differential (see Calvo 1979 and Salop 1979). Worker separations impose costs on the firm, $\lambda$, arising from the loss of training investments, hiring costs that are incurred when the worker is replaced, and other costs such as mandated severance payments. The first-order condition for profit maximization[3] with respect to $\beta$ is:

$$-q'(\beta w^c - w^m)\lambda = 1, \tag{9.3}$$

which defines the enterprise equilibrium with respect to actual wages paid, on average, to workers and includes two endogenous variables ($\beta$ and $w^c$) and one exogenous variable ($w^m$). The total differential of (9.3) gives:

$$-q'[\beta dw^c + w^c d\beta - dw^m]\lambda = 0. \tag{9.4}$$

Assuming that contracted wages are inflexible,[4] for example, due to prohibitive recontracting costs (so that $dw^c = 0$), equation (9.4) yields the result:

$$d\beta/dw^m = 1/w^c > 0 \qquad\qquad\qquad\qquad (9.5)$$

which states that the wage payments compliance rate is higher when a worker faces better expected offers outside the enterprise, that is, wage withholding will be higher among workers with weaker alternative job prospects.

State sector decision makers and enterprise managers were therefore likely to devise strategies of wage nonpayment that best helped them lower wage outlays without losing their best workers. If managers were to withhold the wages of the better-paid, more productive workers, they ran the risk of damaging their productivity through the nonpayment effort disincentive,[5] or their loss to another enterprise. Given the high labor turnover in Russian factories (detailed in chapter 10), employees with marketable skills and opportunities could be expected to move to a better job in another enterprise.[6] Market incentives therefore dictated a pattern of wage withholding skewed in the direction of the less productive workers who faced weaker employment options.

### Markets, Equity, and Wage Arrears

The pretransition tradition of firms acting as production units and providers of social services tended to uneasily coexist as growing market pressures and hardening budget constraints required managers to use wage policies less as mechanisms for fulfilling equity goals than for bottom-line profit calculations. Did managers attempt distributing arrears equitably among workers, i.e. were workers who had their wages withheld in one year less likely to have some of their wages withheld in subsequent years? Again, was the implied "withholding tax" on wages progressive in the sense that a higher percentage of a worker's contracted wage was withheld from higher-wage workers? We investigate these questions in tables 9.1–9.4.

In table 9.1, we utilize the longitudinal structure of the RLMS data for estimating the likelihood of workers suffering wage nonpayment in 1998 as a result of their having been subjected to withholding in 1994, 1995, and 1996.

**Table 9.1**
Persistence in the incidence of wage arrears

|                        | (1)      | (2)      |
| ---------------------- | -------- | -------- |
| $Pjowed_{1996}$        | 0.2840   | 0.2372   |
|                        | (0.034)  | (0.038)  |
| $Pjowed_{1995}$        | 0.1633   | 0.1498   |
|                        | (0.036)  | (0.038)  |
| $Pjowed_{1994}$        | 0.1409   | 0.1821   |
|                        | (0.035)  | (0.037)  |

*Source:* RLMS.
*Note:* The dependent variable is the value of *Pjowed* in 1998. Maximum likelihood probit slope estimates are reported with robust standard errors in parentheses. The lagged values of *Pjowed* are all significant at the 1 percent level. Regression (1) also includes a constant and three year dummies; regression (2) additionally includes variables for age, gender, job tenure, education, monthly wage level, region of residence, occupation, and industry of employment. (These control variables refer to the year 1998.) The sample size is 1,023.

## Was Wage Withholding Inequitable over Time?

If managers allocated wages randomly across their employees, withholding in one year should be unrelated to withholding in subsequent years: The relationship between the dependent variable $Pjowed_{1998}$ and the incidence of prior withholding, $Pjowed_{1994}$, $Pjowed_{1995}$, and $Pjowed_{1996}$ would be statistically insignificant. Alternatively, if managers distributed withholding more equally across their workers so that workers facing withholding in one year were less likely to suffer wage arrears in 1998, then we would expect to observe negative coefficients on some of the prior withholding variables. Finally, if managers systematically allocated arrears to certain workers, especially to those with weakest labor market alternatives as a result of their relatively inferior productivity attributes, then we would expect to find positive coefficients on the prior withholding variables.

The positive estimated effects of $Pjowed_{1994}$, $Pjowed_{1995}$, and $Pjowed_{1996}$ on the dependent variable $Pjowed_{1998}$, in the simple and multivariate specifications in columns (1) and (2), indicate that workers who had their wages withheld in the earlier years were more likely to have their wages withheld in 1998 than workers who did not experience wage nonpayment. For example, the estimates of the multivariate specification (2) indicate that workers who had some portion of their wages withheld in 1994 were 18 percent more likely in row (3) to also face wage arrears in 1998 than workers who did not experience wage withholding in 1994. Similarly, workers facing withholding in 1995 (1996) were 15 percent (24 percent) more likely in rows (2) and (1) to also experience wage arrears in 1998 than workers who did not experience some wage withholding in 1995 (1996). Therefore the pattern of managerial nonpayment decision making was inconsistent with a policy of equitable distribution or sharing of arrears during the 1994–98 period.

## Was Wage Nonpayment a Progressive Tax on Workers?

We assess the progressivity of the implicit withholding tax associated with wage arrears in terms of the impact of the worker wages on the cumulated amount withheld and its duration in table 9.2. The estimated coefficient of the monthly wage variable[7] in regression (1) indicates that a 10 percent increase in monthly real wages was associated, on average, with a 6.6 percent increase in accumulated outstanding debt. When we control for a number of additional factors that influence wage arrears[8] in regression (9.2), this effect (via the estimated parameter 0.5313) declines to 5 percent. The implied taxation of wages, with a positive estimated intercept (not shown), was therefore regressive: Consistent with our finding of chapter 4, a higher percentage of the monthly wage of lower-wage workers was retained by employers as a forced interest-free loan.

In regressions (3) and (4), higher-wage workers tended to suffer a shorter withholding period: A 10 percent increase in monthly wages was associated, on average, with a 2.8 to 3.4 percent decline in the period over which wages were withheld, providing further evidence that generally more productive workers suffered a lesser burden from wage arrears practices.[9]

Thus managerial decisions with regard to the amounts and duration of wage withholding tended to penalize relatively low-paid workers. We now extend our analysis to managerial practices of wage nonpayment in high- versus low-wage industries.

### Incidence of Wage Nonpayment and Worker Industry

Although market pressures influenced managerial behavior, Soviet traditions suggest that managers might also be motivated by welfare considerations with regard to wages actually paid to their workers. If managers allocated arrears with a view to protecting the welfare of

**Table 9.2**
"Progressivity" in the allocation of arrears?

|            | ln(*Amtowed*) (2,917) |          | ln(*Nopaym*) (3,211) |          |
|------------|----------|----------|----------|----------|
|            | (1)      | (2)      | (3)      | (4)      |
| ln(wage)   | 0.6551   | 0.5313   | −0.2763  | −0.3415  |
|            | (0.030)  | (0.036)  | (0.019)  | (0.022)  |

*Source:* RLMS.

*Note:* The dependent variable is ln(*Amtowed*) in regressions (1) and (2), and ln(*Nopaym*) in regressions (3) and (4). All regressions are estimated by ordinary least squares and are restricted to people who reported wage nonpayment (i.e., *Pjowed* = 1). Coefficient estimates are reported with robust standard errors in parentheses. All coefficients are significant at the 1 percent level. Regressions (1) and (3) additionally include a constant and three year dummies; (2) and (4) also include the control variables noted in table 9.1. Sample sizes are listed in parentheses below column headings.

employees most in need, we might expect that in relatively low-wage industries in which workers were worse off, managers would have a stronger (weaker) tendency to withhold wages from higher- (lower-) wage workers; that is, the effect of an individual's wage on the likelihood of wage withholding would be stronger in relatively lower-wage industries.

We investigate managerial behavior from this perspective in table 9.3: How did the impact of an individual's wage on the likelihood of his or her being subjected to wage withholding vary with respect to the level of (real) wages in the industry in which the person worked?[10]

To this end, we calculate the median monthly wage in each industry[11] and estimate (1) the likelihood of wage withholding with respect to an individual's wage relative to the industry median wage, (2) the wage nonpayment likelihood with respect to the median wage in the individual's industry, and finally (3) the effect on wage nonpayment incidence of the interaction between the individual's relative wage and the median wage in his or her industry. As noted above, the redistributive welfare concerns of the traditional, pretransition managerial behavior suggest that an individual's relative wage should have a stronger (weaker) impact on the likelihood of wage withholding in relatively lower- (higher-) paying industries. In other words, managers' concern for fairness in their arrears allocation decision as between low- and high-wage industries should compel them to withhold relatively more wages from the better-paid workers in the textile industry (with a below-median industrial wage) than in the oil industry (with

**Table 9.3**
Regressivity in the incidence of wage arrears

|  | (1) | (2) |
|---|---|---|
| *ir_wage* | −0.4549 | −0.6384 |
|  | (0.177) | (0.185) |
| *m_wage* | −0.1307 | −0.1189 |
|  | (0.027) | (0.029) |
| *ir_wage* × *m_wage* | 0.0378 | 0.0529 |
|  | (0.014) | (0.014) |

*ir_wage* = the ratio of the respondent's wage to the median wage in the respondent's industry

*m_wage* = the logarithm of the median wage in the respondent's industry

*Source:* RLMS.
*Note:* The dependent variable in all four regressions is *Pjowed*. Maximum likelihood probit slope estimates are reported with robust standard errors in parentheses. All coefficients are significant at 1 percent. Both regressions additionally include a constant and year dummies; specification (2) additionally includes variables for age, gender, job tenure, education, occupation, and region of residence. The sample size is 9,435.

the above median industrial wage). We would then expect to find a negative coefficient of the nonpayment incidence with respect to the interaction term of the individual's wage (relative to median wage in the industry) and the median wage in the industry; that is, in lower-paid industries, the incidence of arrears would rise more strongly with individual wages than in the higher-paid industries.

The results of this analysis, reported in table 9.3, do not support the hypothesis of progressive wage withholding practices by managers. First, the negative effect of an individuals' relative wage (*ir_wage*) on the likelihood of withholding (*Pjowed*) in row (1) indicates that the incidence of wage withholding was *higher* for workers in the *lower* half of the wage distribution in the industry in which they were employed. This result is consistent with managerial tendency to allocate wage arrears to the lower-paid, less-skilled employees, those likely to have fewer alternative job prospects and more likely to continue working at substantially lower actual wages.

Next, the negative estimates in row (2) of the effect on wage withholding of the median wage in the respondent's industry (*m_wage*) suggest that workers in *higher*-paying industries were *less* likely to face wage withholding. This was a likely outcome in industries that employed skilled labor with stronger market alternatives and that fared better during the transition.

Finally and most germane to our analysis, the significantly positive signs of the interaction terms (*ir_wage* × *m_wage*) in row (3) suggest that that *lower*-paid workers in *poorer* industries were more likely (relative to workers further up the industrial salary scale) to have their wages withheld. The pronounced managerial tendency to insulate the more productive workers from wage withholding in the poorer industries reflected their fear of losing these workers to jobs in higher-paid industries.

Based on these results, we conclude that managerial practices with regard to the distribution of wage arrears reflected bottom-line considerations of employee retention and wage bill minimization rather than attempts to help the workers most in need: Managers withheld wages from workers who were most likely to accept the implied wage cuts and continue working for them.

We now turn to an analysis of wage nonpayment patterns revealed by RLMS data from the perspective of employees. For example, were workers' personal assessment of their job security and alternative job prospects related to the incidence, amounts, and duration of nonpayment? Did workers subjected to continuing wage nonpayment move to other jobs?

### Labor Market Prospects and Wage Nonpayment

We further assess the influence of labor market pressures on managerial wage nonpayment decision making by relating alternative measures of labor-market options of workers to the likelihood of nonpayment (*Pjowed*), the amount withheld (*Amtowed*), and the duration of outstanding enterprise debt to the worker (*Nopaym*). We use two subjective assessments of labor-market power for the purpose. First, our variable *Findjb* gives the worker's assessment of the ease with which he or she could find comparable work if laid off, is based on the survey question:

Imagine this not very pleasant scene: the enterprise or organization where you work for some reason will close tomorrow, and all workers will be laid off. How certain are you that you will be able to find work, no worse than your present position?

The five possible responses range from a value of 1 for the response "quite confident" to a value of 5 for the response "not at all confident". We code these five responses into the dummy variable *Findjb*, which equals 1 for the "not at all confident" response and 0 for the remaining responses. Second, the variable *Chanj* indicates the worker's concern about being laid off, is based on the survey question:

How concerned are you that you might lose your job?

We code the five possible responses, ranging from a value of 1 for the response "not at all concerned" to a value of 5 for the response "very concerned", into the dummy variable "*Chanj*," which equals 1 for the "very concerned" response to 0 for the remaining responses. Finally, the third variable *Complv*, based on the survey question below, indicates if the worker was ever forced to go on unpaid leave:

Has the administration at any time sent you on compulsory unpaid leave?

Coded as a dummy variable *Complv*, it equals 1 if the response was "yes", and 0 if the response was "no". We thus code our variables *Findjb, Chanj,* and *Complv* as dummies equaling 1 to indicate the absence of perceived market power. To the extent that managers were less hesitant to withhold wages and risk losing employees with weaker market options, we expect to find positive coefficients of these explanatory variables regarding their likely impact on wage nonpayment, *Pjowed*, on the amounts withheld, *Amtowed*, and on their duration, *Nopaym*. In other words, weaker labor market prospects will be associated with workers facing a higher likelihood of wage arrears and, conditional on wage nonpayment, larger amounts withheld for a longer period.

Table 9.4 reports estimates of the relationship between our three measures of labor-market prospects (*Findjb, Chanj,* and *Complv*) and three dependent variables: Nonpayment incidence (*Pjowed*) in column (1), amounts owed (*Amtowed*) in column (2), and duration (*Nopaym*) in column (3). Each cell of the table reports the coefficient estimates from a separate regression of each of the three dependent variables on each of the three explanatory variables, plus a full vector of additional control variables, that is, from nine separate regressions. As predicted, the positive coefficients, each with respect to the workers' assessment of his or her job prospects, *Findjb* in row (1) and *Chanj* in row (2), suggest that wage withholding was higher for workers with lower perceived market power. Similarly, the positive parameter estimates of the forced leave variable *Complv*, in row (3), suggest that managers were less hesitant to subject workers with weak market options, demonstrated by their being put on compulsory leave, to wage withholding.

**Table 9.4**
Effects of labor market prospects on wage arrears

|             | Pjowed              | ln(Amtowed)        | ln(Nopaym)         |
| ----------- | ------------------- | ------------------ | ------------------ |
| Findjb      | 0.0551[a]           | 0 .0850[b]         | 0.0499[b]          |
|             | (0.013)             | (0.037)            | (0.029)            |
|             | [8,066]             | [2,834]            | [2,785]            |
| Chanj       | 0.0400[a]           | 0.0401             | 0.0214             |
|             | (0.012)             | (0.036)            | (0.028)            |
|             | [8,095]             | [2,846]            | [2,796]            |
| Complv      | 0.2243[a]           | 0.0834             | 0.1134[a]          |
|             | (0.025)             | (0.060)            | (0.045)            |
|             | [8,125]             | [2,854]            | [2,804]            |

*Source:* RLMS.
*Note:* Column headings list the dependent variable associated with the column estimates. Cells contain parameter estimates resulting from nine *separate* regressions of the three dependent variables (in the column headings) on the indicated row variable. Each regression additionally contains the control variables listed in the notes to table 9.1. The first regression is estimated by maximum likelihood probit, the second and third regressions are estimated by OLS. Parameter estimates are reported with robust standard errors in parentheses. Sample sizes are listed in square brackets below the standard errors.
a. Denotes significance at 1 percent.
b. Denotes Significance at 5 percent.

In sum, the statistically significant positive estimates indicate that workers who exhibited good market prospects were less likely to be owed wages, the amount owed to them tended to be less, and the duration of nonpayment to them was shorter.[12]

## Wage Arrears and Change of Employer

We have argued that managers allocated wage arrears with an eye to economizing on costly labor turnover. Several questions arise from the workers' perspective: Were workers facing wage nonpayment more likely to change employers in subsequent years? Did workers who moved to other employers tend to experience a lower likelihood of wage withholding on their new jobs? Finally, conditional on being subjected to wage withholding on their new jobs, did the amounts withheld tend to be lower than in the previous jobs? These questions are addressed empirically in tables 9.5 and 9.6, the questions on employer change and its consequence on wage withholding in table 9.5, and the final question on the amounts of arrears on the second job in table 9.6.

The RLMS unfortunately does not explicitly ask questions in Phase II concerning job separations, or distinguish between voluntary and

**Table 9.5**
Effect of wage arrears on employer change (1994–1996)

|                          | (1)                 | (2)                |
| ------------------------ | ------------------- | ------------------ |
| $Pjowed_{t-1}$           | 0.0347[a]           | —                  |
|                          | (0.013)             |                    |
| $\ln(Amtowed_{t-1})$     | —                   | 0.0177[b]          |
|                          |                     | (0.011)            |

*Source:* RLMS.
*Note:* The dependent variable is $Chjob_{t,\,t-1} = 1$ if tenure in year $t$ was less than tenure in year $t-1$ and industry of employment in period $t$ was different from industry in period $t-1$. Maximum likelihood probit slope estimates are reported with robust standard errors in parentheses. Each regression additionally contains a constant and the vector of control variables listed in the note to table 9.1; the control variables take the values of period $t-1$. Sample sizes for regressions (1) and (2) are 2,433 and 596 respectively.
a. Denotes significance at 1 pecent.
b. Denotes significance at 10 percent.


**Table 9.6**
Effect of employer change on wage arrears (1994–1996)

|                      | $Pjowed_t$           | $\ln(Amtowed_t)$    |
|                      | (1)                  | (2)                 |
| -------------------- | -------------------- | ------------------- |
| $Pjowed_{t-1}$       | 0.3705[a]            | —                   |
|                      | (0.025)              |                     |
| $\ln(Amtowed_{t-1})$ | —                    | 0.0306[a]           |
|                      |                      | (0.006)             |
| $Chjob_{t,\,t-1}$    | −0.0932[b]           | −0.2534[c]          |
|                      | (0.039)              | (0.150)             |

*Source:* RLMS.
*Note:* Regression (1) is estimated by maximum likelihood probit, (2) by ordinary least squares. Probit slope estimates are reported with robust standard errors in parentheses. Each regression additionally contains a constant, and the vector of control variables listed in the notes to table 9.1. All control variables take the values of period $t$. The monthly contracted wage for $t$ and $t-1$ is included in regression (2). Sample sizes for regressions (1) and (2) are 2,355 and 772 respectively.
a. Denotes significance at 1 pecent.
b. Denotes significance at 5 percent.
c. Denotes significance at 10 percent.

involuntary turnover, or include employer IDs that would allow us to track employer changes. Given these data limitations, we instead use the longitudinal structure of the survey to create an employer change dummy, $Chjob_{t,t-1}$, which is set equal to 1 if tenure in year $t$ was less than tenure in year $t - 1$ *and* if the industry of employment in period $t$ was different from that in period $t - 1$. We use the joint criteria of tenure decline and industry change as an indicator of employer change so as to be reasonably confident that we are not interpreting job change within the enterprise as turnover to a different employer.[13]

In table 9.5, workers who had a portion of their wages withheld in year $t - 1$ were more likely to have changed employer by year $t$ than workers who did not have a portion of their wages withheld in year $t - 1$. The positive coefficient 0.0347 of $Pjowed_{t-1}$ in regression (1) suggests that the occurrence of wage arrears in year $t - 1$ increased the likelihood of worker turnover between years $t - 1$ and $t$ by 3.5 percent. In the second regression, which focuses on the subset of people who experienced wage withholding in year $t - 1$ (i.e., $Pjowed_{t-1}=1$), the positive coefficient of $\ln(Amtowed_{t-1})$ indicates that the turnover likelihood between years $t - 1$ and $t$ was higher the larger the value of outstanding arrears in year $t - 1$, that is, a 10 percent higher level of outstanding wage debt in year $t - 1$ was associated with a 18 percent increase in turnover likelihood between period $t - 1$ and $t$.[14] Therefore the occurrence of wage withholding per se, and the value of outstanding arrears conditional on their occurrence, tended to increase the likelihood of subsequent labor turnover. As already noted, we cannot empirically assess whether these changes occurred because workers quit their jobs in search of alternative employment or because workers facing wage arrears were more likely to be fired, although given managerial reluctance to fire workers, much of this turnover can be assumed to be worker initiated.

In table 9.6, we address the question of the effects of turnover on the subsequent wage arrears experience of workers. The estimated negative coefficient $-0.0932$ of $Chjob_{t,t-1}$ in regression (1) indicates that workers who changed employers were 9 percent less likely to face wage withholding in their new place of employment. In regression (2), the negative coefficient $-0.2534$ of $Chjob_{t,t-s1}$ again suggests that, among workers who continued to experience wage arrears (i.e., $Pjowed_t=1$), outstanding arrears on the new job tended to be approximately 25 percent lower than the amounts for workers who did not change employers.[15] This result, however, may reflect the relatively short time on the new job. We conclude that job turnover was associated, on average, with a general reduction in the occurrence of wage withholding and perhaps in the amounts withheld, results consistent with our conjecture that much of this turnover was worker initiated.

## Conclusions

In this chapter, we argue that the wage nonpayment decisions by Russian managers reflected managerial strategies aimed at lowering wage outlays while at the same time containing costly labor turnover. Our empirical exercises suggest four conclusions.

First, the incidence of wage withholding was greater, its duration was longer, and its cumulative amount was proportionately higher among relatively low-paid workers, indicating a regressive, (implicit) wage arrears tax. Second, the pattern of wage arrears across industries signals managerial allocation of nonpayment among workers aimed at minimizing the real wage declines of higher-productivity workers. A higher occurrence of wage withholding from relatively low-wage workers in lower-wage industries than in higher-wage industries suggests that wage nonpayment allocation in Russia was influenced more by market impulses in managerial decision making than by traditional (paternalistic), pretransition concerns over equity. Post-Soviet managers responded more strongly to market calculations than to equity considerations in their wage withholding decisions. Third, managerial behavior consistent with a response to market pressures for retaining more productive workers was also reflected in their wage arrears allocation disproportionately toward groups with the weakest market prospects. Finally, managerial concerns about the impact of wage withholding on worker-initiated turnover were well founded: Workers subjected to wage nonpayment tended to move to jobs with other enterprises and, in so doing, reduced the likelihood of their facing continued wage nonpayment.

Did the incidence and amounts of wage nonpayment enforced by enterprise managers affect russia's working woment more severely than working men? We address this issue in the next chapter.

# 10    Did Women Bear Higher Adjustment Costs?

Russia's continuing transformation into a market economy was set to bring about gains for some groups while creating losses for others in the years leading up to 1998 and beyond. Steady inflation control via fiscal and monetary discipline and the restructuring of privatized factories could be expected to result in rising unemployment or declining real wages or both, with a varying impact among different groups and localities. For example, restructuring of large enterprises would endanger the sheltered position of workers who were formerly protected from the competitive pressures of a market economy. Groups that traditionally received relatively low wages, such as women, might gain as firms began competing domestically and internationally, leading them to hire traditionally underpriced labor. On the other hand, factory managers might favor specific groups (for example, an older comrade might be preferred to a new entrant in the workforce) or adhere to traditional social norms (for example, a male worker might be hired and retained instead of a female worker because the former was regarded as the preferred breadwinner). In that case, managerial decisions hobbled by traditional practices rather than nascent market forces would influence the distribution of the transition costs among different social groups. The likelihood of women bearing the brunt of the adjustment costs through job or wage loss was thus largely an empirical question.

The pretransition regime contained significant incentives for managers, including those in the privatized sector reportedly employing 80 percent of the workforce, to retain excess employees. According to Gimpelson and Lippoldt (1996), overstaffing in industry under the old regime varied from 15 to 25 percent; Standing (1996) reported that approximately 8 percent of the industrial labor force was redundant. The combination of soft budget constraints and compensation that was linked to plan fulfillment rather than cost savings provided managers with incentives to overstaff their operations. Managers retained redundant labor because of high severance payments, which could be as high as three months of wages (Layard and Richter 1994), and the political costs of widespread layoffs. However, with (voluntary) separation rates exceeding hiring rates, enterprise workforce downsizing was managed primarily through attrition rather than through disruptive and politically costly layoffs. Some of the separations attributed to quits might have been encouraged by managers through reduced wages or hours or both, unpaid administrative leaves, and unpaid wages.

Faced with surplus labor, high economic and political costs of layoffs, and imperfectly flexible nominal wage reduction, managers tended to opt largely for implicit wage cuts instituted through partial wage withholding and the increased use of unpaid administrative leaves. In this chapter, we analyze if these transition costs were higher for women than for men. We begin by providing a brief account of the hiring and wage-setting practices of Soviet planners leading up to their gradual unraveling under the onset of market reforms, with a view to assessing the relative position of women in the Russian labor force. We also discuss current assessments of the transition's impact on the widening wage and unemployment disparities between male and female workers that have bypassed gender-based analysis of the wage non-payment crisis. We then analyze gender differentials in transition costs arising from frequent nonpayment and cumulated arrears, forced unpaid leave, reduced work hours, and unemployment.

## Labor Allocation and Worker Employment until 1985

Under Stalin's version of the Soviet employment system (*trudoustroystvo*), Soviet citizens were required to work and the state was obliged to provide them with employment. The 1936 constitution declared that " 'work in the USSR is a duty, a matter of honour for every able-bodied citizen—He who does not work shall not eat.' Citizens had the right to work and to 'guaranteed employment'. In the 1977 constitution citizens were not only given the right to work but also the choice of a trade or profession" (Lane 1986, p. 9).

The planners sought to create full employment in the context of fast-paced industrialization geared toward heavy industry and state ownership of productive assets. The process was overadministered from the start: Workers were allocated to specific industries, which in turn were assigned production targets. (The rigors of workforce allocation varied over time, as will be discussed below.) Cadres and specialists were trained by numbers and types according to plan requirements. Youngsters were assigned to higher education or vocational training schools to meet plan targets. Wage and salary scales were fixed by type of work and location of job.[1] Needless to say, employment planning was less than perfect: There were mismatches between job preferences of potential employees and the requirements of prospective employers (Gloeckner 1986; Marnie 1986). At the same time, centrally determined wage guidelines may have been insufficient in explaining workers' job selection, which was influenced by opportunities to earn bonuses and extra incomes elsewhere (Malle 1986).[2] In any case, the planners persisted in managed labor allocation and differentiated wage scales (with periodic variations) until their relaxation in the late 1980s under Gorbachev and their abandonment after 1992.

During the Stalinist industrialization drive (1928–1940), elements of compulsion were present in the system of labour allocation. Millions of forced labourers obviously had no control over the place and nature of their work. . . . The general picture, however, is one of an employment policy still in practice based on a free labour-market. For the majority of Soviet workers in the 1930s, the existence of a highly authoritarian government, willing to use harsh sanctions against its population to achieve its ends, nonetheless did not mean the end of freedom to choose their place of work. The factor which eventually inaugurated the era of compulsory labour direction was not Stalinist industrialisation but war. (Barber 1986, p. 63).

Even under Stalin's authoritarian regime, Soviet planners sought to resolve the dilemma between socialist egalitarianism and market incentives by tipping wage policies in the direction of increased rather than diminished (administered) wage differentials (Bergson 1946; Yanowitch 1963; Chapman 1970, pp. 7–14). "There is evidence that wage differentials were wide and increasing from the early 1930s up to and including the Second World War" (Chapman 1991, p. 179). There was, however, a social contract, which consisted of the provision of a guaranteed job and ". . . low and stable prices for food and housing in return for showing up at work, docility and obedience on the part of the workers" (Chapman 1991, p. 177).

The wartime legislation through which state agencies could freeze workers in their jobs or force them to change their occupations was repealed in 1954. "Once workers were free to change jobs, it became necessary to review the entire structure of wage rates, to bring relative wages into accord with changes that had occurred in the demand for and supply of labour of different sorts and to make the wage system more efficient as an allocator of labour" (Chapman 1991, p. 179). The reforms consisted of changes in the centrally determined basic wage and salary rates and in the rules for compensation for conditions of work and geographical location, and for incentive pay. As a result, an effective minimum wage was introduced in 1957 and a virtual ceiling was set on upper-level salary rates. (Details are in Chapman, 1991, pp. 179–180.) These changes had a dramatic impact: "In industry, salaried workers earned 46 per cent more than wage earners in 1955 but this advantage had fallen to only 9 per cent in 1980 and 6 per cent in 1985. . . . By the late 1970s and early 1980s, some Soviet economists had begun to suggest that wage differentials had become too narrow to provide effective incentives. Concern was increasingly expressed over the fact that some engineers and others with professional education were taking blue-collar jobs for better pay, thus wasting their training" (Chapman 1991, p. 180).

While the skewed wage structure resulted in perverse choices by workers, they nevertheless changed jobs in response to perceived advantages from alternative employment. Of greater concern, however, were problems arising from the "taut" economic plans that plagued factory managers in their workforce utilization. The goal of transforming the economy into "a gigantic building site for projects of capital construction" via physical output targets imposed from the top on managers of factories (especially in machine building and raw materials) created excess demand for inputs[3] and labor.[4] Managers tended to hoard labor and conceal labor reserves (Harrison 1986, pp. 74–75). They expected to profit from this practice.

First, the larger the enterprise labor force, the higher the basic pay scales of management. Second, labor is worth hoarding anyway because of the irregularity of material supplies and the associated need for 'storming'; the possibility that your plan target will be increased during the year; the possibility that the local Party secretary will call up unexpectedly and requisition some of your employees for road-building, road-sweeping, harvest work and the like; and the fundamental fact that bonuses are in practice linked above all to total output. Third, the continued predominance of the output target . . . has a further effect on labour demand. (Hanson 1986, pp. 88–89).

"To the Soviet manager the additional labour has no effective cost since his budget constraints are soft, not hard" (Hanson 1986, p. 94). The economy was thus characterized by overall labor shortage and varying amounts of hidden labor reserves in factories.

Did the Soviet workers manage to beat the system as well? Up to a point. Labor turnover, defined to include workers who quit their jobs voluntarily or who were dismissed for violations of the work rules, had been persistently high and steady in the post-Stalin era beginning the mid-1950s. Such turnover, which Soviet sources described as arising from "dissatisfaction with working conditions," included two out of every ten industrial workers and three out of every ten construction workers (Powell 1981, p. 101). Younger workers were far more apt than their older colleagues to quit their jobs. "In the [former] RSFSR, for example, workers under thirty years of age are responsible for 60–65 percent of all labor turnover . . . ." (Powell 1981, p. 109). One reason may be that approximately one of every five workers under thirty did not do work for which he or she was trained (Powell 1981, p. 111).

It is doubtful if the high turnover by labor (including dismissals of delinquent workers by management) in search of higher pay or better housing or a more attractive job environment prompted more efficient use of labor resources by managers or more productive work effort by workers. Both were constrained by systemic factors: The former concentrated on fulfilling output targets without concern for wage-bill minimization and the latter lacked the incentives to work hard in view of the endemic shortages of consumer goods. The social contract had degenerated into "they pretend to pay us and we pretend to work for them." There was job security but poor utilization of labor resources by managers.

### Women and Employment Policies until 1985

Within the overall pattern of job security marked by poor utilization of the workforce and its significant turnover, the participation of women raised specific issues. Two features in this regard are noteworthy. First, the Soviet-era participation rates of women in the workforce[5] had been among the highest in the world. The overall labor participation rate increased from 65.80 percent in 1950 to 80.52 percent in 1979, having stabilized at that level thereafter. Women's participation rate went up from 59.9 percent in 1950 to 83.1 percent in 1979. "In the Soviet Union the participation rate for women between 20 and 40 years of age, the time of child-birth and care, is . . . very high. In 1970 it reached 85.1 per cent for women between 20 and 29 years of age and 91.2 per cent for women between 30 and 39 years old" (Pietsch 1986, p. 179). Second, in 1970 (which the sex composition of the labor supply was close to normal), women accounted for 50.7 percent of the employed compared to 48.3 percent in 1960. "This was at a time when the proportion of women in the working-age population was steadily falling, continuing the post-war trend, as normal demographic patterns were re-asserted" (Kostakov 1991, p. 88).

The high female participation rates (continuing after the breakup of the former Soviet Union in December 1991) had resulted from several factors, among them official policies to draw housewives into the workplace in the face of mounting labor shortages, continuing economic pressures to earn a second family income, and above all, the ideological emphasis on the intrinsic value of work outside the home.

At the same time, family chores took an unprecedented share of working women's time: "Although men and women devote roughly equal time to paid employment and physiological needs, working women devote on average 28 hours per week to housework, compared to about 12 hours per week for men; it has also been found that men have 50 percent more leisure time than women." (Lapidus 1981, p. 134). Part-time employment was rare because enterprise and administration managers were not interested in such arrangements. Less than 2 percent of employed women had part-time jobs in the late 1980s (Kostakov 1991, p. 90). Again, women had lower enrollment rates in programs to raise professional qualifications and add to their technical skills; women industrial workers also participated less frequently in sociopolitical activities such as attending factory production meetings or becoming Communist Party members (Lapidus 1981, p. 126). The obligatory dual roles inside and outside the home left women less time for upgrading their skills and advancing their job prospects via networking. According to one survey, 85 percent of the male-female earnings differential resulted from unequal opportunities for women to advance their careers. (Details are in Chapman 1991, p. 186.) There is no evidence that the situation has changed in that regard.

But were women discriminated against? Cultural norms reinforced by official policies suggested sexual identification of occupations as "men's work" and "women's work" based on biological and sexual stereotypes. Of the 1,100 occupations for which training had been offered at Soviet technical-vocational institutions for men and women, only 714 had been available to women (Lapidus 1981, p. 129 ). At the same time, the terms of female (and not male) employment had been adjusted by legislation to accommodate household and family responsibilities "as primarily and properly the domain of women." Thus women and women only had dual roles (Lapidus 1981, p. 130).

Explicit gender discrimination in the former Soviet and current Russian workplace is, however, difficult to track down. Was the legal requirement of equal pay for equal work implemented by ensuring that women were placed in positions matching their skills and training? Doubts persist. "Women are . . . frequently overqualified for the jobs they hold. A recent study of industrial enterprises in Taganrog found that 40 percent of all female workers with higher or secondary specialized education occupied low-skill industrial positions, compared to 6 percent of comparable males." (Lapidus 1981, p. 128).

The continuing result of the compulsory dual role for Soviet women was their overrepresentation in jobs with low skill, less responsibility and authority, and more flexible work schedules. Women were concentrated in some occupations that remained female.

The largest share of female labor in the Soviet economy today can be found in agriculture; . . . In industry, as in the economy as a whole, women are heavily concentrated in a relatively small number of areas and are significantly underrepresented in others. Although half of all industrial workers are women, three industrial branches—machine building and metalworking, textiles and the food industry—account for 70 percent of all female industrial employment; women comprise over 80 percent of food and textile workers and over 90 percent of garment workers, but less than 30 percent of the workers in coal, lumber, electric power, and mineral extraction. . . . even as women begin to enter the middle and upper ranks of industry, they continue to predominate in low-level, unmechanized, and unskilled jobs. . . . Between 1962–69, women accounted for 96 percent of the growth in manual employment; women still account for 80 percent of the auxiliary workers in industry, 80 percent of those engaged in packing, and 86 percent of all women workers doing grading and sorting. (Lapidus 1981, pp. 125–126)

The uneven distribution of women in industry and occupations and their underrepresentation in jobs of high skill and responsibility resulted in their relatively lower earnings, at 65 to 70 percent of male earnings. In particular, their underrepresentation in industrial branches with high wage levels and wide differentials—such as heavy industry and construction—and their high concentration in light industry and services with low wage levels and narrower differentials contributed to the earnings gap (Lapidus 1981, p. 127). "In construction, where women constituted 28 percent of the labor force in 1975, monthly earnings averaged 176.8 rubles; in public health and physical culture, where females make up 84 percent of the work force, they averaged 102.3 rubles" (Lapidus 1981, p. 127).

At the time of Gorbachev's rise to Soviet leadership in March 1985, Soviet women's participation rate in the economy was inordinately high at about 85 percent; their employment rate was a little over 50 percent. However, with involuntary dual roles at home and in the workplace, limited opportunities for skill upgrading and job networking, women were heavily concentrated in female jobs with low wages and narrow wage differentials. Their prospects of benefiting from the limited labor market and wage policy changes under Gorbachev, and of safeguarding their job security or advancing their job opportunities under the escalating labor-market changes beginning in January 1992, were conditioned by this dominant feature.

### Gorbachev and Labor-Market Reforms

The main features of the wage reform under Gorbachev, introduced in 1986 and completed in 1989 (except in agriculture), consisted of revisions in wage differentials and centrally mandated wage increases requiring enterprises to finance them from their own funds. (Details are in Chapman 1991, pp. 180–184.) The self-financing of wage bills was intended to discipline enterprise cash flows, compel managers to release hoarded labor, and improve the productivity of the remaining workers.

At the same time, cooperatives and individual labor activity, and leasing arrangements in farms and factories were multiplying, the former creating alternative employment opportunities, and the latter providing incentives to worker collectives. There were no direct controls over incomes and wages in cooperatives. Income from individual labor activity was subject to personal taxation (Chapman 1991, pp. 188–189).

Three results followed from these measures. First, overall earnings and earning differentials increased, especially among cooperative members. By 1987, the rate of growth of employee earnings in industry had outstripped the rate of growth of industrial productivity. Industrial enterprises had failed to exercise hard budget constraints and had to be bailed out via subsidies from the state budget, which added to the budget deficits (Desai 1989, pp. 4–5). Second, overall unemployment in the economy (of those without a job and seeking employment) stood at 2 million or under 2 percent of the employed in 1989 (Chapman 1991,

p. 183). In 1988, however, layoffs were much lower than labor turnover: "In industry, the rate of labour turnover has been nine times greater than that of workers' release (12.6 and 1.4 per cent of employment respectively)" (Maslova 1991, p. 136). Finally, the layoffs initially affected women and workers nearing the pension age, and skilled workers who could not find alternative jobs via placement services. Labor turnover had the expected pattern: Between 1985 and 1987, people under thirty had become more mobile than those over thirty: Again men were slightly more mobile than women, but women's mobility had increased while men's had decreased, the former still remaining lower than the latter. (Details are in Maslova 1991, pp. 137–138.)

The reforms initiated in 1992 by Acting Prime Minister Gaidar were qualitatively different, with critical implications for job security and employment layoffs in the economy. These reforms increasingly enforced hard budget constraints on farms and factories by curtailing budgetary support. The privatization of factories (which were to begin restructuring by mid-1995) was also aimed at belt tightening by managers and the release of redundant workers. At the same time, privately owned businesses in small-scale industry, trade, and services were calculated to create new jobs. Wages and salaries of employees in the state sector and pensions to retirees were raised from time to time. Employee compensation in the rest of the economy was to be determined by employers in response to market forces.[6]

Several researchers have analyzed the differential impact of these dramatic changes on the employment and earnings of women.

## Women's Employment and Earnings: Current Assessments

Using primary information based on monthly surveys of 3,000–4,000 randomly selected individuals in ninety different areas of Russia conducted by the All-Russian Center for Public Opinion Research (VtsIOM) between 1991 and 1994, Elizabeth Brainerd (1996a) concludes that decentralized wage setting had resulted in the doubling of overall wage inequality between 1991 and 1994 and a decline in female wages relative to male wages across all percentiles of the wage distribution. Focusing on the gender gap in wages in Russia from 1992 to 1995, and using data for 3,000 to 6,000 households from the RLMS, Glinskaya and Mroz (1996) suggest that the already marked segregation of the Russian labor market had continued to grow, that the important increase in the gender gap in wages had taken place at the *upper tail* of the wage distributions, and that nearly all of these changes were due to highly paid men's wages increasing more rapidly than those of women. Extending her inquiry to six East European and three post-Soviet economies, Brainerd (1997) observes a remarkable increase in female relative wages in the former and marked declines in Russia and Ukraine, the latter attributable to tremendous widening of their wage distributions.

By contrast, Standing relies on information put together from questionnaires administered by managers in a random sample of 501 factories covered by the Russian Labor Flexibility Survey. He finds that employment decline beginning with voluntary attrition and unfilled vacancies toward the end of 1991 was moving into substantial layoffs in 1992. Again, higher wages for some occupations (accompanied by bonuses and entitlements) and wider wage differentials (with erosion of wages and benefits in the lower end) in some privatized and quasi-private firms had begun to appear in 1992, signaling labor market fragmentation. To make matters worse, the practice of administrative leaves and short-time hours had increased between 1992 and 1994–95 (Standing 1996). As for women's position in the labor market, it was still strong by international standards in early 1992: Women accounted for about half the share in employment; and there was less occupational segregation by gender than existed in most countries, although women probably made up larger proportions of lower-status jobs within each occupational category.

Our analysis based on RLMS sampling rounds from 1994 to1998 goes beyond women's unfolding occupational and earnings situation. We extend our inquiry in two directions: First, were women denied wage payments more frequently and in larger amounts than men? More to the point, were women placed in similar occupations and (contracted) wages as men penalized more severely in terms of these norms? Second, did women bear a higher burden than men in terms of compulsory unpaid leave, reduced work hours, and unemployment? We explore the rich information contained in RLMS for the purpose, proceeding from the simple descriptive features to the more meaningful multivariate estimation of the relevant indicators.

## Gender Patterns in Wage Nonpayment

Were women more likely to have their wages withheld? Among those subjected to wage nonpayment, were the cumulative arrears greater for women than for men? Mean comparisons reported in table 10.1

**Table 10.1**
Nonpayment patterns (mean comparisons)

|  | 1994 | | 1996 | | 1998 | |
|---|---|---|---|---|---|---|
|  | Male | Female | Male | Female | Male | Female |
| Incidence | 27.31 | 26.59 | 44.15[b] | 44.10[b] | 53.22[b] | 54.57[b] |
|  | [1,355] | [1,568] | [632] | [848] | [622] | [821] |
| Amount | 1,016,759 | 572,159.2[a] | 1,254,584[b] | 924,609[a,b] | 1,290,027 | 822,916[a,b] |
|  | [370] | [417] | [279] | [374] | [331] | [448] |

*Source:* RLMS (1994–98).
*Note:* Means are reported with standard deviations in parentheses. These estimates are based on sample observations that have data for variables listed in the note to table 10.2. Sample sizes are listed in square brackets.
a. Denotes a significant difference (at 10 percent or better) between women and men (marked on the female mean).
b. Denotes a significant difference (at 10 percent or better) between 1994 and 1996 (marked on the 1996 mean), and between 1996 and 1998 (marked on the 1998 mean).

indicate that the incidence of wage arrears in row (1) increased for men and women from 27 percent for both in 1994 to 53 percent for men and 55 percent for women in 1998. Amounts withheld in row (2) were smaller for women for the three years, with significant increases between 1994 and 1996 for both men and women. Between 1996 and 1998 there was no change in amounts withheld for men, yet a decline is evident for women.

We analyze these descriptive gender patterns of the incidence and amounts of nonpayments in multivariate specifications in tables 10.2 and 10.3 by controlling for the impact on these indicators of the wage level, the demographic attributes such as education and age, and the occupation and the place of residence of the respondents. In other words, did women having the same demographic features, earning the same wage, being in the same occupation, and working in the same location as men face higher incidence and larger cumulated arrears?

We focus initially on the trends in nonpayment separately for men and women. The year dummies in table 10.2 suggest monotonic increases in the incidence in columns (1) and (2) and amounts of arrears in columns (3) and (4) for men and women between 1994 and 1998. The incidence of nonpayment, having increased in 1995 over 1994 by 2.7 percent for female respondents (3.7 percent for male respondents), had jumped by 33 percent for both in 1998 compared to 1994. The amounts withheld, higher for women and men in 1996 in relation to 1994, had

**Table 10.2**
Gender differences in nonpayment trends

|             | Incidence |           | Amount    |           |
|-------------|-----------|-----------|-----------|-----------|
|             | Female    | Male      | Female    | Male      |
| $d$1995     | 0.0272    | 0.0373[b] | −0.2468[a] | −0.0746   |
|             | (0.018)   | (0.020)   | (0.077)   | (0.079)   |
| $d$1996     | 0.1845[a] | 0.1831[a] | 0.4325[a] | 0.3342[a] |
|             | (0.021)   | (0.024)   | (0.053)   | (0.064)   |
| $d$1998     | 0.3346[a] | 0.3283[a] | 0.6051[a] | 0.5278[a] |
|             | (0.022)   | (0.025)   | (0.055)   | (0.073)   |
| Sample size | 4,481     | 3,649     | 1,583     | 1,273     |

*Note:* Parameter estimates are reported with robust standard errors in parentheses. Each specification additionally contains a constant, and variables to control for education, age, job tenure, wages rates, region of residence, occupation, and industry. The *Incidence* regression is estimated by maximum likelihood probit. We report the resulting slope estimates in the table. The *Amount* regression is estimated by OLS.
a. Denotes significance at 1 percent.
b. Denotes significance at 5 percent.

also jumped substantially for both groups in 1998: by 61 percent for women and 53 percent for men By the same token the *decline* in cumulated arrears in 1995 over 1994 was higher for women by 25 percent and for men by an insignificant amount. The low rise in the incidence and fall in the cumulated arrears in 1995 (based on sample responses collected in the fall) resulted from the easing of wage nonpayment attributable to the political imperative of the December 1995 Duma elections.

The rising incidence and nonpayment of wages from 1994 to 1998 for men and women provide a clue to the actual differential treatment of women in regard to both via a gender dummy variable that we now introduce as the variable "female" in row (1) of table 10.3 with respect to the incidence of nonpayment, and in table 10.5 with respect to its cumulated amount in multivariate specifications.

**Gender Difference in the Incidence of Wage Nonpayment**

The step-by-step estimation of table 10.3 proceeds from specification (1) to specification (2) that additionally includes the wage level as an explanatory variable. Both specifications are estimated on the basis of the explanatory variables shown in the tables. By contrast, specifications (3) and (4) are multivariate, and (4) additionally includes the

**Table 10.3**
Gender differences in the incidence of wage nonpayment

|                | (1) | (2) | (3) | (4) |
|----------------|-----|-----|-----|-----|
| Female | −0.0019 | 0.0400[a] | 0.0525[a] | 0.0562[a] |
|        | (0.013) | (0.013) | (0.016) | (0.021) |
| $d$1995 | 0.0107 | 0.0166 | 0.0312[b] | 0.0372[c] |
|         | (0.013) | (0.013) | (0.013) | (0.020) |
| $d$1996 | 0.1794[a] | 0.1618[a] | 0.1799[a] | 0.1828[a] |
|         | (0.015) | (0.015) | (0.016) | (0.024) |
| $d$1998 | 0.2758[a] | 0.3016[a] | 0.3280[a] | 0.3273[a] |
|         | (0.015) | (0.016) | (0.017) | (0.024) |
| $d$1995 × female | – | – | – | −0.0109 |
|                  |   |   |   | (0.026) |
| $d$1996 × female | – | – | – | −0.0049 |
|                  |   |   |   | (0.029) |
| $d$1998 × female | – | – | – | 0.0011 |
|                  |   |   |   | (0.030) |
| ln(wage) | – | 0.0903[a] | 0.1281[a] | 0.1281[a] |
|          |   | (0.007) | (0.009) | (0.009) |

*Note:* See the note to table 10.2. Maximum likelihood probit slope estimates are reported with robust standard errors in parentheses. Specifications (1) and (2) only include the variables shown; specifications (3) and (4) further include variables to control for age, education, tenure, region of residence, occupation, and industry. The sample size is 8,130.

interaction between the gender dummy and the dummy for each year (the latter suggesting the change in the incidence of wage nonpayment over 1994).

The estimates reveal an interesting pattern. The statistically insignificant estimate of −.0019 of specification (1) in row (1) suggests that there was no difference between men and women in the likelihood that a fraction of their wages was withheld. This result supports the mean comparisons of table 10.1 that also indicated the absence of overall or average difference between men and women in the incidence of wage withholding. These results do not, however, remove the impact of other countervailing factors such as age, education, occupation, and location of respondents on the incidence of wage nonpayment. In other words, men and women in similar employment environment having similar personal attributes might have faced differential incidence of wage withholding.

Specifications (2) and (3) support such an outcome. Regression (2), identical to (1) but for the inclusion of the respondent's wage, suggests in row (1) that, net of the wage effect, women were 4 percent more likely than men to experience wage withholding. The statistical insignificance of the gender effect in specification (1) results from the dual facts of lower-wage workers less likely to experience nonpayment (seen from the positive wage effect on the likelihood of withholding) and women tending to have lower wages than men.[7] In other words, the significantly positive gender effect in specification (2) implies that, for workers at similar wage levels, women were more likely than men to have a fraction of their wages withheld.

When we further introduce age, education, tenure, location, occupation, and industry in specification (3), the gender differential remains significantly positive: For statistically similar male and female workers, women in row (1) were 5.3 percent more likely to experience wage withholding than men.[8]

But did this gender differential in the likelihood of nonpayment incidence change during 1994–98? We examine this question by adding to specification (3) the necessary interaction terms between the female dummy variable and the year dummies reported in specification (4). The estimated interaction terms, all statistically insignificant, suggest that the gender differential of women being subjected to 5.6 percent higher likelihood of wage nonpayment in row (1) remained unchanged during 1994–98.

Our finding that, on average, women with comparable wages as men faced a higher incidence of wage withholding than their male counterparts may have resulted from the occupational distribution of women rather than their lower wage. In other words, if women were concentrated in occupations with lower average wages *and* if these occupations faced higher withholding due to labor demand shifts against these skill groups, then the wage controls in specifications (3) and (4) in table 10.3 may simply be capturing the gender occupational distribution effect rather than the wage effect. We examine this question in tables 10.4a and 10.4b.

## Gender Differential in Wage Nonpayment Incidence and the Impact of Wages versus Occupational Affiliation

In table 10.4a, we report the RLMS occupational distribution of women respondents ranked by the median occupational wage. Although the pattern was not monotonic, women were predominantly represented in occupations with lower median wages. Only 23 percent of plant and machine operators, the second highest-paid occupational group, were

**Table 10.4a**
Occupational wage and gender employment patterns

| Occupation groups (sample size) | Median wage | Percentage female |
|---|---|---|
| Legislators, senior managers, officials (169) | 776,699 | 42.01 |
| Plant and machine operators, assemblers (1,448) | 593,312 | 22.72 |
| Craft and related trades (1,389) | 582,848 | 20.16 |
| Professionals (1,699) | 578,704 | 67.35 |
| Service workers, market workers (672) | 447,427 | 68.60 |
| Technicians and associate professionals (1,414) | 431,383 | 80.98 |
| Clerks (605) | 361,011 | 93.22 |
| Elementary (unskilled) occupations (758) | 320,899 | 66.23 |
| Simple correlation (significance level) | −0.7726 (0.0246) | |

*Note:* Wage and employment patterns by occupation are averaged over the years 1994–98.

women, while 93 percent of clerks, the next to lowest-paid occupational group, were women. The simple correlation coefficient between the last two columns (significant at 5 percent)—the summary measure of the degree of association between median occupational wage level and the presence of women in an occupation—gives the expected negative correlation: Higher median occupational wages were associated with lower female employment percentages.

This correlation between wage levels and occupations in table 10.4a establishes the necessary but not sufficient condition for the possibility that the wage variable in the incidence regressions of table 10.3 simply captures occupational effects. We consider this possibility in table 10.4b by assessing the influence of wage versus occupational variables on gender differences in the wage nonpayment incidence in row (1). There is no gender difference in the incidence of wage arrears in specification (1) that excludes variables for wage level or occupation type: The estimated "female" coefficient of −.0025 in row (1) is statistically not significant. The gender coefficient of 0.0024 in specification (2) turns positive when we introduce occupation type as an explanatory variable but it is still insignificant. In specification (3), the gender effect increases to 0.0505, becoming significantly positive when we additionally control for wages: Women entitled to similar wages as men were 5 percent more likely to be subjected to nonpayment. We would not expect to find these differential patterns in specifications (2) and (3) if the wage variable simply reflected occupation effects.

**Table 10.4b**
Occupation and wage effects on gender differentials in the incidence of wage nonpayment

|                        | (1)              | (2)             | (3)                | (4)                |
|------------------------|------------------|-----------------|--------------------|--------------------|
| Female                 | −0.0025          | 0.0024          | 0.0505[a]          | 0.0525[a]          |
|                        | (0.014)          | (0.016)         | (0.015)            | (0.016)            |
| Controls for wages     | No               | No              | Yes                | Yes                |
| Controls for occupation| No               | Yes             | No                 | Yes                |

*Note:* See notes to table 10.2. Maximum likelihood probit slope estimates are reported with robust standard errors in parentheses. Each specification additionally contains a constant, three year dummies, and variables to control for education, age, job tenure, region of residence, and industry. The sample size is 8,130.

This conclusion is supported unambiguously in specification (4) in which the inclusion of occupation variables has little effect on the gender differential coefficient in specification (3), although the gender effect in (4) is over twice that in (2). In sum, these results do not support the possibility of the higher incidence of wage arrears among statistically similar men and women arising from women's occupational employment patterns.

### Gender Difference in Cumulated Wage Nonpayment

A slightly different story emerges from our analysis of the cumulated outstanding wage debt among workers who had a portion of their wages held back. These results are reported in table 10.5. In specification (1), row (1), the amount withheld was approximately 54 percent lower for women who faced some wage nonpayment. When we introduce the wage variable in the estimation, the gender difference in specification (2) declines to 28 percent in row (1) reflecting the fact of women earning lower wages being again subjected to lower wage nonpayment. Specifications (1) and (2) exclude our oft-repeated set of demographic and occupation, industry, and location variables. When these are included in specification (3), the gender difference shows a 21 percent lower cumulated amount held back from women in row (1), the reason, once again, being the lower average wages paid to women combined with lower wage withholding at lower wages. Finally, as we noticed in table 10.3 with respect to the trend in gender differential in wage nonpayment incidence, the general insignificance of the interaction effects in specifications (4) suggests that gender differentials in the

**Table 10.5**
Gender differences in the amount of wage nonpayment

|  | (1) | (2) | (3) | (4) |
|---|---|---|---|---|
| Female | −0.5443[a] | −0.2758[a] | −0.2145[a] | −0.2344[a] |
|  | (0.045) | (0.040) | (0.045) | (0.063) |
| $d$1995 | −0.2457[a] | −0.1786[a] | −0.1695[a] | −0.1003 |
|  | (0.062) | (0.056) | (0.056) | (0.078) |
| $d$1996 | 0.4122[a] | 0.3556[a] | 0.3853[a] | 0.3119[a] |
|  | (0.047) | (0.041) | (0.040) | (0.063) |
| $d$1998 | 0.3128[a] | 0.5692[a] | 0.5679[a] | 0.5312[a] |
|  | (0.048) | (0.043) | (0.043) | (0.068) |
| $d$1995 × female | − | − | − | −0.1290 |
|  |  |  |  | (0.106) |
| $d$1996 × female | − | − | − | 0.1295[c] |
|  |  |  |  | (0.080) |
| $d$1998 × female | − | − | − | 0.0628 |
|  |  |  |  | (0.085) |
| ln(wage) | − | 0.5938[a] | 0.5178[a] | 0.5151[a] |
|  |  | (0.029) | (0.036) | (0.036) |

*Note:* See notes to table 10.2. The regressions in panel (b) are estimated by OLS. Specifications (1) and (2) only include the variables shown; specifications (3) and (4) further include variables to control for age, education, tenure, region of residence, occupation, and industry. The sample size is 2,856.

cumulated wage nonpayment between 1994 and 1998 remained constant with women experiencing 23 percent lower withheld amount than men.

The above analysis raises the question of the net effect of two factors that influence gender difference in the amount held back, namely the gender difference in the likelihood of the respondents facing wage nonpayment and in the amount owed, conditional on their facing arrears. We address this question by assessing the effect of gender on the outstanding wage debt without restricting the analysis to the subsample of respondents who faced arrears as we did in table 10.5. In other words, the sample of respondents in table 10.6 includes all working women.

The results are reported in table 10.6. In specification (1), which excludes variables other than the three year dummies, the amount owed to women, on average, was no different from that owed to men: The coefficient −0.2125 is statistically insignificant. When we control for personal and job attributes, however, the average amount owed to women in specification (2) was approximately 52 percent higher than

**Table 10.6**
Gender differences in the expected amounts owed

|  | (1) | (2) |
|---|---|---|
| Female | −0.2125 | 0.5181[a] |
|  | (0.164) | (0.193) |

*Note:* See notes to table 10.2. Regression (1) also includes three year dummies; (2) also includes the individual's (contracted) wage rate, age, education, tenure, region of residence, occupation, and industry. The dependent variable is the logarithm of the (real) ruble value of outstanding wage debt, and the sample is not restricted to the sample of respondents who faced wage arrears. The sample size is 8,130.

that owed to men with similar personal and job characteristics.[9] Therefore working women, on average, were owed less than men, but this pattern can be explained by the lower wages received by women and the occupations and industries in which they were predominantly employed. When these and other factors are included in the specification, women were owed a greater amount of wages than their male counterparts, suggesting that the burden of wage withholding fell more strongly on women than on men and that this pattern persisted during 1994–98.

We turn now to an analysis of gender differences arising from the employment experience of women with respect to unpaid leave, monthly hours of work, and unemployment incidence, in that order.

### Gender Differences in Labor Market Experiences

Along with questions on wage arrears, the RLMS asked respondents a series of questions, reported in table 10.7, dealing with their actual employment experiences. Table 10.8 reports mean values of alternative job market measures, separately by year and gender. The respondents' likelihood of experiencing unpaid leave (*Complv*), monthly hours of work (*Hours*), and unemployment incidence (*Unempl*) feature among these indicators.

In 1994, women (at 12 percent ) were more likely than men (at 9 percent) in row (1) to have been forced to take unpaid leave during some time in the past, but by 1996 and extending through 1998, the difference had ceased to be statistically significant.[10] Along with compulsory administrative unpaid leave, reduced work hours constituted another device resulting in hidden unemployment or underemployment. Among working people in the sample with jobs, women worked fewer hours

**Table 10.7**
Job experience variable definitions

| Variable name | Definitions and survey questions |
|---|---|
| *Complv* | "Has the administration at any time sent you on compulsory unpaid leave?", which is coded as 1 if the answer is yes, 0 if the answer is no. |
| *Hours* | "How many hours did you actually work at your primary place of employment in the last thirty days?" |
| *Unempl* | = 1 if the respondent is without a job and indicates that he or she wants to find a job via active search (BLS definition). |

*Source:* RLMS (1994–98).

**Table 10.8**
Job experience patterns (mean comparisons)

| Variable name | 1994 | | 1996 | | 1998 | |
|---|---|---|---|---|---|---|
| | Male | Female | Male | Female | Male | Female |
| *Complv* | 8.88 | 11.68[a] | 6.48[b] | 7.58[b] | 7.66 | 6.64 |
| | [1,441] | [1,627] | [694] | [897] | [679] | [858] |
| *Hours* | 168.66 | 147.55[a] | 178.34[b] | 155.85[a,b] | 172.45[b] | 153.29[a,b] |
| | [2,027] | [1,878] | [1,684] | [1,657] | [1,603] | [1,686] |
| *Unempl* | 5.72 | 6.59[a] | 7.03[b] | 7.89[b] | 8.75[b] | 8.10 |
| | [2,816] | [2,912] | [2,603] | [2,724] | [2,641] | [2,790] |

*Note:* See notes to table 10.1. Sample sizes are listed in square brackets.

averaging nineteen fewer hours per month than men in all years in row (2).[11] Finally, women were significantly more likely then men in row (3) to be unemployed in 1994; however, these gender differences, as with compulsory leave, disappeared by 1996 and did not resurface in 1998. The descriptive features of compulsory leave and work hours in table 10.8 do not reveal a significant trend during the period up to 1998. However, the incidence of unemployment, higher among men, seems to have gone up.

We extend these simple comparisons to a multivariate context in tables 10.9 and 10.10 (beginning with unpaid leave) to see whether there was a worsening trend in women's relative situation with regard to our measures of employment experience in the years 1994 to 1998 when other potentially gender-related explanatory variables are introduced in the specifications.[12] In other words, because these regressions control for personal attributes (such as education and job tenure), region of

Table 10.9
Gender differences in job experience trends

| | Complv | | Hours | | Unempl | |
|---|---|---|---|---|---|---|
| | Female (4,627) | Male (3,810) | Female (4,199) | Male (3,597) | Female (11,175) | Male (10,715) |
| d1995 | −0.0325[a] | −0.0301[a] | 7.070[a] | 9.095[a] | 0.0024 | −0.0028 |
| | (0.006) | (0.007) | (1.756) | (2.338) | (0.006) | (0.006) |
| d1996 | −0.0237[a] | −0.0127 | 6.659[a] | 7.431[a] | 0.0123[c] | 0.0123[b] |
| | (0.006) | (0.008) | (2.036) | (2.473) | (0.007) | (0.007) |
| d1998 | −0.0347[a] | −0.0121 | 7.860[a] | 3.066 | 0.0153[b] | 0.0280[a] |
| | (0.006) | (0.008) | (2.127) | (2.473) | (0.007) | (0.007) |

*Note:* See notes to table 10.2. Each specification additionally contains a constant, and variables to control for education, age, job tenure, wages rates, region of residence, occupation, and industry. The *Unempl* regression only controls for age, education, and region of residence as information on wages, tenure, occupation, and industry was not available for unemployed respondents. The *Hours* regressions are estimated by OLS. The *Complv* and *Unempl* regressions are estimated by maximum likelihood probit. We report slope parameters with robust standard errors in parentheses. Sample sizes are listed in parentheses below column headings.

residence, occupational affiliation, and the industry of current employment, the estimated gender differences in employment experience will exclude the impact of factors such as differences in the occupations that men and women opted for, or the industries in which they found employment in.

### Unpaid Leave and Gender Differences

Unpaid leave, along with flexible wages and work hours, gave Russian firm managers an additional instrument for managing their personnel. The practice shares some features of temporary layoffs in the U.S. economy (see Feldstein 1976): Work can be shared within a given labor force, allowing employers to avoid unpopular layoffs and maintain a labor reserve for meeting unanticipated increases in demand.[13] According to Goskomstat's Labour Force Survey (LFS),[14] administrative leave peaked at 2.3 percent of the labor force during the second quarter of 1994, falling steadily to 1.6 percent in the first quarter of 1996.

The time dummy estimates of table 10.9 with 1994 as the base suggest changes in the likelihood by men and women of being forced to take unpaid leave in the succeeding years. For example, the likelihood of women being forced to take unpaid compulsory leave in row (3)

**Table 10.10**
Trends in gender differences in job experience

|  | Complv (8,608) | Hours (7,796) | Unempl (21,890) |
|---|---|---|---|
| Female | 0.0324[a] | −17.159[a] | 0.0087 |
|  | (0.008) | (2.274) | (0.009) |
| Female × $d$1995 | −0.0026 | −1.6172 | 0.0037 |
|  | (0.011) | (2.891) | (0.009) |
| Female × $d$1996 | −0.0134 | −0.4014 | −0.0024 |
|  | (0.010) | (3.213) | (0.009) |
| Female × $d$1998 | −0.0249$^\beta$ | 5.7449[c] | −0.0134[*] |
|  | (0.009) | (3.156) | (0.008) |

*Note:* See the note to table 10.2. All regressions include three time dummies in addition to the control variables noted in table 10.9. Sample sizes are listed in parentheses below column headings.
* Denotes significant at 15 percent.

declined by 3.5 percent in 1998 compared to 1994. (The estimated year effect is −.0347.) Men were 3 percent less likely in row (1) to be put on forced leave in 1995 than in 1994. (The year effect is −.0301.) Beyond that, there was no change in the enforcement of leave for men. (The dummy parameters are statistically insignificant.)

The trend in gender differences in compulsory leave practices for men and women are given in table 10.10 by the interaction of the gender dummy in row (1) and the relevant time dummy. The significantly positive coefficient of 0.0324 of the female dummy in row (1) suggests that women were 3 percent more likely than men to have been forced to take unpaid leave in 1994. However, the negative coefficient of the interaction term of −.0249 in row (4) suggests that the gender difference had diminished to less than 1 percent (0.0324 − 0.0249), but continued being positive in 1998. Women continued to bear a greater burden of the short-run employment adjustments brought on by the transition.[15]

## Reduced Work Hours and Gender Differences

Labor inputs can also be varied without layoffs via reduced work hours. Along with administrative leaves, this practice constitutes "hidden unemployment" in the official statistics reported by Goskomstat (and reproduced in various issues of *Russian Economic Trends*). Monthly hours[16] in table 10.9 do not trend downward over time for women (the positive year dummies do not show a definite trend) but decline for men between 1995 and 1998. In table 10.10, the negative coefficient on the female dummy in row (1) shows that women worked fewer hours than men in 1994, but the positive interaction term estimated at 5.7449 in row (4) suggests that the gender differential in work hours declined by about six hours per month between 1994 and 1998. Therefore, although women carried a greater burden than men of reduced work hours in response to lower demand for labor services as the transition progressed, the relative burden of the adjustment costs in terms of work hours narrowed in 1998.

*Unemployment and Gender Differences*

We analyze the relative incidence of unemployment using the U.S. Bureau of Labor Statistics (BLS) definition: The respondent was unemployed if he or she was without a job and was actively looking for work (*Unempl*). In table 10.9, men and women experienced increased unemployment incidence between 1994 and 1998. This increase was nearly twice as strong for men relative to that for women in 1998: The 1998 dummy coefficient of 0.0280 for men in row (3) is almost twice as large as 0.0153 for women. This result is also supported in table 10.10 by the statistically significant and negative interaction term of −.0134 in row (4) between the gender dummy and the 1998 dummy. In other words, unemployment incidence increased between 1994 and 1998 for men and women, but the more rapid increase for men led to a relatively higher male unemployment incidence by 1998.

In sum, we find that while the gender differences narrowed over time, women were more likely than men in 1998 to be forced to take unpaid leave and work reduced hours. The incidence of unemployment however fell more heavily on men[17] as the transition progressed.

### Conclusions

Have the costs of Russia's market-oriented transition fallen more severely on women? Our results indicate three major conclusions with respect to the incidence and amounts of nonpayment between men and women. First, women with similar demographic and job market attributes as men were more likely to be subjected to wage nonpayment. Next, for women who had been denied wages, the amounts held back were smaller than for similarly placed men because women earned lower (contracted) wages. Finally, the amounts withheld for working women in general were 52 percent higher than for similarly placed men. On balance, wage nonpayment imposed higher costs on women than on men in similar situations.

This conclusion is strengthened by our estimates relating to women's job market experience. Women were more likely to be put on compulsory unpaid leave and shorter work hours, but as the transition progressed the initial gender difference, unfavorable to women, persisted at lower levels. Men, however, experienced higher unemployment in the latter years of the transition.

To what extent were men and women who were denied wages compensated via barter? We addres this issue in the next chapter, in the context of enterprise barter practices and the problems of accurately measuring them.

# 11    How Much Barter?

Barter arrangements imply exchange of goods in lieu of cash or credit between suppliers and clients. They also refer to supply by factories of goods to workers as payments for their labor services. The definition of barter is stretched in the Russian context to include noncash arrangements used by clients to pay their suppliers (Guriev and Ickes 1999). According to the former two definitions, barter includes shipment of Moskvich cars by the auto manufacturer as payment for the services of a private land reclamation company. The company must find middlemen to sell the cars to recover cash (Yakovlev 1998, p. 2). Workers receiving pots and pans in lieu of wages from a manufacturer are similarly subjected to barter. But would accumulated debts among enterprises classify as barter?

At the very outset, therefore, we highlight the confusion surrounding the definition of barter that has plagued the measurement of the phenomenon in Russia before proceeding to an analysis of the rise of inter-enterprise barter transactions, turning next to our empirical models that establish a link between wage withholding and barter payments to Russian workers.

## Barter: Definition and Measurement

The seriousness of the issue is brought out by two estimates of barter in Russia reported in tables 11.1 and 11.2. According to official data from Goskomstat presented in table 11.1, less than one-third (30.7 percent) of nonpayment between buyers and sellers (i.e., among enterprises and between enterprises and the state) in September 1998 was cleared via noncash money from enterprise bank balances (to be precisely defined below). Another one-third (31.9) was denominated in mutual clearing

**Table 11.1**
Structure of payments (for output and services shipped/rendered by major Russian tax-payers), September 1998

|  | Billion rubles | Percent of total | Percent of total, August 1998 |
|---|---|---|---|
| Output | 65,530 | 100.0 | 100.0 |
| Paid by |  |  |  |
| Cash and noncash money | 24,966 | 38.1 | 34.6 |
| Noncash money | 20,137 | 30.7 | 29.8 |
| Veksels | 5,967 | 9.1 | 10.5 |
| Bonds | 155 | 0.2 | 0.8 |
| Federal | 84 | 0.1 | 0.1 |
| Russian Federation's subjects | 48 | 0.1 | 0.1 |
| Municipal | 17 | 0.03 | 0.1 |
| Corporate | 6 | 0.01 | 0.5 |
| IOUs denominated in noncash rubles | 3,764 | 5.7 | 1.6 |
| Clearing | 20,893 | 31.9 | 36.4 |
| Barter | 5,867 | 9.0 | 9.2 |
| Other types of payments | 3,918 | 6.0 | 6.9 |

*Source:    Sotsial'no-Ekonomicheskoye Polozheniye Rossii,* Moscow: Goskomstat Rossii, Yanvar'-Noyabr' 1998, p. 203.
*Note:* In accordance with government decree 10 of January 6, 1998, Goskomstat carries out a statistical surveillance of financial flows of Russia's major taxpayers including Gazprom, Aeroflot, and federal railroad companies.

transactions. Barter at 9 percent played approximately the same relative role as *veksels* (or debt instruments, to be explained below) and outright cash payments of 7.4 percent.

In table 11.2, we report data from the *Russian Economic Barometer* on trends in barter. This alternative source publishes information on barter based on monthly surveys of approximately 200 Russian enterprises, providing a strikingly different assessment of barter transactions in Russian industry from that reported by Goskomstat in table 11.1. Accordingly, industrial barter in row (1) increased from 6 percent of sales in 1992 to 41 percent in the first half of 1997, a sevenfold increase. Barter increased in all sectors at different rates. Recent data of sales in industry via barter at 42 percent was slightly higher than the 41 percent noted above for the first half 1997. Barter transactions in industry as a fraction of sales in 1998 through November were a substantial 51 percent.

**Table 11.2**
Dynamics of barter (in sales of industrial enterprises – percent)

|  | 1993 | 1994 | 1995 | 1996 | 1997[a] |
|---|---|---|---|---|---|
| All industry | 9 | 17 | 22 | 35 | 41 |
| Electric power | 4 | 13 | 19 | 35 | 46 |
| Fuel | 10 | 17 | 20 | 32 | 33 |
| Metallurgy | 14 | 32 | 37 | 47 | 56 |
| Machine-building and metalworking | 12 | 18 | 23 | 35 | 41 |
| Chemical and petrochemical | 21 | 25 | 23 | 43 | 52 |
| Logging, woodworking, pulp, and paper | 12 | 21 | 18 | 35 | 46 |
| Construction materials | 11 | 24 | 35 | 48 | 59 |
| Light | 8 | 20 | 22 | 40 | 42 |
| Food | 6 | 9 | 11 | 17 | 25 |
| Other | 8 | 11 | 16 | 24 | 27 |
| Sectors of manufacturing |  |  |  |  |  |
| Consumption goods | 7 | 12 | 14 | 26 | 32 |
| Investment goods | 12 | 17 | 20 | 37 | 42 |
| Intermediate goods | 11 | 25 | 30 | 44 | 55 |

*Source:* C. Aukutsionek, "Barter v Rossiskoi Promyshlennosti," *Voprosy Ekonomiki,* February 1998, pp. 51–52.
a. First half of the year.

How can the two barter estimates—9 percent of industry sales in Goskomstat estimation and 51 percent according to the Russian Economic Barometer—be so wide apart? Goskomstat conceded that the share approached 15 percent for major taxpayers. The outlandish measure of barter from the *Barometer* source results from enterprise managers' viewing of noncash mutual arrangements as barter. Obviously, classifying them as indebtedness—what they in fact were— would drag a large number of enterprises into bankruptcy courts, whereas an enterprise claiming to pay a supplier via barter could claim temporary cash-flow problems and continue functioning. The exaggerated inter-industry barter estimate reflecting one managerial survival strategy created an image of Russia's degeneration into a primitive barter economy.

The definitional distortion in tracking barter was noticed by Russian analysts, resulting in a subsequent modified definition of barter by the *Barometer.* Thus the settlement of mutual liabilities by enterprises without a cash transfer, called clearing schemes, was distinguished from barter involving payment in kind (Yakovlev 1998, p. 1).

**Clearing Schemes**

Clearing schemes took place among large enterprises, numbering five to seven, with stable links of commodity circulation as illustrated in the following example:

A Tula Province producer A of dry mixture from mineral gypsum bought electric power from Tulaenergo Corporation. This local power supplier in turn bought power from the wholesale Cherepovets Electric Power Company that in turn purchased cement from a cement plant in Moscow Province. The cement plant bought its raw material, the gypsum dry mixture, from the first Tula Province producer. The four suppliers were thus linked in a mutual chain of transactions requiring payment settlements that the Tula Province producer A, buying electric power from Tulaenergo Corporation, was most anxious to settle for fear of losing its power supply. This Tula Province producer A of gypsum dry mixture initiated a complicated mutual clearing scheme involving all the partners.

The arrangement was marked by following features: The product prices underlying the clearing were settled with mutual negotiations approximating valuations emerging from supply-demand calculations. Second, the negotiation and settlement of the payment arrangements extended over several parties and for several months and were generally not linked with current liabilities of a customer to the supplier. In other words, the arrangements were part of the enterprise financial planning occasionally undertaken in advance with a view to linking financial flows among several major parties. Third, the clearing arrangements bypassed cash payments, but they differed from barter deals involving direct commodity exchanges between two parties with matching needs. The net liability of a customer might be carried over to the next period. By contrast, physical exchange of commodities between two parties without elaborate financial planning among several parties took place when mutual needs could be assessed and satisfied.

**Barter Deals**

For example, the Tula Province producer of gypsum mixture exchanged it for pipes from a pipe supplier because he needed pipes for upgrading water and heat facilities in the factory. Or the Tulaenergo Corporation, unwilling to continue waiting for the settlement of outstanding liabilities of the Tula Province gypsum mixture producer, cleared the debt by accepting any product from the latter that could be sold. Among such readily salable items were chocolates, beverages, chewing gum, computers, and office supplies (Yakovlev 1998, p. 2).

Such barter deals were "spot and occasional." In fact, a questionnaire-based survey of 800 industrial enterprises undertaken by the Center of Economic Analysis and Forecasting of the Russian Federation government revealed that only 20 percent of the total noncash transactions (i.e., clearing schemes plus pure barter) among enterprises involved barter. The remaining 80 percent were clearing schemes among several enterprises linked by mutual pairwise needs (Yakovlev 1998, p. 2). Toward the end of 1998, clearing schemes were presumably 31.9 percent of the total inter-enterprise transactions in table 11.1. A major disadvantage of such arrangements was that enterprises were unable to break away from traditional ties in search of new partners.

**Payment Arrangements in Lieu of Cash**

Although barter represented 10 to 15 percent of inter-enterprise transactions, the net indebtedness resulting from mutually agreed upon clearing arrangements among a chain of enterprises was among the variety of stratagems for evading cash payments adopted by cash-strapped Russian governments at various levels and by privatized enterprises. These arrangements took many forms, including mutual offsets and an assortment of interest-bearing notes that were devised to handle the nonpayment problem.

*Offsets between the Government and Suppliers to the Ministries*

The offsets discussed at length in chapter 2 occurred when the Ministry of Finance allowed write-offs of the tax liabilities of the railways, for example, against the failure of the Ministry of Defense to pay the railways for hauling defense hardware, or balanced the overdue tax payments of construction enterprises against charges owed by a government department for the services of the construction companies. The Ministry of Finance began disallowing the practice in 1997; it was discontinued from January 1, 1998 via a presidential decree of mid-November 1997.

*Simple* **Veksels** *(Promissory Notes) and Transferable* **Veksels** *(Bills of Exchange)*

*Veksels,* also noted in chapter 2, issued by banks and financial institutions, enterprises, and regional and municipal authorities, performed routine commercial functions of debt instruments such as certificates of deposit, commercial paper, simple IOUs, and bonds (Hendley, Ickes, and Ryterman 1998). Federal authorities also issued debt instruments for financing procurement of defense hardware. A hierarchy of risk premiums on *veksels* reflected varying assessments by their holders regarding the solvency or trustworthiness of the issuers.

Interest-bearing notes issued by private banks and guaranteed by the Ministry of Finance appeared when the ministry borrowed from a bank to pay a defense industry plant with the note. Ultimately the bank paid the plant when the government settled its account with the bank with cash. These notes were accepted by local budgets to settle their debts with local enterprises, the notes' creditworthiness depending on the issuing bank. Russia was being divided into regions in which banks issued surrogate money in the form of interest-bearing notes linking its regions with captive enterprises.[1]

How was the mountain of debts, generally unmatched by real resources, eventually cleared? Enterprises assigned their debtors' debts to creditors in a chain of transactions that was completed when the final debtor agreed to pay his creditor with goods at prices with a heavy discount. The manager of the creditor company seized the opportunity of settling a debt at a heavy discount on which he would not have otherwise earned a kopeck, scoring a personal cut for himself in the bargain.[2]

*Veksels* also played an important role in tax procurement. Although receipts from profit and VAT taxes were divided in legislated proportions between the federal and regional budgets, as noted in chapter 5, *veksels* were accepted as tax payments only by regions. By deliberately promoting the use of *veksels* as instruments of tax clearance, regional administrations helped assure themselves a larger share of (undercollected) tax revenues than was prescribed by law. In other words, tax payments via veksels in local budgets signaled to the center greater local need for tax revenue and the inability of local authorities to collect it. According to the 1997 and 1998 OECD Economic Surveys, regions that collected a bigger share of taxes in noncash instruments kept a larger fraction of all tax revenues.[3]

## IOUs

These written documents promising to pay (as a rule, in noncash bank deposits), in full or in part, the value of the purchases were open-ended with respect to their duration between the date of a transaction and the date of payment.

## Cash Money versus Noncash Money

Russian enterprises and other legal entities continued facing restrictions on their access to, and use of, cash.[4] The law required all legal entities to deposit their cash income in current accounts, allowing them limited sums on hand. Beyond the prescribed limits, they could hold cash sufficient to cover wages, pensions, stipends, and insurance payments for a period of no more than three days, including the day on which it was received or withdrawn from banks. Enterprises could withdraw cash from their current accounts in limited amounts and for specified purposes. These included the payment of wages, expenditures connected with business trips, and "commercial necessities" such as the purchase of agricultural produce on a retail basis from the population, office supplies, and urgent repair work (for example, plumbing problems).

As late as 1993, all inter-enterprise transactions had to be conducted on a noncash basis. Inter-enterprise cash transactions under 500,000 rubles were allowed in 1994. Beginning in 1995, transactions among legal persons, as well as between legal and physical persons, in amounts exceeding 2 million rubles were permitted on a noncash basis only. Russian banks were charged with the task of systematically verifying their clients' compliance with these rules and could be held responsible along with their customers for their violation.

## The Separation of Cash and Noncash Transactions

Why were cash and noncash transactions separated by law? Three reasons were advanced by the government for the partitioning. First, until the unilateral dissolution of the ruble zone in July 1993 by the Central Bank of Russia, only the Russian central bank, having a monopoly on the emission of ruble cash, issued currency. The non-Russian central banks could issue only noncash money by extending credits to clients, a privilege they resorted to generously, thereby contributing to inflation in the ruble zone. With the abolition of the ruble zone, this argument for separating cash from noncash rubles disappeared. The post-Soviet states acquired their own central banks and currencies. Second, wages were paid in cash. Restrictions on the conversion of noncash into cash was calculated to impose hard budget constraints and an incomes policy on enterprises. The Soviet-era practice was continued because, unlike in the old days, wages were freed. Third, cash shortages were a weapon of inflation control. Because the economy was increasingly flooded with credit instruments that the authorities could not control and even promoted, they considered a deliberate enforcement of cash shortages as anti-inflationary.

According to Tompson (1997), the enduring reason for retaining the cash/noncash distinction was the government's dire need for tax revenue. Taxes were collected by banks from enterprise noncash bank accounts. Retention of the dual circuit was calculated to ease tax collection by limiting enterprise managers' opportunities for financing unrecorded cash transactions that were the familiar device for tax evasion. Restricting their access to, and use of, cash was intended to lock them within the payment system. In Tompson's view, the other arguments for retaining the cash/noncash distinction had disappeared. The ruble zone was history; enforcing wage restraint on irresponsible enterprises was no longer a policy priority; and the emission of noncash credits via central bank money creation that characterized 1992–93 had slowed. On the other hand, fiscal necessity required that the dual circuit remain.

Not only did tax collection remain a major problem, but managerial attempts to reduce the amount of cash coming into company accounts to avoid paying taxes created the shortage of funds to pay wages (Tompson 1997, pp. 1162–1165). A large percentage of tax liabilities were instead paid via tax write-offs.

A side effect of the dual circuit was a decline in the ruble's unit of account value to below its cash value: In accounting terms, cash in the bank could be worth substantially less than cash in hand. When noncash credit was relatively easy in 1992–93, one noncash ruble was worth 33 percent of a cash ruble; by the end of 1996, the differential had fallen to about 4 percent (Tompson 1997, p. 1163).

Was there an increasing shortage of noncash rubles with enterprises limiting their ability to remit taxes to the state, clear bills with their suppliers, and pay wages to their workers? We explore this issue by relating enterprise noncash rubles in their bank balances with their payment obligations (to each other, to the workforce, and to the state) and by linking the varying impact of price liberalization on cash-flow pressures for enterprises and sectors.

## Enterprise Payment Obligations, Noncash Shortage, and the Impact of Relative Price Shifts

### Enterprise Payment Obligations and Noncash Shortage

Enterprises could replenish their balances by borrowing from banks; however, the interest charges were prohibitive in view of the fact that returns from investing the cash in the real economy were uncertain. The replenishment of noncash balances via central bank monetary emission, which was used for financial bailout of enterprises in the early years of the transition in 1992 and 1993, became increasingly difficult as monetary control became effective. Finally, enterprises could enlarge their noncash bank balances by effective downsizing, producing saleable items, and receiving cash from clients, in the process moving their bank balances in tandem with their overdue payment obligations (to suppliers, to the budget, and to off-budget funds and the workforce). Rather than provide an ideal norm of enterprise financial viability in terms of the relationship between these two magnitudes, we underline the plummeting ratio of enterprise bank balances to their total overdue payment obligations: In figure 11.1, it had sunk from 9.6 percent in January 1998 to 6 percent in July 1998 as Russia's financial crisis escalated. Increasingly, enterprises resorted to mutual clearing, debt accumulation, tax write-offs, barter, and wage nonpayment. As economic activity picked up following the August 1998 devaluation of the ruble, enterprise bank balances improved in relation to their overdue payment obligations: The ratio had moved up from a low of 6 percent in October 1998 to 11 percent in December 1998. The liquidity crunch[5] signaled by declining noncash bank balances as a fraction of enterprise overdue payment obligations was also in all likelihood aggravated by the diversion of funds by managers to other uses in the midst of crumbling supervisory and surveillance activities by banks authorized to do so. Joint ownership of banks and large businesses facilitated such diversion via conversion of funds into hard currency or their placement into government bills and bonds, both offering high returns.

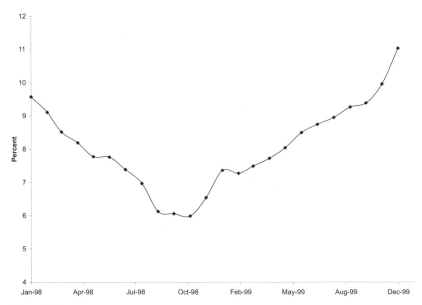

**Figure 11.1**
Ratio of enterprise noncash bank balances to enterprise overdue payment obligations
*Source*: Goskomstat.
*Note*: Enterprise payment obligations are to suppliers, the budget and off-budget funds, and the workforce. Enterprises include units in nine sectors of the economy, namely industry, construction, transport, agriculture, communications, retail trade and catering, wholesale trade, housing, and "other sectors." Enterprise noncash bank balances were on average 35 percent of total bank deposits in the economy during January 1998–December 1999. The breakdown for earlier years is not available, requiring us to exclude the pre-January 1998 pattern.

## Relative Price Shifts and Noncash Shortage

At the same time, the relative price shifts following the price liberalization measures begun in 1992 aggravated enterprise cash flow problems with varying intensity. Price decontrol measures moved relative prices in favor of Russia's three leading monopolies: Gazprom that supplied natural gas, the railways that carried freight, and the Unified Power System that generated and distributed electric power.

As argued at length in chapter 3, the producer price indexes in figure 11.1 from January 1995 until the collapse of the ruble that began in August 1998 100 placed electric power, fuel (including natural gas), and construction material sectors at the top; processed food, light industry, and nonferrous metallurgy at the bottom; and the remaining industry groups in the middle. Not surprisingly, the power and fuel sectors emerged as major payment claimants vis-à-vis the remaining sectors as price decontrol took hold in the economy.

David Woodruff (1996, p. 4) notes that between 1993 and 1994, overdue debt to electric power companies rose from 5 percent to 17 percent of all overdue debt in Russian industry. The cutback of power to nonpaying customers, prohibited by law, threatened the continuing operation of the companies in question, eliminating any chances of collecting on their debts because bankruptcy mechanism might fail to compensate creditors from company assets in the event of a company shutdown. Power companies had the same legal claims as tax authorities to directly withdraw funds from enterprise bank accounts, with the result that enterprise managers took recourse to creating artificial cash shortages and piling up debts against the power suppliers.

Accelerated nonpayments also appeared between the state and the three monopolies: Government agencies that could not pay the three "fat boys" for providing electricity to hospitals and gas heat to state factories or for hauling tanks to Chechnya accumulated debts with them. Privatized factories in the manufacturing sector that could not pay the high tariffs of the three monopolists also amassed debts with them; about half of all nonpayment in industry was owed to the energy sector toward the end of 1996.[6]

Agriculture and the agro-industrial complex were severely affected by the relative shift of oil prices, prompting the government to deliberately encourage barter or semibarter transactions in their favor. In figure 11.2, the producer price indexes for livestock output and processed food compared unfavorably with those for industry and the energy sector. To enable farms to overcome the unfavorable terms of trade, the federal budget began assigning funds to farms and the agro-industrial complex for purchases of fuel and lubricants. The arrangement worked as follows: Having received crude oil from YUKOS, the oil company, without payment, the company's refineries in Samara refined it into gasoline and lubricating oil, shipped the products without payment to their marketing organizations, which in turn delivered them to the farms that agreed to repay the organizations after harvesting. Occasionally local administrators seized the products en route, shipping them to farms and using up the cash payments from farms for the province's urgent needs. Oil refineries diverted sales to prospective nonfarm clients in exchange for cement and pipes. At times, farms paid gasoline suppliers a year later via shipments of sugar, butter, or meat.[7]

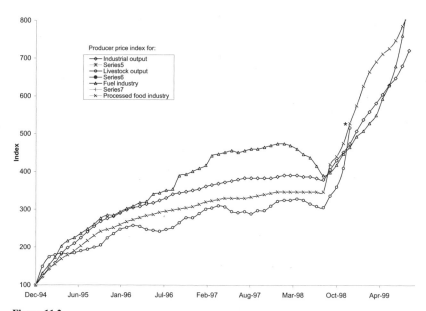

**Figure 11.2**
Producer price indexes by sectors of the economy
*Source*: Goskomstat.
*Note*: December 1994 = 100. * The series was discontinued in January 1999. Separate price index for grain is not available. The new series of producer price index for agricultural produce in the aggregate starting in 1999 does not include data for the earlier years.

The practice begun in 1994 continued in 1995. The agrarian lobby failed to procure trillions of rubles in credit from the budget for planting and sowing by farms. Oil companies were once again instructed to supply oil to farms that agreed to make advance payments for only 10 percent of oil deliveries. The farms also were required to pay off the partial tax payment exemption of the companies in the budget (plus 10 percent interest charge) at the end of harvesting. Farms "borrowed" 6 trillion rubles in commodity credits of the 11 trillion rubles offered to them despite doubts about their ability to repay the loans given their poor loan repayment record in the past.[8]

In a vigorously functioning market economy, monetary brakes and relative price movements would separate inefficient from efficient enterprises, creating substantial unemployment and industrial overhaul that in turn would restore the chain of financial payments among the robust survivors. In Russia, by contrast, the process was marked by recourse to "funny money" in the form of credit instruments, mutual payment clearing, and barter (although inter-enterprise barter, in our view, contributed far less to the survival mechanism) than recourse to borrowing and mutual clearing arrangements. More important, inter-enterprise cash nonpayment marched hand in hand with nonpayment to the workforce along with cutback in work hours and forced unpaid leave, practices analyzed at length in chapter 9. At the same time, barter payment to workers by factory managers was not substantial enough to counter the accumulated wage debts. However, countless examples of barter arrangements between workers and enterprises as alternatives to monetary payments circulated in the press.

## Barter Payments and Workers: The Anecdotes

An extreme example of barter was reported in the *Chicago Tribune* (October 12, 1997): "Russian seamstresses, owed two years of back wages, refused to accept coffins as barter payments, asking for grocery carts instead, the Itar-Tass news agency reported. The workers at the Voskhod clothing plant in Yaya, about 1,900 miles east of Moscow, would use the carts—worth about $21 each—to transport vegetables from their land plots. 'They are refusing to take the coffins in advance, explaining that they want to live and not to die,' the news agency said."

An article in the *BBC Online Network* (August 24, 1998) cited the following case: "One factory in the City of Perm regularly pays its workforce in bicycles—which they then have to try and sell on the streets in direct competition with their employers."

Yet another piece from the BBC News documented the plight of teachers:

Teachers in part of western Siberia are being paid in bottles of vodka, because the authorities have no money to meet their wages bill. The teachers in the most populous Maima district of the Altai republic are getting 15 bottles each. They have not been paid their proper salaries since February or March. An Itar-Tass news agency correspondent in the region says the teachers reckon it is better to get the vodka – which can be sold in local markets – than nothing at all. An attempt to pay them in toilet paper and funeral accessories provoked indignation. (*BBC Online Network*, September 22, 1998)

Occasionally barter tended to increase arrears to social funds and even facilitate theft. In a discussion on Russian public TV, correspondents discussed the embezzlement of local pension funds in the Tyumen region facilitated by the manner in which the funds were collected:

The procuracy here believes that the pension payments problems are due not only to the crisis. It is also interested in how money is collected for pension organizations. One of the companies doing that was the Tyumen-based Zashchita [Protection] charitable fund. Under an agreement with the Pension Fund, it was entitled to collect debts from businesses, which in the absence of live money settled up with petroleum products, building materials, IOUs or railway haulage services. But while it was doing this, Zashchita was not thinking about clearing those companies' debts to the Pension fund. All the property it received in this way was sold off and the money thus raised it spent on itself. (*BBC Worldwide Monitoring*, November 19, 1998)

The examples point to enterprises engaging in barter activities for clearing payments to workers and contributions to pension funds. But did barter between employers and workers increase sufficiently to compensate for wage nonpayment? To what extent did the monetary value of the goods and services arrest the upward trend in outstanding debt to workers? The abundant anecdotal evidence on workers being paid in kind rather than in cash does not address the question of an empirical link between wage arrears and enterprises resorting to partial wage payment to workers in the form of goods. We analyze this question by using RLMS questionnaire responses from 1994 to 1998 for measuring the trends in the incidence and magnitude of barter, and the relationship between wage arrears and barter payments.

### Wage Arrears and Barter Payments via RLMS

To track the incidence of barter payments, we created an indicator (dummy) variable, *Goodsp*, based on the survey question: "Have you received in the last thirty days at this enterprise in lieu of payment for your labor something from its production or from the production of another enterprise?" The response was coded as 1 if the respondent said "yes" and as 0 if the respondent said "no". Next we created a variable for the monetary value of these barter payment, *Goodsv*, based on the survey question: "Estimate, please, how much the product you received cost in rubles, regardless of what you did with it?" Respondents skipped this question if they answered that they did not receive goods in lieu of wages, that is, if the value of the indicator variable *Goodsp* was equal to zero.

The results in row (1) of table 11.3 suggest that 7.7 percent of the working population received part of their compensation in the form of goods in 1994, the ratio dropping to 6.5 percent in 1995, then rising to 9.3 percent in 1996 and again to 13.6 percent in 1998. Thus the fraction

Table 11.3
Trends in barter and percentage of people facing wage arrears

|  | 1994 | 1995 | 1996 | 1998 |
|---|---|---|---|---|
| *Goodsp*: percentage of people facing wage arrears who received barter | 7.70 (0.27) [3,260] | 6.49* (0.25) [2,819] | 9.25* (0.29) [2,303] | 13.62* (0.34) [2,378] |
| *Goodsv*: value of barter received | 231,947 (324,727) [130] | 199,634 (421,143) [76] | 201,656 (233,846) [155] | 127,380* (179,701) [228] |

Source: RLMS.
Note: Annual averages are reported with standard deviations in parentheses. * Denotes a significant difference at 5 percent between adjacent columns (years). Sample sizes are listed in square brackets below the standard errors.

of the working population receiving part payment in barter had jumped by nearly 77 percent in 1998 from the 1994 level.

However, increased *prevalence* of barter was not associated with a higher ruble value of barter payments, *Goodsv*, in row (2), which fell by 1998 to nearly one-half of the 1994 value. This decline in the average magnitude of barter payments indicates that, while the increased prevalence of barter helped ameliorate the adverse effects of the widespread wage withholding over time, barter payments only partially mitigated the upward trend in the value of outstanding debt to workers. Additional support for this conclusion is provided by the estimates of table 11.4.

These simple, average patterns in the incidence and magnitude of barter generally persist in table 11.4 when we analyze them below in a multivariate context. The prevalence of barter significantly increased between 1994 and 1998, and although there was no change in the value of barter between 1994 and 1996, it significantly declined in 1998.

## Did Barter Respond to Wage Nonpayment and Compensate Adequately?

Although trends in barter between 1994 and 1998 are relevant for our analysis, our central focus is to check if barter transactions responded to the presence of wage arrears. Regression (1) of table 11.4 analyzes the likelihood of barter payment in the presence of wage nonpayment. In regression (2), we estimate the responsiveness of barter payments with respect to the magnitude of wage arrears for workers who were owed wages. The final regression (3) investigates the relationship between

**Table 11.4**
Effect of wage arrears on barter

|  | Goodsp | | Goodsv |
| --- | --- | --- | --- |
|  | (1) | (2) | (3) |
| Pjowed | 0.0541* | — | — |
|  | (0.006) |  |  |
| ln(Amtowed) | — | 0.0244* | 0.1427* |
|  |  | (0.010) | (0.069) |
| d1995 | −0.0102 | −0.0191 | −0.1385 |
|  | (0.006) | (0.016) | (0.176) |
| d1996 | 0.0155* | 0.0572* | 0.0972 |
|  | (0.007) | (0.020) | (0.155) |
| d1998 | 0.0267* | 0.0496* | −0.3070* |
|  | (0.008) | (0.020) | (0.165) |
| $R^2$ | 0.1981 | 0.2153 | 0.2449 |
| Sample size | 8,423 | 2,854 | 390 |

*Source:* RLMS.
*Note:* We report slope estimates in the *Goodsp* regressions estimated by maximum likelihood probit. The ln(*Goodsv*) regression is estimated by ordinary least squares. Parameter estimates are reported with robust standard errors in parentheses. Each regression includes a constant and control variables for age, wages, gender, tenure, education, region, occupation, and industry. * Denotes significance at 5 percent.

the ruble value of barter and the ruble value of cumulative wage debt for those workers who experienced wage arrears *and* who received goods instead of cash.

In specification (1), the positive coefficient of *Pjowed* (the dummy variable that signals that a respondent was owed wages) indicates that the likelihood of receiving barter payment was higher by 5.41 percent for respondents who were owed wages in contrast to those who were not denied wages.

In specification (2), the positive coefficient of ln(*Amtowed*), 0.0244, suggests that among individuals who were owed wages, the likelihood of receiving goods increased by 2.4 percent with a 10 percent increase in the ruble value of outstanding arrears. We restrict our analysis in regression (2) to respondents who were currently owed wages by their employers (*Pjowed* = 1), so that the value of accumulated outstanding wage debt to the worker (the variable *Amtowed*) was positive. Therefore the estimate of the coefficient of the variable ln(*Amtowed*) reflects the effect of the change in the value of outstanding debt to a worker per se rather than a combination of this effect and the likelihood of having his wage withheld, that is, of observing a positive value for the variable *Amtowed*.

In the last regression, the positive coefficient of ln(*Amtowed*) suggests that the value of the goods received, conditional on receipt of goods (the regression is limited to people who reported receiving goods in lieu of wage payments, i.e., *Goodsp* = 1), increased with the ruble value of outstanding arrears. This result provides evidence that barter transactions arose at least in part as a response to wage arrears. The coefficient of 0.1427 suggests, however, that a 10 percent increase in the value of outstanding wage debt was associated, on average, with only a 1.4 percent increase in the value of payment in the form of goods. Therefore although barter payments could potentially mitigate the hardships to employees associated with wage withholding, the magnitude of these payments in lieu of wages to the sampled Russian households had a small mitigating effect on the adverse impact of wage arrears.

## Conclusions

Our analysis of barter practices among Russian enterprises, and between enterprises and workers (based on RLMS data), throws up two major conclusions. Russian enterprises created liquidity shortages by accumulating payment obligations rather than streamlining their production routines. The structural impact of relative price shifts (contributing to the unfavorable charges imposed by the monopoly power and fuel sectors) also aggravated their cash-flow problems. As a result, they employed a multifaceted survival strategy consisting of resort to a variety of debt instruments, tax write-offs, inter-enterprise barter, wage nonpayment to workers (including shorter work hours and forced unpaid leave), and barter payment to workers.

In the context of this many-pronged survival strategy, exceptional to Russia's market transition, barter strictly defined as exchange of goods and services in lieu of cash played a limited role in inter-enterprise and employer-employee transactions. Inter-enterprise barter transactions as a proportion of sales in September and November, 1998 were closer to the Goskomstat range of 9 to 15 percent than to the alternative measure of 51 percent (including mutual payment clearing among a chain of large enterprises).

By the same token and despite abundant anecdotal evidence, although employers did pay workers in goods and services, the amounts were by no means adequate to mitigate the hardships imposed on working men and women by wage nonpayment and the accumulated wage arrears. Workers' responses to wage denial via protest activities (including strikes) and a variety of survival strategies to maintain family well-being form the substance of the following two chapters.

In Soviet days, factory trade unions, controlled by the Communist Party of the Soviet Union (CPSU), looked after workers' welfare without playing a role in wage setting. Following the dissolution of the USSR in 1991 and emasculation of the Communist Party thereafter, trade unions and factory committees professing to protect workers' rights proliferated. So did laws guaranteeing wages and laying down punitive measures for managers withholding wages from working men and women. Wage arrears nevertheless accumulated.

In this chapter, we provide a brief survey of trade union activity in Soviet days and address three related issues, namely, the role of Russian trade unions in settling wages owed to workers; the set of laws they invoked for the purpose; and workers' resort to legal action and protest activity, including strikes, for extracting payment from employers. In conclusion, we conclude that the recourse to laws was ineffective, and strikes were largely uncoordinated over time and territory. Although wage arrears led to increased strike activity reflected in lost man-days in factories, strikes did not result in a lowering of accumulated wage arrears.

**The Legacy of Trade Union Activity**

Russia's original trade unions at the turn of the century, calculated to spread Marxist ideas among the proletariat and serve as instruments of revolutionary activity in the land of the czars, were overtaken by Lenin's view of trade unions as "transmission belts." They were supposed to convey proletarian grievances from below and required to transmit party decisions from above. During the brief New Economic Policy (NEP) phase of the early 1920s, they organized workers in private industry and led strikes in the state sector. Under Stalin, they helped in the planners' drive for industrialization by enforcing labor discipline.

With Stalin's passing from the scene in 1953, Soviet trade unions acquired a broad array of rights and responsibilities. Management could not dismiss workers without trade union consent. They monitored occupational, health, and safety conditions in factories in accordance with the prevailing labor laws. When these were transgressed, they tried enforcing closure of production sites and shops, and removal of managers. In the 1980s, they demanded dismissals of up to 10,000 managers for violating labor laws (Kanaev 1991, p. 260).

They carried out these functions, however, under the strict day-to-day control of the CPSU. The Party gave formal rights to the unions and their members via a maze of elaborate laws, but "the employment relation was not regulated by law and contract but by political administrative structures, of which trade unions and the judiciary were specialized parts and for which the law and constitution served as a mere resource" (Clarke 1998, p. 2). Rule of the Party-state rather than rule of law governed relations between employers and workers. More specifically, workers' rights were overridden by the supreme objective of boosting production. At the plant level, management often pressured trade unions "to subordinate their activities to the priority of meeting plan targets" (Clarke 1998, p. 2).

A major function of Soviet trade unions consisted in looking after the welfare of workers. They administered state and enterprise-funded welfare benefits and managed state-owned network of sanitariums and rest homes. They controlled substantial funds accruing from union dues and from a payroll levy supplemented by a budget subsidy. They distributed vouchers and allocated housing to employees.

The role and organization of the trade unions changed with the sweeping political changes initiated by Mikhail Gorbachev, who became General Secretary of the CPSU in March 1985. The first steps were slow and the signals were mixed. In 1986, the 27th Congress of the CPSU invoked trade union committees to be "the real rather than compliant partners of management" (Kanaev 1991, p. 261). In 1987, the 18th Congress of the Soviet Trade Unions, interpreting the trade union role in traditional terms, called upon unions to implement the social policies as laid down by the president before the Central Committee of the CPSU at the 27th Congress. The president, the Party, and its central committee were still the navigators of trade union activity.

The winds of change gathered pace slowly. The All Union Central Council of Trade Unions (AUCCTU), the national trade union organization, sought release from CPSU control. Workers, encouraged by mounting freedoms and dissatisfied with wages and working conditions, resorted to widespread strikes in June 1989. The AUCCTU, while endorsing workers' right to strike, emphasized the "tripartite system" of dialogue between trade unions, employers, and the government. The stage was set for a proliferation of trade unions, a loosening of collective bargaining procedures and adoption of new laws.

## More Trade Unions

Sotsprof, an umbrella organization combining unions of journalists, lawyers, local government employees, scientific workers, and an assortment of white-collar workers, was set up in August 1989. The Confederation of Labor, organized in the city of Novokuznets in May 1990, emphasized political activity to improve workers' welfare and called for a struggle against the domination of CPSU and AUCCTU. Occasionally, unions with competing tactics vied for workers' loyalty and dealt with factory management: In the huge Samara Ball Bearing Corporation, the pro-management and pliable Avtoselkhozmash Committee was pitted against the reformist Solidarnost that sought wage payment for workers along with factory restructuring. The mining region of Kuzbass witnessed the birth of several trade unions with miners, teachers, and health workers as members. Strike committees sprouted in factories all over Russia. The Russia-wide organization, linking the numerous trade unions, old and new, titled the Federation of Independent Trade Unions of Russia (FiTUR), had 60 million members according to its president, Mikhail Shmakov.

## Wage Setting, Collective Bargaining, and Labor-Market Policies

The proliferation of trade unions, increasingly independent of political control, set the stage for collective bargaining procedures that departed in principle from Soviet practices. In their wage setting practices, Soviet planners were conflicted by the desire to control income inequality and the need to provide work incentive. The detailed paraphernalia of wage tariffs in the productive sectors ranged from basic rates of the least to the most skilled workers in each branch, the rates in the job hierarchy varying by skill scales that reflected the differential with respect to the lowest skill. Arduous work and inhospitable job location in a given job entitled workers to a wage supplement. Wages in the "nonproductive" sectors of services, health care, and administration were set in relation to similar jobs in the productive sector. Collective farmers were guaranteed minimum wages.

The 1987 Law on Enterprises changed these arrangements by introducing an incomes policy. Nonbudget enterprises were freed to fix their wages, the floor determined by the existing wage tariff structure and the ceiling constrained by a tax penalizing excessive wage increases. The excess wage tax was abolished in 1995.

### Legal Provisions: The Soviet Legacy

Along with procedural changes in wage setting, new legislative provisions defining collective bargaining for wage negotiations and work conditions appeared in rapid succession, differing radically from Soviet laws.

Soviet labor law was noted for its solid tradition of comprehensiveness. The 1970 Principles of Labor Law and the 1971 Labor Code were painstakingly elaborate in specifying the rights and duties of employers and employees and the role of trade unions and courts in resolving disputes. These contained "all permissible disciplinary sanctions and provide(d) a complete list of grounds for dismissal" (Lampert 1986, p. 257). An employee could appeal within the norms of the law against arbitrary action by management over "payment of wages, salaries and bonuses; holiday entitlements; and compensation for damages" (Lampert 1986, p. 258). Collective industrial action by workers was ruled out. Soviet workers did not strike.

In practice, however, trade union officials lacked the independence to defend a worker's rights when conflicts developed and employee rights were threatened. First, enterprise management, the Party committee, and trade union officials were collectively responsible for enterprise performance and plan fulfillment. If the manager said a worker was a troublemaker, union officials were unlikely to dispute that judgment. Second, trade union officials, nominated and selected by the management in alliance with the Party secretary, were beholden to both. Finally, the material benefits and career advantages from being successful negotiators of labor disputes compelled trade union officials to adopt low-profile, conciliatory roles (Lampert 1986, pp. 264–265).

The new Russian laws departed from the old artifacts in allowing worker collectives to select their own trade union representatives and to initiate collective as well as individual action against management. But the tradition of "informal understandings and reciprocal favors" within the enterprise and the subordination of courts to "local political influences," which put employees at a disadvantage, persisted. In stark contrast to job security that arose from guaranteed employment in the Soviet days, the potential job loss in reforming Russia predisposed working men and women and their unions and committees to generally compromise over the issue of nonpayment.

### Legal Provisions: The Russian Laws

The 1987 Law on Enterprises empowered the worker collectives to decide on the need, if any, for a collective bargaining agreement with management; to select a trade union or a committee or any organization to engage in collective bargaining on their behalf; to agree on its provisions; and to ratify it. The law also recognized the rights of these bodies to conclude agreements with union, provincial, and local government agencies relating to wage formation guidelines, social security provisions, minimum wage guarantees, and wage indexation.

Subsequent legislation including the Russian Labor Code extended these provisions with a view to guaranteeing wage payments to workers in the privatized and budget sectors. The Russian Labor Code requires that wages be paid "no less than fortnightly," holiday pay be made in advance, and overdue wages be cleared on the workers' departure. The Federal Labor Inspectorate (Rostrudinspektsiya), the State Prosecutor, and their agencies are responsible for enforcing the legislation.

With escalating wage nonpayments in the budget sector, presidential decrees and government resolutions proliferated. The presidential decree of March 10, 1994, "instructing the state prosecutor to pursue those responsible for late payment" was followed by a succession of decrees instructing Rostrudinspektsiya "to verify the observance of the law, to impose fines for violations (regardless of property form) and hold personally responsible all federal leaders and officials" accountable for paying wages and transferring budgetary funds for such payments. A government commission was charged with the task of following the wage payments schedule from the budget on a weekly basis, punishing officials responsible for payment delays, and working up proposals for indexation of unpaid wages (Clarke 1998, p. 8).

Wage nonpayment in privatized factories that overshadowed budget sector arrears in scale and speed presented serious challenges as well. First, the right of workers to form a trade union was threatened with their privatization, managers increasingly taking the position that employee-shareholders—owners rather than employees—were not entitled to protection against themselves. The presidential decree of January 12, 1996, sought to close this loophole. It reaffirmed the right of workers, foreign and domestic, to form trade unions empowered to negotiate wage and contract terms with managers and conclude collective bargaining agreements on behalf of the workers. Employers were required to issue written notices to trade unions of not less than three months prior to closure or partial shutdown of factories or deterioration of employment terms. Unions could negotiate proposals, seeking delays of mass layoffs with local administrations. They could enforce provisions of labor laws aimed at ensuring the safety and health of workers (*The Moscow Times*, December 17, 1996).

Even before the adoption of this presidential decree, measures were in place calculated to extract payments from delinquent enterprises. Rostrudinspektsiya was empowered by the presidential decree of July 20, 1994, to secure the necessary information on payment delays and impose fines and sanctions on managers and officials alike. Failure to carry out a court order to pay wages, however, did not amount to criminal liability, the Duma having rejected a June 1995 amendment to the Criminal Code to that effect as "draconian" (Clarke 1998, p. 10).

Armed with the decrees, Rostrudinspektsiya went to work identifying culprits and imposing fines. Vladimir Varov, deputy labor minister and head of the agency, found 14,500 violations from 22,000 inquiries (Interview, *Novosti News Agency*, July 25, 1994). Most of the infringements in the budget sector arose because heads of universities and research institutes had misused funds allotted for staff and teachers. Commercial banks had failed to transfer funds to entrepreneurs that would enable them to make wage payments. Rostrudinspektsiya had imposed fines on 3,000 entrepreneurs and hauled up more than 1,000 managers for administrative and criminal accountability.

The president and the government too displayed bouts of resolve. The president sacked the administrative heads of Arkhangelsk and Saratov oblasts for misuse of funds, their removal coinciding with the presidential election campaign of spring 1996. Prime Minister Chernomyrdin promised to cut public sector wage arrears by half by December 31, 1997, and pay the rest by the middle of 1998. The actual performance (described in chapters 2 and 5) fell short of the promise due to limited commitment by the regions. The president instructed the prime minister on July 2, 1997, to pay arrears to the armed forces within two months. As noted in chapter 6, these were cleared with funds acquired from sale of state stock in the telecommunication company Svyazinvest. Withheld pensions were paid off the same year with World Bank credits provided for the purpose. However, nonpayment to the army and pensioners was to reappear soon thereafter, leading a desperate Prime Minister Yevgenii Primakov to plead before the legislators in September 1998: "Kill me, cut me"—words unbecoming the head of a government.

Although the obligations of employers to pay wages in exchange for labor services were laid down in law, the actual record lagged woefully behind. The creation of independent trade unions that could enforce these obligations, enlist members, protect their rights against employers, and take employers to court for wage nonpayment proved an uphill task involving time, resources, and skill. Unions caved in to management concerns that court action or a strike would paralyze the enterprise and threaten its revival. Occasionally competing unions and committees played off rival groups of workers. They were unable to implement court decrees for lack of funds or the necessary technical expertise or the weight of authority. The government tended to support official trade unions with entrenched traditions of ensuring social peace rather than guaranteeing employee rights. As a result, Russian trade unions, having failed to enforce workers' rights via contracts and laws, sought to extract wage payments to workers via protests exhibiting special features that, in turn, reflected the legal constraints within which they operated.

## Conciliatory Trade Unions and Strike Committees

At most enterprises, unions and committees initially sought to resolve wage nonpayment via direct negotiation with management, knowing well that persuasion did not work, managers made vague promises, and the nonpayment problem would continue.

Having failed at persuasion, employees and their committees held back from initiating court action for two reasons. The enterprise was in the red either because it was not able to sell its output or because it was not producing much due to material shortage. A worker at a chemical factory summed up the situation: "We come here every day to discover shortage of butylphenol leading to work stoppage. How can we expect to get paid if there is no production?" Plant management assured workers that if production could be revived by securing raw materials and cutting current debts, wages could be paid in the future. In that case, workers opted for a wait-and-see attitude rather than risk plant closure by insisting on wage payment via court action.

## Trade Union Rivalry

Decision making was occasionally embroiled in competing unions seeking worker allegiance and forcing managerial choices, at times resulting in benign outcomes. The events at the Samara Ball Bearing Corporation, which produced 80 percent of ball bearings for the military, was a case in point.

The plant, barely functioning during 1992–96, had stabilized by March 1997. The April 1993 workforce of 26,000 was slashed to 7,500 by September 1997. Some property was sold off. Housing was gradually transferred to the town municipality. The remaining was only partially subsidized. The tourist center, children's summer camp, and sports stadium, all self-sustaining, were kept under plant management. A number of workshops were locked up; their power and water supply was stopped. Wages were frozen at low levels. The plant received half of its 8 billion ruble monthly income in early 1997 in kind. with which it paid 70 percent of its power supply and 70 percent of raw material costs. The management opened a store at the plant where workers could get products in lieu of wages.

Despite the fine tuning, wage arrears accumulated. So wage payments were staggered. Workers at the main assembly workshops received payment first, followed by those at the auxiliary workshops, ending with employees of departments and services.

The arrears split the response of two competing unions. Avtoselkhozmash Committee sided with the administration that had revived the plant after the financial collapse of 1992–96. It wanted to turn around the unit, preserve current jobs, and support management. By contrast, Solidarnost, the Independent Workers Union, launched in 1992, adopted radical tactics within the legislative guidelines. It favored streamlining of production activity, sale of assets, and worker layoffs. It organized protests in 1995 and 1996, financially the most stressful years for management. It blocked the Moscow highway passing through Samara on June 26, 1996, forcing the company to take out a loan and clear arrears. It filed eleven collective lawsuits beginning 1994 by securing partial clearance of back wages. On balance, Solidarnost activism and management response contributed to an effective retooling of the plant and downsizing of the workforce.

## Unions Lacking Resources and Clout

Occasionally trade union committees, having gone beyond negotiations and persuasion and filed collective lawsuits for clearing wage arrears, faced technical chores and administrative details they were incapable of handling.

Thus, on getting a successful court decree at the end of 1996 ordering management to clear wage arrears, the trade union committee of Novokuibyshevsk Oil and Chemical Integrated Plant faced a string of problems: Union accountants and treasurers, unable to handle financial details of the court award, sought the help of outsiders, inflating their budget for the purpose in the process; the committee had no guarantee that the commercial bank would release the necessary funds from the plant account without exorbitant charges, or that the plant cashiers would distribute the funds. Two remedies were available to workers if employers failed to pay wages. They could file a lawsuit or declare a strike.

## Workers and Lawsuits

Faced with wage nonpayment, workers could resort to court action. A worker could submit an individual petition to a court claiming payment of withheld wages without linking it to inflation-based indexation or compensation for moral damage arising from nonpayment. If, on submission of the necessary documents, the court issued a payment decree, the corresponding amount had to be withdrawn from the enterprise bank account to clear the back pay.

The union committee could also file a collective statement of claim on behalf of the workers, sparing them a complicated procedural and court battle. The courts, however, preferred to hear cases on an individual basis and award claims to a litigant rather than the entire workforce. Occasionally they awarded damages to litigants for "moral loss" under Article 151 of the Civil Code and indexation of unpaid wages under Article 395 of the Civil Code.

Therefore, although collective action was possible in principle, it was ruled out in practice as in the Soviet days. In any case, having issued a ruling, courts did not enforce payment if an enterprise was short of cash in its bank account (Clarke 1998, p. 9). Instances of cash diversion to clear back payment also came to light. Teachers in Sysert' region in Sverdlovsk province were paid after a four months' delay in March 1997 from funds siphoned off from kindergartens. If the collective agreement with management included a clause specifying the date for wage payment, failure on management's part to pay wages on time constituted a legal ground for a strike.

**Workers and Strikes**

Under prevailing law, "a strike is only legal if it is in pursuit of a collective labor dispute (i.e., in relation to the terms of the collective agreement), if it has been endorsed by a ballot, if due notice is given, and if appropriate conciliation and arbitration procedures have been undertaken" (Clarke 1998, p. 8). Since managers generally refused collective contracts and strikes involved complex procedures, most strikes were illegal, officially defined as "unauthorized absence from work." They were marked by three features.

*Disorganized Strikes and Disunited Strikers*

Strikes frequent spread from the budget-sector employees, among them teachers, doctors, and scientists, to other sectors and regions. They were neither open-ended nor coordinated over time and place among strikers. Most strikes were organized by enterprise or organization strike committees rather than by trade unions, who apparently supported them. Strikes at factory gates were rare because half the factories were idle.

The machine builders, aircraft technicians, workers at a shipbuilding plant, and defense industry employees either demonstrated on streets or went on a hunger strike. Strikers at the Zvezda submarine repair plant in the Far East blocked the Trans-Siberian Railway on July 1, 1997. Doctors, who were on strike less frequently than teachers, organized rallies. Strikes at atomic power stations were restricted to refusals to maintain the reactors, because the law forbade a complete shutdown of reactors which could put them out of commission. Several thousand nuclear power plant workers from Smolensk, Kalinin, Leningrad oblast, Kola, and Novovoronezh converged on Moscow on July 16, 1997, demanding funds for plant maintenance and withheld wages. Penniless pensioners disrupted traffic in the center of Samara and blocked the bridges over the Volga.

The strikers were not united despite a common grievance. Solidarity was absent even among groups with traditional "guild" awareness.

When physicians, joined by their colleagues from far-off Kostroma and Yaroslavl', demonstrated in front of the White House, their better-off colleagues in the capital kept away.[1]

The discord among strikers represented by their unions was illustrated by union activity in the Kuzbass coal basin in the Kemerovo Province of Western Siberia. The Kuzbass miners, the vanguard of the workers' movement, gradually lost their pioneering role by refusing cooperation with other unions, having won a wage increase for themselves in 1989. At the same time, Rosugol and the coal industry management dealt with the coal miners in a cloak-and-dagger fashion, rushing cash to Sudzhenskaya miners in Anzhero-Sudzhensk who blocked the Trans-Siberian Railway in April 1997 while closing Tsentral'naya mine in Prokop'evsk in March 1997, a painful closure brought about by a prolonged strike.

The trade unions of teachers and health workers by contrast grew in numbers and discipline. They owed their dominance to the fact that they faced a single administration, city or regional, unlike the miners whose ultimate employer was Rosugol stationed in Moscow. They were more educated, better organized, and highly disciplined, maintaining careful records of the wages owed to them, and ready to devote time and energy to union activity.

It is not clear if teachers and health workers incurred lower incidence and amounts of wage withholding than miners because they were better organized. Our estimates in chapter 4 suggest that miners were the worst sufferers in terms of these criteria.

## Workers and Managers Striking against the State

Protests in large Russian factories, in sharp contrast to labor disputes elsewhere in the industrial world, were marked by an open alliance between labor and management against the state. Indeed, the strategy of the trade unions was to bombard the president, the Russian government, the Federation Council (upper house of the parliament), and the Duma with messages, demands, and occasional threats to settle wage arrears that could have been cleared via direct negotiations with enterprise management and local authorities. Managers provided the strategic input because they could extract concessions from the government. Following Soviet-era tradition, a law enacted by the Duma barred managers from union membership, providing them with opportunities for self-serving activity. Disgruntled managers, denied membership, were often in the forefront of strikes for settling wage disputes. At the same time, they victimized and dismissed workers for initiating strikes.

*Predictable Annual Strike Pattern*

Kuzbass miners sought concessions from the industry or the government at the start of the year before the cumulative burden got out of control. Teachers by contrast got active on the eve of the summer vacation, facing the prospect of a three-month vacation without pay during which they held odd jobs. The employers played off one group against the other, paying the more vocal while postponing a systematic resolution of the problem.

Local administrators responsible for paying teachers used a gradual, step-by-halting-step payment schedule and sought to break the resolve of striking teachers, who worried about the social responsibility of educating children. In early June 1997, Sverdlovsk teachers served notice demanding back wages and school repairs without which, they insisted, school would not open in September. On the first day of the strike, the striking teachers received wages for the previous February. At the end of the first week, they were paid for March with funds borrowed from a bank at 28 percent interest. As the strike wore on, their resolve weakened, differences developed, and some worried about the children's education. Soon thereafter, schools were back to normal. Teachers and administrators staged similar routines in other parts of the country.

The annual protest ritual in the federal and local budget sectors was predictable and even manageable. The government responded to a potential strike scheduled toward the end of the year—the 'working-people's autumn rallies"—by putting together a payment schedule from next year's budget, thereby restoring a social partnership. The strike was postponed. As new debts appeared by March of next year and negotiations for settling them dragged on into the summer, the government proposed a schedule of payment based on the economy's performance in the first half and prospective tax collection. Once again the strike was averted.[2]

However, the period of nonpayment had become longer. The two-weeks payment delay of 1992 had stretched to two months by the start of 1996. The two-month-delay formula was extended to the nonbudget sector in November 1996: The leaders of the Federation of Independent

Trade Unions (FiTUR) and the Russian Trilateral Commission on Labor Disputes decided (following the one-day, Russia-wide protest action on November 5, 1996), that enterprises that did not pay wages and salaries for three months (the utmost permissible limit) should be subjected to bankruptcies. Thus the consensus model between employees, the budget sector, and the trade union leaders was in effect extended to the privatized enterprises: Workers were willing to put up with a delay in wage payment of up to three months. The substantive outcome of the November 1996 agreement therefore was that wage arrears would not disappear in the future, but would not stretch beyond three months.[3]

The accommodating stance was evident also in activities of FiTUR, which organized successive day-long, Russia-wide protest rallies. Its chairman, Mikhail Shmakov, supported acting Prime Minister Kiriyenko by rescheduling the FiTUR rally on April 9, 1998, separating it from the protests of the Communist Party of the Russian Federation (RFCP) on that day. It conveyed FiTUR's concerns for wage payment, unemployment reduction, and legislative protection of the workers to the government without politicizing its demands into antigovernment channels.

The government for its part adopted the tactic of plugging holes and allocating money to those who protested the loudest. Systematic bankruptcies and an effective restructuring or closure of nonviable units were postponed to the future.

Strikes, scattered over time and territory, and organized by a motley group of inexperienced strike committees, lacked a sustained momentum designed to pressure employers to clear wage arrears in the budget sector and in factories. The strikers modulated their demands in recognition of the inability of employers to pay them fully. They demonstrated against nonpayment without successfully solving the problem. What kind of association do the available data suggest between strikes and nonpayment?

## Strikes and Nonpayment

We utilize monthly data on man-days lost in strikes from February 1997 to October 1999 for analyzing the following questions: Did wage nonpayment during the period, represented by monthly real wage arrears in December 1997 prices, contribute to a significant rise in strike activity? Alternatively, did strikes lead to lower wage arrears?

**Table 12.1**
Relationship between strike activity and wage arrears

|                    | (1)          | (2)          |
|--------------------|--------------|--------------|
| ln(*arrears*)      | 2.718[b]     | 2.161[b]     |
|                    | (1.08)       | (0.88)       |
| ln(*wages*)        | −2.875       | −7.586[a]    |
|                    | (2.07)       | (2.02)       |
| Trend              | −            | −0.146[a]    |
|                    |              | (0.04)       |
| Adjusted $R^2$     | 0.1493       | 0.4473       |

*Source: Russian Economic Trends*, various issues.
*Note:* The analysis is based on thirty-three months of data ($n = 33$) from February 1977 through October 1999. Ordinary least squares parameter estimates are reported with standard errors in parentheses (both regressions additionally include a constant). The dependent variable is the logarithm of man-days lost per month (MDL) in all sectors of the Russian economy. Explanatory variables are monthly wage arrears (in billions of December 1997 new rubles) in four major sectors of the economy; wages are monthly real wages due to workers in December 1997 rubles; "Trend" is a linear time trend.
a. Denotes significance at 1 percent.
b. Denotes significance at 5 percent.

The regression results in table 12.1 support our qualitative analysis: While wage arrears did lead to increased strike activity measured in lost man-days, it failed in whittling down wage nonpayment. We measure strike activity in man-days lost due to strikes, rather than the number of strikes per se to assess the impact of strikes on wage nonpayment. Data on man-days lost, however, are available only for the entire economy and not by specific sectors, so that we are unable to establish a statistical relationship between wage arrears and union actions in, for example, the coal sector or for striking teachers.

The estimates reported in table 12.1 suggest that from early 1997 to late 1999, man-days lost to strikes were positively associated with the real monthly wage debt. In specification (2), a 1 percent increase in the real monthly arrears increased the monthly man-days lost due to strikes, on average, by 2.16 percent over the period. Again, a 1 percent increase in real monthly wages, ceteris paribus, decreased man days lost by 7.59 percent.

But did arrears lead to increased strike activity? Did strikes in turn prompt officials and managers to undertake actions aimed at reducing wage arrears? To establish a general, systematic cause-and-effect pattern, we carry out a simple Granger causality test.[4] Specifically, we run the following two OLS regressions:

$$MDL_t = \beta_0 + \beta_1 MDL_{t-1} + K + \beta_m MDL_{t-m}$$
$$+ \alpha_1 WA_{t-1} + K + \alpha_m WA_{t-m} + \varepsilon_t \qquad (1)$$

$$WA_t = \delta_0 + \delta_1 WA_{t-1} + K + \delta_m WA_{t-m}$$
$$+ \gamma_1 MDL_{t-1} + K + \gamma_m MDL_{t-m} + \mu_t \qquad (2)$$

where $MDL$ represents man-days lost due to strikes, and WA represents real monthly wage arrears. When we use four lags ($m = 4$), our test of whether the group of coefficients $\alpha_1$, $\alpha_2$, $\alpha_3$, and $\alpha_4$ in (1) is significantly different from zero yields an $F$-statistic of 2.33, which has a $P$-value of 0.0916; we therefore reject the null hypothesis (at 10 percent significance) that wage arrears do not "cause" man-days lost. On the other hand, testing whether the group of coefficients $\gamma_1$, $\gamma_2$, $\gamma_3$, and $\gamma_4$ in (2) is significantly different from zero yields and $F$-statistic of 0.22, which has a $P$-value of 0.9263, so that we are unable to reject the null hypothesis that man-days lost do not "cause" reduced wage arrears.[5] Thus the Granger causality test supports our conclusion that wage arrears resulted in greater levels of strike activity. While the government may have responded to strikes by allocating additional funds for reducing outstanding arrears in a specific activity, we do not notice a systematic feedback from strikes to lower arrears. However, the availability of data on specific sectors and occupations, such as coal and teaching, might have helped us establish a cause-and-effect relationship from strike activity to reduced arrears.

## Conclusions

Our analysis in this chapter raises a substantive issue, beyond the scope of this book, with regard to the social and historical roots of the failure of protests, rallies, and uncoordinated strike activity to materialize into a sustained mass movement. Russia, potentially on the verge of a revolution, was devoid of revolutionary activity. How does one explain the enigma?

We addressed this issue here from the limited perspective of the lack of institutional means in workplaces enabling workers to mount an organized protest movement. In the Soviet days, discontent was ventilated through party cells in the factories and organizations that were disbanded in reforming Russia. Under perestroika, the citizens gained individual freedoms but lost the apparatus for collective action. The factory strike committees, hastily put together by activist groups, were manipulated by managers and regional bosses, who, while responsible for wage arrears, pitted workers against the federal authorities. At the same time, the Communist Party of the Russian Federation led by Gennady Zyuganov, had a countrywide organization, but failed to offer a new vision and a credible alternative.

A more persuasive argument in support of the failure of a socially explosive situation to develop into a mass movement consisted in the readiness of the masses to channel their time, resources, and energies into the monumental task of survival in the midst of acute deprivation. People sought out opportunities to alleviate hardships and discover ways to supplement their incomes. Those denied wages found second jobs and informal paid activity. Almost half the population started growing a variety of food items for self-consumption and sale. Pensioners sought out jobs. People ran down savings and sold family heirlooms. Adult children transferred incomes to parents and vice versa.

A rigorous analysis of these alternative survival strategies that people adopted from day to day while being denied wages forms the substance of our next chapter.

# 13 Wage Arrears, Poverty, and Family Survival Strategies

Did wage withholding push people below the poverty line, defined in terms of a minimum living standard? How did families survive when they were denied wages for months at a time? In this chapter, we analyze the likely impact of wage arrears on family poverty and household responses to wage nonpayment, ranging from multiple job holding to home production of food, to borrowing and selling family assets in attempts to maintain family well-being. We use the rich information elicited by the RLMS questionnaires for the purpose, beginning with a discussion of the complex issue of defining a minimum living standard for Russia in the midst of its chaotic transition, then turning to the string of Russia-wide opinion polls that complement our statistical analysis with their empirical patterns.

## Measuring Minimum Living Standard in Russia

The measurement of poverty itself raised tricky questions that were actively debated by Russian analysts. The council of ministers was instructed in mid-1993 to devise a social standard defining the basic needs of the population for food, medical care, education, housing and utility charges, and purchase of durable goods. This minimum living standard (*prozhitochny minimum*) was to serve as the basis for future changes in payments to the public and assistance to the needy.[1]

The minimum living standard was derived separately for each Russian region on the basis of a basket of nineteen food items, with a percentage supplement depending on the climate. The concept of the minimum living standard, however, was not clear. Not only was there no law on the minimum living standard, but there was no unique method for calculating it. The Federation of Independent Trade Unions of Russia, the Ministry of Labor, and the Trade Union for Defense

Industry Workers had three different versions of a minimum living standard. Even in Moscow, the figure varied from 450,000 rubles to 1.2 million rubles a month in mid-1997.[2]

The average minimum living standard for Russia in 1996, according to the Ministry of Labor, was 317,000 rubles a month, less than the 367,000 rubles for Moscow. Almost 32 million Russian citizens, 21.6 percent of the population, had monthly per capita incomes below the minimum living standard.[3] The critical issue was defining the minimum standard in terms of changing realities.

### Defining Poverty in the Midst of a Chaotic Transition

The method of computing the minimum standard, adopted in 1992, reflected the gravest period of economic crisis, which was expected to last a year or a year and half. It assumed that citizens would spend 68.3 percent of the budget on food and postpone purchases of items of necessity such as clothes, shoes, and dishes.

The temporary method remained in force, so the minimum standard was inadequate for basic survival. For example, the minimum standard based on the labor ministry's calculation for Moscow for August 1996 was 462,000 rubles a month, including 297,000 rubles for food, which left 165,000 for everything else. But bus and subway rides to work cost 132,000 rubles for monthly transportation, leaving little for utilities including rent (which cost more than food in 1996) and essential items such as a tube of toothpaste, a bar of soap, and a roll of toilet paper. Therefore the poverty threshold for Moscow was 695,000 rubles a month and not 462,000 rubles. Adjustment of food expenses to 58.9 percent of the budget gave an average minimum living standard for Russia in August 1996 of 432,000 rubles a month, putting 40 million people in poverty instead of 30 million.[4]

These measurement problems did not deter the Duma from passing a law (with 326 votes out of 450 in favor) requiring all social payments from January 1, 1996, to be calculated on the basis of the minimum living standard. This implied that individuals whose incomes fell below the standard had a right to apply for the difference.[5]

The public, unaware of the debates surrounding the measurement of poverty norms, adopted several ways of overcoming a decline in living standards brought on by the Gaidar price decontrol measures of January 1992, having practiced the art of survival long before wage withholding contributed further to the hardships.

## Survival Strategies and Public Opinion Polls

The immediate impact of the Gaidar reforms and the people's strategies of coping with the resulting turmoil were brought out in a series of 1993 countrywide opinion polls of 1,500 to 2,000 people representing Russia's adult population by social and demographic features.

Eighty-six percent of those surveyed complained of their family incomes lagging behind price rises. Nine out of ten were dissatisfied with their families' economic condition. Food outlays in poor and better-off families made up 60 to 70 percent of family budgets. More than 80 percent lacked cash to buy a durable good, and 72 percent held off buying clothes and footwear.

People lacked money to bury their loved ones. Such "refuseniks," a category increasingly identified by morgues, were a new group on the Russian landscape, requiring the state to bury the dead. The 10,000 ruble voucher did not pay for a funeral that required 12,000 rubles up front.[6]

Respondents of a January 1993 survey managed to mitigate the impact of price increases by selectively storing everything worth stocking, home growing and processing food products, and undertaking supplementary jobs and new economic activity. By August 1992, almost half (47 percent) of Russian families had garden plots that they cultivated; every sixth person in the survey earned extra income by holding a second job or working under a temporary contract or personal arrangement; 5 percent were busy with street vending. Such supplementary work, requiring 21.4 hours a week including Sundays, brought extra income comparable to their regular earnings for one-third of the additionally active. The respondents, expecting prices to go up, spent the extra cash immediately but selectively. Twelve percent also adapted to the hardships by taking up totally new activities in lease-holding enterprises, joint-stock companies, and private enterprises, enjoying in the process a better life than state employees.[7]

This pattern of surviving and overcoming hardships continued as wage nonpayment appeared and became a routine for most families. By 1996, the number of fruit growers had almost tripled and the number of vegetable gardeners had nearly doubled in nine years, half the city dwellers having plots on which they grew 25 percent of potatoes and vegetables and 40 percent of fruits and berries in the economy. Dacha gardening activity, however, was increasingly taxed by local bureaucrats and rural administrators in a hierarchy of budget claims in the form of contributions to employment, education, and pension funds, and increased cost of transportation. A bus trip for a couple on a city bus in Rostov-on-Don to a distant plot cost 10,000 rubles.[8]

At the same time, the economy was increasingly moving underground, with people concealing their incomes from official reporting and taxes and avoiding open settlement of accounts with customers and suppliers. By 1996, the shadow sector was estimated at 20 to 40 percent of the open economy.[9]

A similar pattern of adjustment was reported in a 1997 survey of 2,200 people, eighteen years and older, representing eleven broad social/occupation groups and matching the composition of Russia's population in terms of sex, age, and ethnic affiliation (the results had a margin of error of 3 to 4 percent.): Only a minuscule 3.2 percent managed to buy everything, living well and meeting all their needs. The next 12.2 percent had enough cash to eat, dress well, and buy a variety of goods excluding expensive items such as a dacha, a car, or an apartment. 60 percent of the respondents lived from payday to payday, spending their earnings on food and other necessities without borrowing. Twenty percent regularly borrowed money or sold personal items to scrape through. According to the survey, 80 percent of the population managed to survive.[10]

Almost half, 46.8 percent, of these survivors sought opportunities for supplementary temporary work or multiple jobs. Roughly the same number met their food needs from personal auxiliary plots, orchards, or gardens, and 13 percent of the food growers sold some of the produce. Some 10.2 percent got financial help from relatives and friends; 7 percent traded items including secondhand goods, or leased their dwellings' garages or dachas. Only 1.8 percent received benefits from local administrations, and a tiny 0.3 percent got help from charitable organizations.[11]

If life continued to deteriorate, about one-third was willing to put up with the deprivations, but more than 50 percent were against tolerating a further deterioration: 80 percent of these were ready to seek additional ways of making money, whereas 30 percent would engage in political protest consisting of rallies, demonstrations, and strikes. Almost 60 percent of the respondents believed that Russian authorities could not be positively influenced.[12]

Finally, a substantial 40 percent in the survey would have liked to live in the Brezhnev era, 3.4 percent in the Gorbachev period, and 11.6 percent in the Yeltsin years. Twenty-three percent of respondents, twenty years and younger, preferred the choice of living under Yeltsin as against a smaller 17 percent of the same age under Brezhnev. Again, 34 percent of entrepreneurs and 39 percent of students surveyed exceeded by a large margin their respective cohorts at 8 and 9 percent who would have liked to revert to the past. The remaining occupations clearly preferred the Brezhnev years.[13]

In a later Public Opinion Foundation survey, only 6 percent believed that Russia was moving in the right direction, whereas 54 percent thought that the country was "taking a wrong path." A majority of 58 percent was against privatization. In the continuing dispute between the Duma and the president over land ownership, 52 percent supported the Duma's preference for collective farms against 27 percent supporting the president's choice for private ownership of land.[14]

The survey results suggest that, disillusioned with the reforms and nostalgic about the Brezhnev era, people continued with their innovative efforts at supplementing their rapidly deteriorating living standards. The opinion polls, however, did not differentiate between the survival strategies of those who were subjected to wage withholding and those who were not. Did the former group, for example, resort to multiple job holding or supplemental paid activity more frequently? Were they more likely to grow their own food or borrow money, sell assets or draw down their savings? Was the group denied wages more likely to be rendered poor than the group that continued receiving wages? Were the survival strategies of supplementing the material resources of the wage-deprived group more likely to rescue it from being pushed into poverty? We use data from the RLMS to analyze these question in depth.

We first assess the effect of wage arrears on the incidence of family poverty and then investigate family responses to wage nonpayment for maintaining family welfare. Among the survival strategies were multiple job holding and less formal, paid economic activity; home production of food for consumption and sale; various forms of dissaving such as taking out loans, withdrawing savings, and selling family assets; and intrafamily transfers from relatives to people experiencing nonpayment. Finally, we consider the role of home production and these income transfers in mitigating the impact of wage arrears on poverty incidence.

## Wage Arrears and Poverty

Clearly the incomes of families who were not being fully paid for work were lower than those of people receiving their contracted wages.

**Table 13.1**
Wage arrears and the incidence of poverty

|                | 1994     | 1995     | 1996    | 1998    |
|----------------|----------|----------|---------|---------|
| Owed wages     | 11.89    | 26.87    | 25.93   | 34.42   |
|                | [875]    | [722]    | [729]   | [813]   |
| Not owed wages | 8.13     | 15.98    | 13.89   | 22.43   |
|                | [2,017]  | [1,589]  | [799]   | [633]   |

*Note:* The sample is restricted to currently employed wage earners. Each cell entry gives the percentage of respondents in families with family incomes below regional poverty thresholds. The first row gives poverty percentages for respondents who reported that they were owed wages by their employers; the second row gives poverty percentages for people who did not report that they were owed wages by their employers. Poverty rates are significantly different at 1 percent in all years between respondents based on their having been owed wages or otherwise in each year. Sample sizes are listed in square brackets.

While reduced income unambiguously cut back family welfare, it was not clear if it actually pushed families into poverty.[15] The results of our analysis, focusing on the relationship between wage arrears and the incidence of poverty among Russian families, are reported in tables 13.1 and 13.2. Empirically, we define families as poor in terms of an indicator variable that is set equal to 1 if family income (adjusted for the structure of the family, i.e., number and age of children, number and gender of adults, and number of the elderly) falls below regional poverty thresholds; the variable is set at 0 if family income does not fall below the poverty threshold. RLMS researchers calculated regional poverty thresholds on the basis of a subsistence minimum consumption bundle, using subsistence food amounts for approximately fifty-five food items for five demographic groups (young children, older children, adult males, adult females, and the elderly) and regional average prices for each item (for ten regions).

Mean comparisons of table 13.1 suggest three principal conclusions. First, the percentage of people in poverty increased in Russia during the transition irrespective of whether people were owed wages.[16] Second, this percentage was higher in all years for people who were owed wages in row (1) at 12 percent in 1994, in contrast to 8 percent for those not experiencing wage nonpayment. Finally, the incidence of poverty increased faster, by 189 percent, between 1994 and 1998, for people denied wages as against 176 percent for those not owed wages.

The multivariate analysis reported in table 13.2 focuses on the impact of wage arrears, captured by the indicator variable *Pjowed* in row (1), on poverty incidence. We see that poverty rates were higher in 1994

**Table 13.2**
Trends in the relationship between wage arrears and the incidence of poverty

| Explanatory variables | (1) | (2) | (3) |
|---|---|---|---|
| Pjowed | 0.0555[a] | 0.0545[a] | 0.0969[a] |
| | (0.018) | (0.018) | (0.017) |
| Pjowed × d1995 | 0.0603[a] | 0.0428[c] | 0.0316[d] |
| | (0.026) | (0.026) | (0.023) |
| Pjowed × d1996 | 0.0698[a] | 0.0602[b] | 0.0448[c] |
| | (0.028) | (0.029) | (0.026) |
| Pjowed × d1998 | 0.0582[a] | 0.0367[d] | −0.0070 |
| | (0.026) | (0.027) | (0.021) |
| d1995 | 0.1022 | 0.1074[a] | 0.0973[a] |
| | (0.015) | (0.015) | (0.014) |
| d1996 | 0.0829[a] | 0.0841[a] | 0.1139[a] |
| | (0.017) | (0.020) | (0.020) |
| d1998 | 0.1968[a] | 0.1875[a] | 0.1667[a] |
| | (0.019) | (0.023) | (0.022) |
| (psuedo) $R^2$ | 0.0594 | 0.0519 | 0.2140 |

*Note:* Regression (1) includes all respondents, while (2) is restricted to currently employed wage earners. Maximum likelihood probit slope coefficient estimates are reported with robust standard errors in parentheses. The dependent variable is defined as 1 if the family income (adjusted for family structure) fell below the poverty threshold and as 0 if the family income did not fall below the poverty threshold. Regression (3) additionally includes a constant and control variables for age, tenure, gender, education, region, occupation, and industry. The sample size for regression (1) is 10,302 and 8,195 for (2) and (3).
a. Denotes significance at 1 percent.
b. Denotes significance at 5 percent.
c. Denotes significance at 10 percent.
d. Denotes significance at 15 percent.

for those denied wages among all respondents (regression 1), among the subsample of wage earners (regression 2), and finally, among wage earners (regression 3) when we control for demographic and job market attributes of the respondents. In regression 3, the 1994 poverty rate in row (1) among wage earners (on payroll) denied wages was 10 percent higher.

The interaction effects in the table help us assess the differential impact over time of wage arrears on the likelihood of an individual being in poverty, that is, being a member of a family with an income below the regional poverty threshold. A positive interaction effect indicates a stronger effect relative to that in the 1994 base year. In specification (1) for all respondents, the impact of wage arrears on poverty incidence in rows (2)–(4) was higher by an almost constant 6 to 7 percent in

1995–1998 than in 1994. When we restrict the analysis to currently employed wage earners in specification (2), wage nonpayment increased the likelihood of being in poverty by 5.5 percent in 1994 (once again, relative to people who did not have some portion of their wages withheld), by 9.7 percent (0.0545 + 0.0428) in 1995, by 11.5 percent (0.0545 + 0.0602) in 1996, and by 9.1 percent (0.0545 + 0.0367) in 1998 (although this differential effect is significant at 15 percent).

When we additionally control for demographic and job market attributes in specification (3), wage nonpayment (net of the influence of these factors) increased the likelihood of a person being in poverty by 9.7 percent in 1994 (once again, relative to people who did not have some portion of their wages withheld), by 12.9 percent (0.0969 + 0.0316) in 1995 (although this differential is significant at 15 percent), and by 14.2 percent (0.0969 + 0.0448) in 1996. It remained unchanged in 1998 at (the 1994) 10 percent higher for those denied wages (the interaction parameter is statistically not significant).

Two major conclusions emerge from this analysis. First, wage arrears not only reduced family incomes via wage nonpayment during 1994–98, but drove an increasing number of people into poverty. Second, among wage earners (who received partial wage payments), the poverty impact of wage nonpayment fell back to the 1994 levels in 1998.[17]

### Responses to Wage Arrears

How did families get by when they were not paid? We examine below the impact of a number of survival mechanisms at play in Russia on the incidence of household poverty.

#### *Secondary Job Holding and Informal Paid Work*

People responded to wage nonpayment by taking secondary jobs and by engaging in informal, supplemental work for pay.[18] Traditional models of moonlighting behavior argue that workers take second jobs when they are underemployed on their main job, underemployment being defined as workers desiring more work hours than their main employers make available to them. In other words, the wage rate on their main job is higher than their marginal rate of substitution between earnings (consumption) and leisure at current hours of work (see Shisko and Rostker 1976). This framework assumes that workers are paid for hours of work: They are underemployed if they want to earn more income by working more (paid) hours.

Wage nonpayment in Russia can be seen in a similar light: Workers, unable to generate desired income on their primary jobs,[19] engaged in supplemental employment to meet their income goals. From that perspective, the wage arrears crisis evidently had real effects on the economy by inducing labor supply responses in the form of supplemental economic activity[20] in addition to those generated by expenditure shifts.

We consider two forms of secondary economic activity—multiple job holding and less formal supplemental work for pay. We analyze the effect of wage arrears on multiple job holding by using a dummy that indicates if a person held a second, formal job for pay. We use the following survey question for the purpose:

Tell me, please, do you have some other kind of work?

The multiple job holding dummy is coded as 1 if the answer to the above question is "yes", and coded as 0 if the answer is "no." By contrast, we analyze informal secondary job holding via a dummy indicating a respondent's engagement in less formal, largely self-employment activities:

Tell me, please, in the last thirty days did you engage in some additional kind of work for which you got paid? Maybe you sewed someone a dress, gave someone a ride in a car, assisted someone with apartment or car repairs, purchased and delivered food, looked after a sick person, or did something else that you were paid for?

The informal economic activity variable is coded as 1 if the answer is "yes", and as 0 if the answer is "no".

As a result of the RLMS sampling procedure, the former question was only asked of people who reported that they currently held a job, whereas the latter was asked of all respondents. However, we include identical sets of respondents in both cases by restricting our samples to those who received positive wage payments during the surveys. This sample restriction may bias our estimates of supplemental work activity and the effects of arrears on supplemental labor supply decisions, because people on leave will tend to have different incentives for engaging in supplemental work from those currently receiving wages. The direction of the bias, however, is not obvious because those on voluntary leave, including maternity leave, having relatively high reservation wages during their leave, might be less likely to find alternative work, while those on involuntary leave might be in greater need of supplemental income.

**Table 13.3**
Wage arrears and secondary economic activity

| Explanatory variable | Multiple job holding (8,507) | Informal economic activity (8,545) |
|---|---|---|
| *Pjowed* | 0.0057 | 0.0205[a] |
|  | (0.005) | (0.006) |

*Note:* See the note to table 13.2. These regressions, and all regressions in tables 13.4–13.6, additionally include a constant, three-year dummies, and control variables for age, tenure, gender, education, region, occupation, and industry of employment. The dependent variable for the first regression is a dummy equal to 1 if the respondent held a second job for pay; the dependent variable for the second regression is a dummy equal to 1 if the respondent was engaged in informal economic activity for pay. Sample sizes are listed in parentheses under column headings.
a. Denotes significance at 1 percent.

The results of this analysis are reported in table 13.3. The coefficient of *Pjowed*, the wage nonpayment incidence variable, with respect to multiple job holding in the first regression is statistically not significant. Wage withholding had no effect on the tendency of workers to hold more than one formal job for pay. By contrast, the significantly positive coefficient of *Pjowed* in the second regression suggests that wage nonpayment had distinct labor supply effects with respect to less formal supplemental work.

These differential labor supply effects occurred because workers received housing and an array of entitlements from their primary job regardless of their being subjected to wage nonpayment; therefore the net return from taking another formal job might have been relatively small. They might have also found it difficult to locate another job. By contrast, informal work agreements brought in extra cash or prearranged barter payments, in turn facilitating tax avoidance and mitigating nonpayment problems. On balance, it would seem that wage arrears not only provided downward wage flexibility, allowing firms to retain redundant workers, but also stimulated employment and output through these induced labor supply effects.[21]

*Intrafamily Transfers*

Were people subjected to wage nonpayment likely to receive help from relatives? Such transactions played an important social dynamic in Russia during the transition. Cox et al. (1997) found that such transfers were pervasive in Russia in 1992 and 1993, and served to reduce poverty. The following excerpt from an ICFTU (International Conference of Free Trade Unions) newsletter on the wage arrears crisis illustrates the intergenerational concern for family well-being:

> How do people manage to survive for months without receiving any wages?" is the question regularly asked by visitors from the West. So we asked Larisa Seliverstova, the chairperson of the trade union committee of school number 10 in Prokop'evsk, Kemerovo oblast, about the budget of her own family. "How do you survive? Does someone help you?" "Our parents help: my husband has two and I have one. My father gives us all of his pension—he is still working. My husband's mother helps us with food. Grandpa and grandma completely support our child. They live in a private house which has a garden, and they also have an allotment." (ICFTU Campaign on the Non-payment of Wages in Russia, *Newsletter No. 2*, September 1997).

We begin by analyzing income supplements received from family members by workers with wage arrears. These include parents giving money to working (adult) children, adults giving money to working parents, and relatives, among them aunts, uncles, and grandparents, providing support to cash-strapped relatives. We use the following survey question to create a dummy variable to indicate if a transfer of resources was received from a family member:

> Has your family received money, food, clothes, or other goods in the last thirty days and, if so, how would you assess this aid in rubles?

Aid from either spouse's parents, children, grandparents, grandchildren, or other relatives is counted as intrafamily transfers.

Next, we analyze if wage nonpayment resulted in people giving reduced material support to family members. We use the following survey question to create a dummy to indicate the presence of a transfer to a family member:

> Has your family or one of its members given or sent money or goods – food, clothes, other items—without obligation to people who are not members of your household—children, parents, other relatives, friends, or simply strangers—in the last thirty days?

Transfers to either spouse's parents, children, grandparents, or grandchildren are included in the measure.

In table 13.4, the significantly negative coefficient −0.0211 of *Pjowed* indicates that, net of a number of demographic attributes and job-related variables, respondents who experienced wage nonpayment were 2 percent less likely to give money and/or goods to relatives. Consistent with this pattern of intrafamily interactions, the

**Table 13.4**
Wage arrears and intrafamily transfers

| Explanatory variable | Gave money to relatives (9,446) | Received money from relatives (9,772) |
|---|---|---|
| Pjowed | −0.0211[b] | 0.0352[a] |
|  | (0.009) | (0.010) |

Note: See notes to tables 13.2 and 13.3. The dependent variable for the first regression is a dummy equal to 1 if the respondent *gave* money to relatives; the dependent variable for the second regression is a dummy equal to 1 if the respondent *received* money from relatives. Sample sizes are listed in parentheses under column headings.
a. Denotes significance at 1 percent.
b. Denotes significance at 5 percent.

significantly positive coefficient 0.0352 of *Pjowed*, again net of a number of demographic attributes and other variables, suggests that the likelihood of receiving a transfer was 4 percent higher for people who faced arrears than for those who were fully paid.[22] It appears that intrafamily transfers served to mitigate the adverse impact of wage arrears on Russian families.

*Home Production*

Families also engaged in production of goods for consumption and/or for sale to maintain their standard of living. Panel (a) of table 13.5 analyzes the relationship between wage arrears and the consumption and sale of home-produced agricultural goods.[23] The significantly positive *Pjowed* effects in both regressions indicate that home production of harvested food for own-consumption was higher by 7 percent among people who were owed wages; production of agricultural items for sale was also higher by 4 percent among people who were owed wages.[24] Because we have controlled for a series of demographic, regional, and job characteristics, these patterns are unlikely to reflect secondary relationships associated with the incidence of wage arrears, such as higher levels of wage arrears in regions where the use of private plots for agricultural cultivation was more widespread.

*Dissaving*

Families also maintained consumption levels by varying their saving rates and by engaging in various forms of dissaving including borrowing, selling family consumer durable items and other assets, and

**Table 13.5**
Incidence of wage arrears and family survival responses

(a) Home production—consumption and sales

| Explanatory variable | Consumed own food production (9,826) | Sold own food production (9,826) |
|---|---|---|
| Pjowed | 0.0705[a] | 0.0413[a] |
| | (0.012) | (0.007) |

(b) Sale of family assets and debt

| Explanatory variable | Sold family assets (9,808) | Took out a loan (9,826) |
|---|---|---|
| Pjowed | 0.0160[a] | 0.0831[a] |
| | (0.005) | (0.010) |

(c) Saving and dissaving

| Explanatory variable | If saved any money (9,795) | Took money out of savings (9,795) |
|---|---|---|
| Pjowed | −0.0244[a] | 0.0088[b] |
| | (0.006) | (0.006) |

*Note:* See notes to tables 13.2 and 13.3. The dependent variable for each regression is a dummy equal to 1 if the respondent undertook or experienced the activity in the column heading.
a. Denotes significance at 1 percent.
b. Denotes significance at 15 percent.

drawing down accumulated savings. The significantly positive *Pjowed* effects in panel (b) of table 13.5 indicate that people who were owed wages were more likely, by 2 percent, to sell family assets[25] and more prone, by 8 percent, to take out loans than people who had been fully paid. The negative *Pjowed* effect in the first regression of panel (c) suggests that wage arrears tended to reduce the likelihood of people saving money by 2 percent; the positive *Pjowed* effect in the second regression indicates a less than 1 percent likelihood of wage arrears leading people to take money out of their savings. This latter effect, however, is statistically significant at 15 percent, reflecting low or nonexistent savings for many people.

These wage arrears effects are evident despite our having controlled for a wide range of demographic, location, and job-related factors; the survival mechanisms represented a genuine response to the arrears crisis, ruling out the coincidence of nonpayment in regions or industries with pronounced traditions or opportunities for home production and intrafamily transfers.

Wage arrears therefore were positively associated with the incidence of poverty. They also contributed to greater transfers from relatives and increased home production. Did the higher intrafamily transfers and home production mitigate the effect of wage arrears on the incidence of family poverty?

### Intrafamily Transfers, Home Production, and the Incidence of Poverty

We create three poverty indicators (dummies) for addressing this question, each defining poverty status by the usual condition of family income falling below specified (regional) income thresholds or poverty lines. The first measure (*Poverty 1*) uses actual family income,[26] defining the dummy *Poverty 1* equal to 1 if family income fell below regional poverty thresholds. The second dummy (*Poverty 2*) supplements actual family income by the monetary value of intrafamily transfers; the third measure (*Poverty 3*) supplements actual family income by the monetary value of home production. Because receipt of intrafamily transfers and/or home production increased family income, the *Poverty 2* and *Poverty 3* variables should give lower poverty incidence per se than that produced by *Poverty 1*. Moreover, and most germane to our analysis, because transfers and home production were more prevalent among people experiencing wage nonpayment, we expect this differential effect to be greater for people facing wage arrears than for those who were fully paid. In other words, wage nonpayment should have a smaller positive effect on poverty incidence with respect to the second and third poverty dummies than with respect to the first poverty dummy.

We next define two variables for supplementing our analysis: *Comparison 1* is a dummy equal to 1 if a person is classified as poor based on *Poverty 1* index but is not classified as poor in terms of *Poverty 2* index; it equals zero when *Poverty 1* and *Poverty 2* yield the same poverty classification. The variable *Comparison 1* thus signals if the monetary value of intrafamily transfers raised total family income (including transfers) above the regional poverty threshold, that is, if the value of intrafamily transfers was sufficient to move the individual out of poverty. The variable *Comparison 2* is similarly a dummy equal to 1 if a

**Table 13.6a**
Intrafamily transfers, home production, and poverty rates

|                                               | 1994     | 1995     | 1996     |
| --------------------------------------------- | -------- | -------- | -------- |
| *Owed wages*                                  | [810]    | [746]    | [915]    |
| Intrafamily transfer effects (*Comparison 1*) | 3.92*    | 3.75     | 5.25*    |
| Home production effects (*Comparison 2*)       | 2.94*    | 2.82*    | 3.17*    |
|                                               |          |          |          |
| *Not owed wages*                              | [1,878]  | [1,782]  | [1,127]  |
| Intrafamily transfer effects                  | 2.93     | 4.43     | 3.82     |
| Home production effects                        | 1.06     | 1.12     | 1.15     |

*Note:* Cells contain mean values for an indicator variable, which equals 1 if a person is classified as living in a family that has income below the regional poverty threshold when family transfers (rows 1), or home production (rows 2) are not included, but is not classified as poor when transfers or home production are included, and equals 0 when transfers or home production do not alter the person's poverty classification. Sample sizes are listed in square brackets.
* Indicates a significant difference (at 10 percent or better) in the reclassification of poverty status due to the inclusion of intrafamily transfers or home production for people based on whether or not they experienced wage arrears.

person was classified as poor based on *Poverty 1* but was not classified as poor in terms of *Poverty 3*. *Comparison 2* indicates if the monetary value of home production raised total family income (including home production) above the regional poverty threshold. Given our earlier finding that people who experienced wage arrears were more likely to receive transfers from relatives and engage in home production, we expect the inclusion of these supplemental forms of income to more strongly move people out of poverty when they experienced wage arrears than for people who were fully paid.[27]

The results of our exercise are reported in tables 13.6a and 13.6b. (We restrict our analysis to 1994–96 because RLMS information on the ruble values of home production and intrafamily transfers in 1998 is not fully consistent with earlier years.) Table 13.6a provides simple comparisons of mean values for the variables *Comparison 1* and *Comparison 2*. *Comparison 1* in row (1) is significantly larger in 1994 and 1996 for people who were owed wages, suggesting that intrafamily transfers had a greater effect on moving people out of poverty when they experienced wage arrears than for those who were fully paid. For example, 5 percent of the sampled people in 1996, who experienced pay delays, were classified as poor based on the poverty index that uses family income (*Poverty 1*), but were not classified as poor if intrafamily transfers were

**Table 13.6b**
Do intrafamily transfers and home production mitigate the effect of wage arrears on the incidence of poverty?

**(a) Incidence of poverty (alternative income definitions)**

| Explanatory variable | Poverty 1 | Poverty 2 | Poverty 3 |
|---|---|---|---|
| Pjowed | 0.2284[a] | 0.1986[a] | 0.2012[a] |
|  | (0.016) | (0.016) | (0.016) |

**(b) Incidence of poverty (alternative classification schemes)**

| Explanatory variable | Comparison 1 | Comparison 2 |
|---|---|---|
| Pjowed | 0.0131[a] | 0.0078[a] |
|  | (0.005) | (0.002) |

*Note:* See notes to tables 13.2 and 13.3. Panel (a) reports probit slope estimates for three alternative regressions, each for a different dependent variable: *Poverty 1* defines poverty status based on actual family income; *Poverty 2* uses actual family income supplemented by the monetary value of intrafamily transfers for defining family poverty status; *Poverty 3* uses actual family income supplemented by the monetary value of home production for defining family poverty status. Sample size for panel (a) is 6,299. Panel (b) reports probit slope estimates for two alternative regressions, each using as the dependent variable an indicator variable, which equals 1 if a person is classified as living in a family that has income below the regional poverty threshold when family transfers (*Comparison 1*), or home production (*Comparison 2*), are not included, but is not classified as poor when transfers or home production are included, and equals 0 when transfers or home production do not alter the person's poverty classification. Sample sizes for panel (b) are 6,387 for *Comparison 1* and 6,039 for *Comparison 2*. Robust standard errors for the estimates are reported in parentheses.

included in family income (*Poverty* 2). In other words, the inclusion of intrafamily transfers moved 5 percent of the poor, who suffered wage arrears, out of poverty. However, among those who did not experience pay delays, intrafamily transfers moved 4 percent out of poverty. We observe similar patterns for home production in all years: The inclusion of home production in row (2) moved a higher percentage of people out of poverty when they experienced wage arrears (3 percent in 1996) than those who were fully paid in row (4) (1 percent in 1996).

Panel (b) of table 13.6b provides the multivariate counterpart to the results in table 13.6a. The significantly positive coefficients of *Pjowed* indicate that intra-family transfers and home production were more likely to alleviate poverty when people experienced wage arrears than when they were fully paid. As a complement to the above test, in panel (a) of table 13.6b, we estimate the effect of wage nonpayment on the likelihood of poverty for each of our three poverty indicators. Our expectation is that *Pjowed* will be a weaker (positive) predictor of poverty incidence when intrafamily transfers (*Poverty 2*) or home production (*Poverty 3*) are included than when they are not taken into account (*Poverty 1*). The estimate in column (1) indicates that, when we use actual family income to calculate poverty incidence, wage nonpayment increased the likelihood of a respondent being in poverty by 23 percent relative to statistically similar people who did not experience wage nonpayment. When we supplement our family income measure by the value of intrafamily transfers, the likelihood drops to approximately 20 percent in column (2); if we supplement family income by the value of home production, the likelihood again drops to 20.1 percent in column (3). Therefore these differential coefficients of *Pjowed* indicate that wage arrears had a weaker effect on the likelihood of being in poverty when intra-family transfers or home production are included as part of family income. In conclusion our findings build on our initial results of tables 13.4 and 13.5, which documented a positive relationship between arrears and intrafamily transfers and home production, suggesting that these responses to wage arrears significantly reduced the likelihood of a family experiencing poverty.

## Conclusions

Did wage nonpayment reduce family incomes to such an extent that an increasing number of families were pushed into poverty? How did families respond to their members not being fully paid for their work? Did these responses alleviate the adverse impact of pay delays on family well-being?

We find that the practice of nonpayment increased the likelihood of families living in poverty. Nonpayment was positively associated with families undertaking informal paid activity. Families subjected to wage arrears were also more likely to compensate for their lost earnings by selling family assets, reducing savings rates, and engaging in home production for consumption and sale. Finally, transfers of goods and cash from relatives and home production served to fill a portion of the gap in family income due to wage withholding. They also alleviated the positive effect of wage arrears on the likelihood of families falling into poverty.

# 14　　　　　　　　　Conclusions

Russia's nonpayment crisis from 1994 to 1998 was an extended and exceptional feature of its continuing market transition. Confronted with the challenges of price liberalization, inflation control, and a rapid opening of the economy,the government decision makers, managers of privatized industry, and households devised survival strategies that defied expectations of rational responses on their part to the policy measures. The cash-flow problems in the budget sector and in enterprises and the breakdown of contractual obligations resulted in escalating nonpayments by enterprises of their tax obligations to the budget, by the governments at all levels to their employees, by enterprises to one another and to their workforce. A variety of financial instruments, which became a reckless free-for-all that participants used to accommodate their financial mismanagement, proliferated in the economy. Enterprise managers imposed forced leave, shorter work hours, and barter payments on their workers. The Soviet command economy, in ruins, struck back at the emerging market forces with its own devices.

Within this overall survival mechanism, we find specific features that are supported by empirical evidence and our statistical analysis. In their wage nonpayment practices, managers seemed to have departed from traditional fairness considerations and discriminated against lower-paid workers in the frequency, amounts, and length of nonpayment. Women with similar job market and demographic attributes as men were more likely to be subjected to nonpayment. Although employees received goods in lieu of wages, such barter activity was not sufficient to compensate them for the nonpayment arrears.

We also find that denial of wages and pensions tended to push people into poverty, compared to those who were not so subjected. But they managed to survive by growing food for consumption and sale, selling family heirlooms, borrowing, and relying on intrafamily transfers that, in turn, tended to keep them above the poverty level. Wage nonpayment also induced them to undertake protest activity, including strikes, that were not, however, sufficiently organized over time and territory to result in a lowering of wage arrears.

We notice that political clout, management muscle, and trade union activity had varying impact on a group's ability to fight reformist encroachments on the status quo. The coal sector, led by a militant trade union and protected by the Soviet-era management agency, Rosugol, held back a World Bank–financed plan to reshape it. The pensioners, an active political force, prevented further impoverishment by extracting frequent pension hikes that were not, however, matched by Pension Fund resources. The conversion of the Soviet-era pay-as-you go, employer-financed pension system to an employee-contribution arrangement too was shelved. By contrast the military, devoid of solid political support, experienced a loss of status, demobilization, and devastation that went far beyond denial of wages to the servicemen.

The revival of the economy following the substantial ruble devaluation of August 1998, which favored import substitutes, and the flow of tax revenues to the budget from the oil companies, resulting from higher oil prices, have eased the nonpayment problem. Arrears to pensioners and military personnel were partially cleared on the eve of the March 2000 presidential elections. total overdue payment obligations of enterprises to suppliers, budget and off-budget funds, and the workforce (defined in figure 11.1) grew less rapidly in 1999 and actually declined toward the end of the year (*Russian Economic Trends,* March 2000). Wage arrears had dropped from 76 billion (new) rubles in January 1999 to 40 billion rubles in March 2000 (*Russian Economic Trends,* March 2000). Strikes and protests, measured in the loss of mandays in the economy, had slumped from 577,000 in January 1999 to 27,000 in March 2000 (*Russian Economic Trends,* March 2000).

The permanent solution of the nonpayment crisis will, however, depend on the economy's continuing growth with stable prices and a restoration of contractual obligations by employers to working men and women. The December 1999 parliamentary elections, which put an end to the Communist-left majority of the previous Duma, hold out prospects for a policy consensus between the government and the lawmakers, resulting in the adoption of the necessary legislation on improved bankruptcy and taxation provisions. The election of Vladimir Putin, a believer in a law-based state (*pravovoye gosudarstvo*), raises hopes for a tightening of contractual enforcement that would gradually ease nonpayment practices all around. The legacy of the massive structural rigidities and imbalances in the economy, however, and the absence of an active labor market dampen the prospects of a rapid economic over-haul. The economy's structural turnaround, requiring substantial inflows of investment and technologies from outside, will extend over a number of years even as the nonpayment crisis of 1994–98 analyzed by us has eased and disappeared.

# Notes

## Chapter 2

1. *Rossiskaya gazeta*, October 22, 1996, p. 1; cited in *The Current Digest of the Soviet press*, vol. XLVIII, no. 42, November 13, 1996, p. 11.

2. *Izvestiya*, December 14, 1993, p. 4; cited in *The Current Digest of the Post-Soviet Press*, vol. XLV, no. 50, January 12, 1994, p. 20.

3. *Kommersant-daily*, February 21, 1996, p. 1; cited in *The Current Digest of the Post-Soviet Press*, vol. XLVIII, no. 8, March 20, 1996, p. 15.

4. *Sevodnya*, February 23, 1996, p. 2; cited in *The Current Digest of the Post-Soviet Press*, vol. XLVIII, no. 8, March 20, 1996, p. 15.

5. *Sevodnya*, February 4, 1995, p. 2; cited in *the Current Digest of the Post-Soviet Press*, vol. XLVII, no. 5, March 1, 1995, p. 20.

6. *Kommersant-daily*, June 5, 1997, p. 1: cited in *The Current Digest of the Post-Soviet Press*, vol. XLIX. No. 23, July 9. 1997, p. 12.

7. *Sevodnya*, February 4, 1995, p. 2; cited in *The Current Digest of the Post-Soviet Press*, vol. XLVII, no. 5, March 1, 1995, p. 20.

8. *Izvestiya*, July 21, 1994, p. 1; cited in *The Current Digest of the Post-Soviet Press*, vol. XLVI, no. 29, August 17, 1994, p. 8.

9. *Izvestiya*, November 15, 1997, p. 2; cited in *The Current Digest of the Post-Soviet Press*, vol. XLIX, no. 46, December 17, 1997, p. 13.

10. *Rossiskiye vesti*, August 30, 1994, pp. 1–2; cited in *The Current Digest of the Post-Soviet Press*, vol. XLVI, no. 36, October 5, 1994, pp. 8–9.

11. *Rossiskiye vesti*, August 25, 1994, p. 1; cited in *The Current Digest of the Post-Soviet Press*, vol. XLVI, no. 36, October 5, 1994, p. 8.

12. *Kommersant-daily*, September 13, 1994, p. 3; cited in *The Current Digest of the Post-Soviet Press*, vol. XLVI, no. 37, October 12, 1994, p. 18.

13. *Sevodnya*, November 3, 1997, p. 1; cited in *The Current Digest of the Post-Soviet Press*, vol. XLIX, no. 44, December 3, 1997, p. 8.

14. *Kommersant-daily*, June 14, 1997, p. 2; cited in *The Current Digest of the Post-Soviet Press*, vol. XLIX, no. 24, July 16, 1997, p. 16.

15. *Sevodnya*, December 24, 1997, p. 1; cited in *The Current Digest of the Post-Soviet Press*, vol. XLIX, no. 51, 1998, p. 14.

16. *Sevodnya*, October 16, 1996, p. 1; cited in *The Current Digest of the Post-Soviet Press*, vol. XLVIII, no. 42, November 13, 1996, pp.. 17–18.

17. *Sevodnya*, January 16, 1996, p. 3; cited in *The Current Digest of the Post-Soviet Press*, vol. XLVIII, no. 2, February 7, 1996, p. 22.

18. *Nezavisimaya gazeta*, June 5, 1997, p. 1; cited in *The Current Digest of the Post-Soviet Press*, vol. XLIX, no. 23, July 9, 1997, p. 11.

19. *Izvestiya*, July 7, 1998, p. 2; cited in *The Current Digest of the Post-Soviet Press*, vol. XLX, no. 27, August 5, 1998, p. 7.

20. *Kommersant-daily*, July 15, 1998, p. 7; cited in *The Current Digest of the Post-Soviet Press*, vol. XLX, no. 28, August 12, 1998, p. 13.

21. *Izvestiya*, November 15, 1994, p. 1; cited in *The Current Digest of the Post-Soviet Press*, vol. XLVI, no. 46, December 14, 1994, pp. 24–25.

22. *Sevodnya*, October 7, 1993, p. 2; cited in *The Current Digest of the Post-Soviet Press*, vol. XLV, no. 40, November 3, 1993, p. 28.

22. *Sevodnya*, January 21, 1994, p. 2; cited in *The Current Digest of the Post-Soviet Press*, vol. XLVI, no. 3, February 16, 1994, p. 21.

24. *Sevodnya*, February 23, 1996, p. 2; cited in *The Current Digest of the Post-Soviet Press*, vol. XLVIII, no. 8, March 20, 1996, p. 15.

25. *Sevodnya*, January 9, 1998, p. 4; cited in *The Current Digest of the Post-Soviet Press*, vol. XLX, no. 1, February 4, 1998, p. 7.

26. *Sevodnya*, April 15, 1998, pp. 1–3; cited in *The Current Digest of the Post-Soviet Press*, vol. XLX, no. 15, May 13, 1998, p. 9.

27. *Sevodnya*, April 15, 1998, pp. 1–3; cited in *The Current Digest of the Post-Soviet Press*, vol. XLX, no. 15, May 13, 1998, p. 9.

28. *Megapolis-express, no. 1*, January 5, 1994, p. 11; cited in *The Current Digest of the Post-Soviet Press*, vol. XLVI, February 2, 1994, p. 5.

29. *Rossiskiye vesti*, March 11, 1997, p. 2; cited in *The Current Digest of the Post-Soviet Press*, vol. XLIX, no. 10, April 9, 1997, p. 3.

## Chapter 3

1. *Izvestiya*, February 4, 1993, p. 2; cited in *The Current Digest of the Post-Soviet Press*, vol. XLV, no. 5, March 3, 1993, pp. 21–22.

2. *Izvestiya*, March 20, 1993, p. 2; cited in *The Current Digest of the Post-Soviet Press*, vol. XLV, no. 12, April 21, 1993, p. 29.

3. *Rossiskiye vesti*, April 30, 1993, p. 2; cited in *The Current Digest of the Post-Soviet Press*, vol. XLV, no. 17, May 26, 1993, p. 10.

4. *Izvestiya*, April 3, 1993, p. 2; cited in *The Current Digest of the Post-Soviet Press*, vol. XLV, no. 14, May 5, 1993, p. 28.

5. *Sevodnya*, April 22, 1994, p. 1; cited in *The Current Digest of the Post-Soviet Press*, vol. XLVI, no. 16, May 18, 1994, pp. 19–20.

6. *Izvestiya*, February 4, 1993, p. 2; cited in *The Current Digest of the Post-Soviet Press*, vol. XLV, no. 5, March 3, 1993, p. 21.

7. *Izvestiya*, June 4, 1994, p. 1; cited in *The Current Digest of the Post-Soviet Press*, vol. XLVI, no. 22, June 29, 1994, p. 11.

8. *Sevodnya, June 7, 1994, p. 2; cited in The Current Digest of the Post-Soviet Press, vol. XLVI, no. 23, July 6, 1994, p. 14.*

9. *Kommersant –daily*, February 16, 1996, pp. 1–2; cited in *The Current Digest of the Post-Soviet Press*, vol. XLVII, no. 18, May 31, 1995, p. 15.

10. *Kommersant-daily*, February 16, 1996, pp. 1–2; cited in *The Current Digest of the Post-Soviet Press*, vol. XLVIII, no. 7, March 13, 1996, p. 16.

11. *Rossiskaya gazeta*, April 18, 1996, p. 2; cited in *The Current Digest of the Post-Soviet Press*, vol. XLVIII, no. 16, May 15, 1996, p. 19.

12. *Sevodnya*, June 4, 1994, p. 1; cited in *The Current Digest of the Post-Soviet Press*, vol. XLVI, no. 22, June 29, 1994, p. 12.

13. *Izvestiya*, February 27, 1998, p. 2; cite in *The Current Digest of the Post-Soviet Press*, vol. 50, no. 9, April 1, 1998, p. 17.

14. *Rossiskaya gazeta*, April 18, 1996, p. 2; cited in *The Current Digest of the Post-Soviet Press*, vol. XLVIII, no. 16, May 15, 1996, p. 9.

15. *Sevodnya*, Decemebr 30, 1994, p. 2; cited in *The Current Digest of the Post-Soviet Press*, vol. XLVI, no. 52, January 25, 1995, p. 16.

16. *Sevodnya*, February 13, 1998, p. 4; cited in *The Current Digest of the Post-Soviet Press*, vol. XLX, no. 7, March 18, 1998, p. 15.

17. *Izvestiya*, August 25, 1994, pp. 1–2; cited in *The Current Digest of the Post-Soviet Press*, vol. XLVI, no. 34, September 21, 1994, pp. 18–19.

18. *Sevodnya*, February 16, 1995, p. 2; cited in *The Current Digest of the Post-Soviet Press*, vol. XLVII, no. 7, March 15, 1995, p. 19.

19. *Sevodnya*, January 16, 1996, p. 3; cited in *The Current Digest of the Post-Soviet Press*, vol. XLVIII, no. 2, February 7, 1996, p. 22.

20. *Sevodnya*, February 16, 1995, p. 2; cited in *The Current Digest of the Post-Soviet Press*, vol. XLVII, no. 7, March 15, 1995, p. 19.

21. *Sevodnya*, February 16, 1995, p. 2; cited in *The Current Digest of the Post-Soviet Press*, vol. XLVII, no. 7, March 15, 1995, p. 19.

22. *Sevodnya*, January 15, 1997, p. 5; cited in *The Current Digest of the Post-Soviet Press*, vol. XLIX, no. 2, February 12, 1997, pp. 15–16.

23. *Sevodnya*, February 18, 1995, p. 3; cited in *The Current Digest of the Post-Soviet Press*, vol. XLVII, no. 10, April 5, 1995, p. 7.

24. *Izvestiya*, September 1, 1993, p. 4; cited in *The Current Digest of the Post-Soviet Press*, vol. XLV, no. 35, September 29, 1993, p. 23.

25. *Nezavisimaya gazeta*, July 4, 1997, p. 1; cited in *The Current Digest of the Post-Soviet Press*, vol. XLIX, no. 27, August 6, 1997, p. 13.

26. *Sevodnya*, August 8, 1995, p. 1; cited in *The Current Digest of the Post-Soviet Press*, vol. XLVII, no. 32, September 6, 1995, p. 22.

27. *Sevodnya*, April 16, 1997, p. 1; cited in *The Current Digest of the Post-Soviet Press*, vol. XLIX, no. 15, May 14, 1997, pp. 4–5.

28. *Izvestiya*, May 13, 1998, p. 4; cited in *The Current Digest of the Post-Soviet Press*, vol. XLX, no. 19, June 10, 1998, pp. 5–7.

29. *Sevodnya*, May 31, 1997,p. 6; cited in *The Current Digest of the Post-Soviet Press*, vol. XLIX, no. 22, July 2, 1997, p. 19.

30. *Kommersant-daily*, April 10, 1997, p. 9; cited in *The Current Digest of the Post-Soviet Press*, vol. XLIX, no. 15, May 14, 1997, p. 4.

31. *Sevodnya*, April 16, 1997, p. 1; cited in *The Current Digest of the Post-Soviet Press*, vol. XLIX, no. 15, May 14, 1997, p. 5.

32. *Izvestiya*, August 24, 1995, p. 1; cited in *The Current Digest of the Post-Soviet Press*, vol. XLVII, no. 34, September 20, 1995, p. 22.

33. Peck and Richardson 1991, p. 65.

34. Peck and Richardson 1991, p. 63.

35. *Izvestiya*, July 13, 1993, p. 2.

36. The seven regions of Russia, adopted by us, are defined in chapter 5 and are represented in the map in the chapter.

## Chapter 4

1. These figures are based on eight sectors (industry, agriculture, construction, transportation, education, culture, health care, and science) for which Goskomstat reports wage arrears beginning in 1996, and which constitute approximately 78 percent of total official employment in 1995. They do not cover the large military sector in which wage arrears were quite substantial.

2. Contrary to the impression given in much of the popular press, the government's failure to fully pay its employees is only a fraction of the wage nonpayment problem. In June 1997, wage arrears in the eight sectors of the economy noted in note 1 amounted to 53.9 trillion rubles, of which 11 trillion rubles (20.4 percent of the total) were due to nonpayment from local and federal budgets. Wage arrears to the military were estimated separately at 5.4 trillion rubles.

3. Information on the structure of the survey, the questionnaires, and data sources may be obtained at http://www.cpc.unc.edu/rlms.

4. See Heeringa (1997) for an analysis of sample design considerations and sample attrition in the RLMS.

5. Note that this procedure will be subject to measurement error because we do not know the amount of the outstanding cumulated debt which was incurred in the past thirty days.

6. For a discussion of job turnover in Russian enterprises, see Gimpelson and Lippoldt (1996). In the Russian context, job turnover usually implies moving to a different job within the enterprise (without abrogating the wage contract) rather than quitting the job altogether and moving to a different enterprise or location. The intra-enterprise job turnover has been high in Russia from the Soviet days.

7. "General secondary" education consists of ten to eleven years of schooling; "professional courses" include instruction in areas such as typing, accounting, and chauffeuring; "ordinary vocational" education represents vocational training for those who have not completed secondary schooling, and may be in the form of PTU, FZU, or FZO programs, representing professional/technical trade school, factory/manufacturing trade school (a training program located in factories), and factory/manufacturing department (a specific type of training program) respectively; "secondary vocational" qualification represents vocational training along with secondary education; "specialized secondary" education includes general secondary education and specialized technical, medical, pedagogical, and art training.

8. See Pindyck and Rubinfeld (1991), chapter 10, for a relatively nontechnical discussion of the probit model. Our probit models are estimated using the dprobit procedure in STATA.

9. See Pindyck and Rubinfeld, (1991), chapter 5, for a discussion of the use of dummy variable interactions.

10. Although the more exact calculation of the effect of a dummy in a logarithmic specification is given by $e^{\beta-1}$, where $\beta$ is the estimated coefficient of the dummy, we do not use this formula to generate the numbers discussed in the text as the differences are generally small.

11. The estimated intercept in the ln(amount) regression is 5.793 with a standard error of 0.444.

## Chapter 5

1. These figures are based on data from the *RLMS* for current wage earners from ages sixteen to sixt-four.

2. *Izvestiya*, February 13, 1993, p. 4; cited in *The Current Digest of the Post-Soviet Press*, vol. XLV, no. 7, March 17, 1993, p. 29.

3. *Nezavisimaya gazeta*, July 31, 1993, p. 2; cited in *The Current Digest of the Post Soviet Press*, vol. XLV, no. 31, September 1, 1993, p. 22.

4. *Izvestiya*, February 13, 1993, p. 4; cited in *The Current Digest of the Post-Soviet Press*, vol. XLV, no. 7, March 17, 1993, p. 29.

5. *Sevodnya*, May 14, 1994, p. 3; cited in *The Current Digest of the Post-Soviet Press*, vol. XLVI, no. 9, June 8, 1994, pp. 9–10.

6. *Izvestiya*, October 9, 1993, p. 6; cited in *The Current Digest of the Post-Soviet Press*, vol. XLV, no. 47, December 22, 1993, pp. 13–15).

7. *Izvesitya*, July 1, 1994, p. 1; cited in *The Current Digest of the Post-Soviet Press*, vol. XLVI, no. 26, July 27, 1994, p. 17.

8. *Izvestiya*, January 5, 1993, pp. 1–2; cited in *The Current Digest of the Post-Soviet Press*, vol. XLV, no. 1, February 3, 1993, p. 22.

9. *Moskovskiye novosti, no. 28*, July 11, 1993, p. A8; cited in *The Current Digest of the Post-Soviet Press*, vol. XLV, no. 27, August 4, 1993, p. 6.

10. Ibid.

11. *Sevodnya*, September 9, 1993, p. 2; cited in *The Current Digest of the Post-Soviet Press*, vol. XLV, no. 36, October 6, 1993, p. 25.

12. *Izvestiya*, August 27, 1993, p. 4; cited in *The Current Digest of the Post-Soviet Press*, vol. XLV, no. 34, September 22, 1993, pp. 25–26.

13. *Sevodnya*, September 21, 1993, p. 3; cited in *The Current Digest of the Post-Soviet Press*, vol. XLV, no. 38, October 20, 1993, p. 25.

14. Stephanie Baker-Said, "Regions Get Loans for Back Wages." *Moscow Times*, July 19, 1997.

15. See Daniel Treisman (1999) chapter 4, tables 2–4.

16. *Kommersant-Daily*, September 14, 1995 p. 3; *Izvestiya*, September 17, 1995, p. 2; *Sevodnya*, September 5, 1996, p. 2; September 13, 1996, p. 2; cited in various issues of *The Current Digest of the Post-Soviet Press*.

17. *Izvestiya*, October 29, 1993, p. 1; cited in *The Current Digest of the Post-Soviet Press*, vol. XLV, no. 43, November 24, 1993, p. 20.

18. *Kommersant-Daily*, April 26, 1996, p. 2; cited in *The Current Digest of the Post-Soviet Press*, vol. XLVIII, no. 17, May 22, 1996, pp. 23–24.

19. *Sevodnya*, August 13, 1997, pp. 1,6; cited in *The Current Digest of the Post-Soviet Press*, vol. XLIX, no. 32, September 10, 1997, p. 7.

20. *Izvestiya*, November 25, 1997, p. 1; cited in *The Current Digest of the Post-Soviet Press*, vol. XLIX, no. 47, December 24, 1997, p. 17.

21. Regional identifiers provided by the RLMS bracket Moscow and St. Petersburg in a single group, classifying them as major urban centers with ostensibly similar characteristics. Although the two cities are distinct, we find (using finer regional identifiers provided to us by RLMS researchers) that significant differences in the incidence and amounts of wage arrears between the two are absent. We therefore adopt the original RLMS grouping.

22. Instead of reporting the maximum likelihood probit coefficients for the incidence regressions, we present the change in the probability of nonpayment incidence with respect to an infinitesimal change in each independent continuous variable and with respect to discrete change in the dummy variables.

23. Similar patterns emerge when we use a finer regional classification of thirty-eight regional groups.

24. As in table 5.4, the results of table 5.5 do not significantly differ when we use thirty-eight rather than eight regional groups.

25. This is calculated as outstanding ruble arrears in the region divided by the number of employed workers. Our results remain unchanged with slightly smaller effects when we use the ratio of outstanding arrears to the regional population as our dependent variable.

26. We find similar results in alternative regressions employing the ratio of per capita regional arrears to the regional median wage as the dependent variable. We report the estimates of table 5.5 because the specification, being more flexible, does not implicitly restrict the estimated effect of the regional wage.

27. Using firm level data, Earle and Sabirianova (1998) find that wage arrears tend to exhibit regional concentration. The practice of wage withholding by one firm creates an externality for other firms, making it easier for them to withhold payment from their workers because alternative employment prospects are less attractive. The authors demonstrate that wage nonpayment by firms is strongly correlated with regional nonpayment levels, and that the resulting worker quit disincentives are the primary factors sustaining wage withholding practices by these firms.

28. We formally state the managerial objective and empirically assess this argument in chapter 9.

29. By itself, the alternative specification in terms of the vector of industrial sectors as the explanatory variable can explain approximately 48 percent of the variation in average arrears across regions. The vector of industry variables includes the following sectors – energy; fuel; nonferrous metals; chemical and petrochemical products; machine building and metalworking; logging, woodworking, paper and pulp; construction materials; light industry; and processed food. The inclusion in the specification of each sector, one at a time, has a significant effect on arrears with the exception of logging, woodworking, paper, and pulp, and processed food. When entered as a group, the variables tend to become individually insignificant but remain jointly significant at 5 percent.

## Chapter 6

1. *Izvestiya*, January 18, 1993, p. 5; cited in *The Current Digest of the Post-Soviet Press*, vol. XLV, no. 4, February 24, 1993, p. 12.

2. *Sevodnya*, May 17, 1994, p. 2; cited in *The Current Digest of the Post-Soviet Press*, vol. XLVI, no. 20, June 15, 1994, p. 19.

3. *Nezavisimaya gazeta*, December 4, 1998, p. 4.

4. *Vremya*, June 11, 1999, p. 3.

5. *Izvestiya*, June 10, 1999, p. 3.

6. *Nezavisimaya gazeta*, December 4, 1998, p. 4.

7. *Nezavisimaya gazeta*, June 8, 1993, pp. 5, and *Izvestiya*, June 8, 1993, p. 4; cited in *The Current Digest of he Post-Soviet Press*; vol. XLV, no. 23. July 7, 1993, pp. 26–27.

8. *Federal New Service*, February 9, 1998.

9. Ibid.

10. *Vremya*, May 28, 1999, p. 2.

11. Ibid.

12. *Federal New Service,* February 9, 1998.

13. *Vecherny Stavropol',* December 4, 1998, p. 1.

14. *Nezavisimaya gazeta,* August 27, 1993, p. 1; cited in *The Current Digest of the Post-Soviet Press,* vol. XLV, no. 35, September 29, 1993, p. 12.

15. *Izvestiya,* September 16, 1993, p. 4; cited in *The Current Digest of the Post-Soviet Press,* vol. XLV, no. 37, October 13, 1993, p. 28.

16. *Sevodnya,* June 10, 1994, p. 2; cited in *The Current Digest of the Post-Soviet Press,* vol. XLVI, no. 23, July 6, 1994, p. 7.

17. *Sevodnya,* January 10, 1998, p. 3; cited in *The Current Digest of the Post-Soviet Press,* vol. XLX, no. 2, February 11, 1998, p. 14.

18. *Nezavisimaya gazeta,* December 4, 1998, p. 4.

## Chapter 7

1. *Izvestiya,* September 1, 1995, p. 2; cited in *The Current Digest of the Post-Soviet Press,* vol. XLVII, no. 36, October 4, 1995, p. 14.

2. *Sevodnya,* November 21, 1995, p. 2; cited in *The Current Digest of the Post-Soviet Press,* vol. XLVII, no. 47, December 20, 1995, p. 9.

3. Ibid.

4. Izvestiya, November 16, 1996, pp. 1; cited in *The Current Digest of the Post-Soviet Press,* vol. XLVIII, no. 46, December 11, 1996, p. 8.

5. *Sevodnya,* November 21, 1995, p. 2; cited in *The Current Digest of the Post-Soviet Press,* vol. XLVII, no. 47, December 20, 1995, p. 9.

6. *Sevodnya,* November 21, 1995, p. 2; cited in *The Current Digest of the Post-Soviet Press,* vol. XLV, no. 47, December 20, 1995, p. 9.

7. *Izvestiya,* September 1, 1995, pp. 1; cited in *The Current Digest of the Post-Soviet Press,* vol. XLVII, no. 36, October 4, 1995, pp. 13.

8. *Sevodnya,* November 21, 1995, p. 2; cited in *The Current Digest of the Post-Soviet Press,* vol. XLVII, no. 47, December 20, 1995, p. 9.

9. *Sevodnya,* February 11, 1997, p. 3; cited in *The Current Digest of the post-Soviet Press,* vol. XLIX, no. 6, March 12, 1997, p. 15.

10. *Sevodnya,* February 7, 1997, p. 3; cited in *The Current Digest of the Post-Soviet Press,* vol. XLIX, no. 6, March 12, 1997, p. 15.

11. *Sevodnya,* July 17, 1996, p. 3; cited in *The Current Digest of the Post-Soviet Press,* vol. XLVIII, no. 31, August 28, 1996, pp. 7–8.

12. *Sevodnya,* May 20, 1995, p. 2; cited in *The Current Digest of the Post-Soviet Press,* vol. XLVII, no. 20, June 14, 1995, p. 15.

13. *Sevodnya,* May 8, 1996, p. 2; cited in *The Current Digest of the Post-Soviet Press,* vol. XLVIII, no. 19, June 1996, p. 15.

14. *Sevodnya*, December 19, 1997, pp. 1–6; cited in *The Current Digest of the Post-Soviet Press*, vol. XLIX, no. 51, January 21, 1998, p. 16.

15. *Trud*, January 16, 1998, p. 2; cited in *The Current Digest of the Post-Soviet Press*, vol. XLX, no. 3, February 18, 1998, p. 15.

16. *Izvestiya*, June 20, 1998, p. 2; cited in *The Current Digest of the Post-Soviet Press*, vol. XLX, no. 25, July 22, 1998, p. 16.

17. *Izvestiya*, July 23, 1998, p. 1; cited in *The Current Digest of the Post-Soviet Press*, vol. XLX, no. 29, August 1998, p. 7.

18. *Sevodnya*, June 16, 1997, p. 5; cited in *The Current Digest of the Post-Soviet Press*, vol. XLIX, no. 24, July 16, 1997, p. 15.

19. The percentage of the population with incomes below the subsistence minimum averaged 24 percent in 1992. Poverty rates increased in 1993 with monthly variations between 25 to 36 percent. Rates declined in 1994, often dipping below the 1992 levels, only to rise again during the first half of 1995, then falling to the low 20 percent range in the last quarter of the year. Detailed information is in Braithwaite (1997), Tables 2–6.

20. RLMS data indicate that 12.4 percent of retirees, who reported being employed at the time of the survey, also received a pension; similarly, 10.4 percent of non-retirees responded that they were receiving a pension. (These results are averaged over the 1994–98 period.)

21. We exclude monthly wage, occupation, and industry variables from our specifications of tables 7.2, 7.3, and 7.4 because we focus on retired pensioners.

## Chapter 8

1. We thank Elena Kondratieva for collecting monthly time series data on coal prices, wages and employment, and wage arrears in the two regions from mid-1997 to mid-1999.Kemerovskoya oblast is located in the Kuznetsk Basin of Western Siberia, and Krasnoyarskii krai is in Eastern Siberia.

2. *Sevodnya*, August 21, 1997, p. 6; cited in *The Current Digest of the Post-Soviet Press*, vol. XLIX, no. 34, September 24, 1997, p. 11.

3. Ibid.

4. *Izvestiya*, June 23, 1993, p. 1; cited in *The Current Digest of the Post-Soviet Press*, vol. XLV, no. 25, July 1993, p. 26.

5. *Nezavisimaya gazeta*, February 13, 1997, p. 4; cited in *The Current Digest of the Post Soviet Press*, vol. XLIX, no. 7, March 19, 1997, p. 22.

6. *Izvestiya*, March 3, 1993, p. 2; cited in *The Current Digest of the Post-Soviet Press*, vol. XLV, no. 9, March 31, 1993, p. 30.

7. *Izvestiya*, February 13, 1996, p. 2; cited in *The Current Digest of the Post-Soviet Press*, vol. XLVIII, no. 6, March 6, 1996, pp. 9–10.

8. *Izvestiya*, Janaury 30, 1996, p. 1; cited in *The Current Digest of the Post-Soviet Press*, vol. XLVIII, no. 4, February 21, 1996, p. 16.

9. *Izvestiya*, August 15, 1998, p. 2; cited in *The Current Digest of the Post-Soviet Press*, vol. 50, no. 33, September 16, 1998, p. 13.

10. *Sevodnya*, November 21, 1996, p. 3; cited in *The Current Digest of the Post-Soviet Press*, vol. XLVIII, no. 47, December 18, 1996, p. 19.

11. *Sevodnya*, November 10, 1996, p. 3; cited in *The Current Digest of the Post-Soviet Press*, vol. XLVIII, no. 46, December 11, 1996, p. 6.

12. *Izvestiya*, November 12, 1996, p. 4; cited in *The Current Digest of the Post-Soviet Press*, vol. XLVIII, no. 46, December 11, 1996, pp. 6–7.

13. *Izvestiya*, July 3, 1998, p. 2; cited in *The Current Digest of the Post-Soviet Press*, vol. 50, no. 27, August 5, 1998, p. 13.

14. *Rossiskiye vesti*, February 5, 1998, p. 2; cited in *The Current Digest of the Post-Soviet Press*, vol. 50, no. 6, march 11, 1998, p. 9.

15. Ibid.

16. *Sevodnya*, January 31, 1998, p. 4; cited in *The Current Digest of the Post-Soviet Press*, vol. 50, no. 6, March 11, 1998, pp. 8–9.

17. Ibid.

18. Our data on coal prices are specific for each region, whereas electric power and ferrous metallurgy prices are producer prices in the sectors for the economy.

19. We analyze the impact of relative prices on arrears in the coal sector separately by region because the data on arrears, employment, and relative prices exhibit substantial differences between the two regions. We also introduce the two relative price variables separately in two regressions due to the high degree of collinearity we observed when we introduced both relative prices in a single regression.

## Chapter 9

1. Although benefits tied workers to the firms, wage withholding nevertheless exposed employers to the risks of losing their employees with the most marketable skills and the best alternative employment prospects.

2. The negative effect of noncompliance on labor productivity via work disincentives does not qualitatively change the results that follow (see endnote 5).

3. Given the tax implications of cash profits, Russian managers might choose to maximize the rents that accrue to them rather than maximize profits. If we alternatively interpret (2) as a function describing managerial rents rather than enterprise profits, the comparative static result in (5) is unchanged. That is, rent-seeking managers would still respond to the market options of their more productive workers by paying them a higher percentage of the wages owed to them to discourage costly (rent-reducing) turnover.

4. This is a reasonable assumption: If wages were fully downwardly flexible, firms would lower wage rates in the face of surplus labor rather than withhold wage payments.

5. If we allow labor productivity $\alpha$ to be a concave function of the compliance rate $\beta$, that is, $\alpha = \alpha(\beta)$, $\alpha' > 0$, $\alpha'' < 0$, then it follows that $d\beta/dw^m = q''/[q'' \cdot (w^c)^2 - a''] > 0$. Alternatively, if we specify labor productivity to be a concave function of actual wage payments relative to market alternatives, that is, if $\alpha = \alpha(\beta w^c - w^m)$, then we get an identical result as in (5).

6. For a discussion of job turnover in Russian enterprises, see Gimpelson and Lippoldt (1996).

7. The wage variable used, in table 9.2 and the subsequent tables, is an estimate of contracted wages, which are actual wages paid plus an estimate of the monthly outstanding wage obligations by the employers, the latter calculated as the cumulated nonpayments divided by the number of months for which these wages were owed. (Note that this procedure is subject to a measurement error because we do not know the debt that was incurred in the past thirty days.) Monthly wages are taken from the questionnaire item, "How much money in the last thirty days did you receive from your primary workplace after taxes? If you received all or part of the money in foreign currency, please convert all into rubles, and name the total sum."

8. Because specification (2) additionally includes productivity proxies such as education and employment tenure, the estimated wage variable effects reflect the productivity of unobserved labor quality, rents accruing to workers, and the measurement errors in the included proxies.

9. Alternatively, the more productive workers were less affected by wage arrears because they had moved into more profitable firms. Lack of firm-level data unfortunately prevents us from testing this hypothesis.

10. Ideally, we need enterprise-level data on the allocation of arrears to individuals employed by the enterprise for this analysis; unfortunately, this information is not available to us.

11. Although the RLMS fielded questions on industry of employment, these responses were not translated from Russian and were therefore not distributed to the public for analysis. After discussions with RLMS project directors, we were able to obtain and translate the original industry responses (with the assistance of Anna Demidova and Anatoly Kandel) and group them into twenty-one broad industry groups corresponding roughly to the categories used by Goskomstat in its reporting of industry level statistics.

12. The regressions in columns (3) and (4) are for people who are owed wages, that is, for people with $Pjowed = 1$, so that the results are not picking up the pattern of occurrence of arrears found in column (2).

13. We have restricted our analysis of employer change to the years 1994–96. Given the absence of information for 1997, the two-year period between 1996 and 1998 increases the likelihood of incorrect classification of job changers. Specifically, since our coding scheme requires that job changers must have shorter tenures in period $t$ than in period $t - 1$, we run the risk in all years of missing employer changes in cases where the jobs in period $t - 1$ were relatively short and the workers started their new jobs shortly after their interviews in year $t - 1$. For the 1996–98 period, we are even more likely to miss these employer changers due to the longer period over which individuals may accumulate job tenures on their new jobs, potentially misclassifying a higher percentage of actual employer changers as stayers.

14. The explanatory variables in both regressions are year $t - 1$ *values.*

15. The explanatory variables in both regressions are year $t$ *values.*

# Chapter 10

1. "The tariff system is designed to reward the 'scientifically measurable' contribution of each worker, in accordance with the principle of 'equal pay for equal work', by means of

a system of national job evaluation, supplemented by coefficients for unpleasant conditions, inhospi table regions, training, industrial sector, and so on. The drawing up of tariff scales is such a centralized and bureaucratic process that the incentive impact of the tariff wage is barely discernible on the shop floor" (Rutland 1986, p. 195).

2. "Material rewards (i.e., wages) consist of two elements: the tariff wage (about 70 percent of total earnings) and the various bonuses for overfulfilment, innovation, and so on" (Rutland, 1986 p. 195).

3. The reasons for this are well known. "The more inputs the enterprise can have allocated to it, the better, so far as the management is concerned. If these inputs are incorporated in the production plan, they will be covered in the enterprise's financial plan, even if planned losses are involved. In general, the enterprise cannot be penalized for high costs incorporated in its plan: there are no competitors to undercut it, and no fear of business failure" (Hanson 1986, p. 88).

4. "Soviet planners regularly underestimate labour demand by large amounts. In other words the sum of enterprise labour-force plans (certainly after 'corrections' within the plan period, and probably even after that) tends to exceed any aggregate labour-force plan [by planners] for the state sector as a whole. The actual demand for labour therefore probably exceeds the available supply. Vacancies outnumber unemployed job-seekers; or to put it differently, the average vacancy remains unfilled longer than the average job-seeker remains out of work" (Hanson 1986, p. 94).

5. The labor participation rates are calculated by dividing the people employed in state enterprises and administration and collective farms with the population between sixteen and fifty-four to fifty-nine years of age.

6. Worker mobility between 1992 and 1995 was high: Goskomstat estimated that approximately 31 percent of employees left their jobs every year. Details are in Gimpelson and Lippoldt (1996), p. 12.

7. Data from the RLMS indicate that women on average earned approximately 60 percent less than men during 1994–98.

8. When we include the three interaction terms of specification (4) in specification (2), they turn out to be statistically insignificant, indicating that the overall gender differential in the likelihood of wage withholding did not change during 1994–98.

9. Interaction effects of gender and the three year dummies, statistically insignificant, suggest that these gender patterns were relatively constant during 1994–98.

10. The 1994 pattern is consistent with a greater reliance by employers on laying off women as a way of absorbing the unemployment shocks associated with macroeconomic brakes and enterprise restructuring during the transition.

11. These calculations of work hours relate only to the respondents' main job and ignore the influence of secondary jobs: Increased multiple job holding during the transition would tend to mitigate our reported trend in hours.

12. With the exception of the analysis of the incidence of unemployment, the regressions in tables 10.9 and 10.10 only include respondents who held jobs at the time of the interviews.

13. The observation by Gimpelson and Lippoldt (1996) in one of the four firms they studied is relevant here: "Since 1993 some if its core workers (mostly women working on the assembly lines) have been on unpaid vacations on a rotating basis. Thus, for the

individual employee the firm has sought to minimize the duration of unpaid leave; at the same time it maintained the overall numbers on unpaid leave." While these work-sharing practices have some of the characteristics of temporary layoffs, the absence of unemployment benefits for workers on administrative leave means that these practices play a different role from that played by temporary layoffs in the United States. Russian workers were likely to favor contracts that have flexible wages rather than unemployment risks (see Azariadis 1983).

14. Data on underemployment is collected for medium and large-sized firms only, covering roughly 75 percent of the labor force. Smaller firms were perhaps less able and willing to engage in work sharing of this form, especially if they were relatively newer firms with fewer redundant workers. Therefore the official statistics may overstate the prevalence of administrative leave.

15. The cyclical sensitivity of female employment is greater than that of male employment in some European economies, the United States and Japan (see Tachibanaki 1987), results consistent with the gender patterns of unpaid leave observed in Russia.

16. Observations with monthly hours in excess of 360 were deleted.

17. According to Foley (1996), women in Russia experienced a longer average duration of unemployment than men, and were generally less likely to change their status from unemployed to employed by returning to work.

## Chapter 11

1. *Izvestiya*, January 30, 1997, p. 4.

2. ibid.

3. OECD Economic Surveys, 1997–1998. Russian Federation, pp. 117–118.

4. See, for example, Thompson (1997), pp. 1162–1165.

5. Pendergast and Stole (1996) provide arguments for barter within organizations that are not based on liquidity constraints per se. Among these are the ability of enterprises to reduce excess inventories creating negotiations between enterprises and workers for mutually beneficial barter arrangements (according to Roha and Schulhof 1996) and use of goods as a source of price flexibility (according to Stigler 1969).

6. *Izvestiya,* January 30, 1997, p. 4.

7. *Sevodnya,* March 21, 1995, p. 3; cited in *The Current Digest of the Post-Soviet Press,* vol. XLVII, no. 12, April 19, 1995, p. 8)

8. *Izvestiya,* September 21, p. 2.

## Chapter 12

1. *Moskovskiye novosti, no. 44,* November 3–10, 1996, p. 4; cited in *The Current Digest of the Post-Soviet Press,* vol. XLVIII, no. 44, November 27, 1996, pp. 1–4.

2. *Sevodnya,* November 10, 1996, p. 3; cited in *The Current Digest of the Post Soviet Press,* vol. XLVIII, no. 45, December 4, 1996, p. 16.

3. Ibid.

4. See Granger 1969, pp. 424–38. For a simple description of the test, see Pindyck and Rubinfeld (op. cit.), pp. 216–219.

5. Granger tests based on $m = 2$ and $m = 7$ yield results similar to those reported for the $m = 4$ period lag.

## Chapter 13

1. *Izvestiya,* April 20, 1993, p. 4; cited in *The Current Digest of the Post-Soviet Press,* vol. XLV, no. 16, May 19, 1993, p. 29).

2. *Sevodnya,* June 18, 1997, p. 3; cited in *The Current Digest of the Post-Soviet Press,* vol. XLIX, no. 24, July 16, 1997, p. 16.

3. *Sevodnya,* June 16, 1997, p. 5; cited in *The Current Digest of the Post-Soviet Press,* vol. XLIX, no. 24, July 16, 1997, p. 15.

4. *Trud,* October 10, 1996, pp. 1–4; cited in *The Current Digest of the Post-Soviet Press,* vol. XLVIII, no. 44, November 26, 1997, pp. 18–19.

5. *Izvestiya,* April 28, 1995, p. 2; cited in *The current Digest of the Post-Soviet Press,* vol. XLVII, no. 17, May 24, 1995, p. 18.

6. *Izvestiya,* January 27, 1993, p. 5; cited in *The Current Digest of the Post-Soviet Press,* vol. XLV, no. 4, February 24, 1993, p. 5.

7. *Izvestiya,* February 9, 1993, p. 2; cited in *The Current Digest of the Post-Soviet Press,* vol. XLV, no. 6, march 10, 1993, p. 22.

8. *Izvestiya,* April 28, 1995, p. 2; cited in *The Current Digest of the Post-Soviet Press,* vol. XLVII, no. 17, May 24, 1995, p. 18.

9. *Trud,* October 10, 1996, p. 4; cited in *The Current Digest of the Post-Soviet Press,* vol. XLVIII, no. 44, November 26, 1997, p. 19.

10. *Nezavisimaya gazeta,* October 17, 1997, p. 5: cited in *The Current Digest of the Post-Soviet Press,* vol. XLIX, no. 41, November 12, 1997, pp. 2–5.

11. Ibid.

12. Ibid.

13. Ibid.

14. *Sevodnya,* October 18, 1997, p. 3; cited in *The Current Digest of the Post-Soviet Press,* vol. XLIX, no. 41, November 12, 1997, p. 5 .

15. Wage nonpayment not only reduces family disposable income directly but also cuts into family wealth because wage arrears are not indexed. This means that even if Russian workers were to be eventually repaid, they would have suffered a significant loss given the high monthly inflation rates that persisted during the years considered here.

16. See also Popkin and Mroz (1995), Mikhalev (1996), Milanovic (1998), Gregory (1997), and Klugman (1997) for discussions of trends in Russian poverty and issues relating to its measurement.

17. This latter effect may well have been the result of wage nonpayment, pushing more people into unemployment or out of the labor force by 1998, thereby removing the worst hit from our wage earners' sample in 1998.

18. See Foley (1997) for a study of multiple job holding patterns in Russia during the transition.

19. Labor supply effects of wage arrears may more accurately be modeled, depending on management behavior, as a cut in wage rates (when managers withheld pay based on a percentage of earnings) or a limitation on available paid hours (when they stopped payments after a certain threshold of earnings was reached).

20. In all likelihood, wage arrears produced labor supply effects in primary employment via increased quits from enterprises and sectors that failed to fully pay their wage obligations. The Soviet-era linkage of social services and housing to the employing enterprise limited these mobility responses.

21. We also find, in results not reported here, that women were less likely than men to engage in supplemental work activities, perhaps due to family obligations. When we split the sample by gender, we again find that wage arrears had a significant and positive effect on supplemental labor supply for men, but an insignificant (though positive) effect for women, possibly reflecting family constraints and/or gender differences in secondary job market opportunities.

22. We also find in results not reproduced here that these relationships between arrears and transfers were constant during the 1994–98 period.

23. These goods include any of twenty-five different foods that were grown/harvested on land that the family owned or leased. (A detailed list of food items is available on request.)

24. These goods include items referred to in note 23, plus sales of livestock, poultry, bees/honey, wool/down, milk, eggs, hides, mushrooms, nuts, berries, and fish.

25. Respondents were asked if they owned an item in a list of seven different consumer durables, plus cars, boats, apartments, and houses, and then were asked: "In the last three months has your family sold any of their things in order to get enough money for food and clothing?"

26. We use the responses to the survey question: "How much did your family receive (from a primary or additional place of work) after taxes and other deductions in the last thirty days? If you were paid in the form of goods or services, what was the approximate value in rubles?"

27. While intrafamily transfers and home production might reduce the *depth* of poverty experienced by wage nonpayment victims, they might be insufficient to move them above the given thresholds.

# References

Alfandari, G., and M.E. Schaffer. 1996. "Arrears in the Russian Enterprise Sector." In S. Commander, Q. Fan, and M.E. Schaffer, eds., *Enterprise Restructuring and Economic Policy in Russia*. Washington, D.C.: EDI (Economic Development Institute), World Bank.

Aukutsionek, Sergei, and Rostislav Kapeliushnikov. 1997. "Why Do Russian Enterprises Hoard Labor?" Paper presented at the 23rd CIRET (Center for International Research on Economic Tendency Surveys) Conference, August.

Aukutsionek, Sergei. 1998. "On Types of Barter." *Russian Economic Barometer* 7(2).

Azariadis, Costas. 1975. "Implicit Contracts and Underemployment Equilibria." *Journal of Political Economy* 83(6):1183–1202.

Baranets, Victor. 1998. *Poteryannaya Armiya: Zapiski Polkovnika Genshtaba*. Moscow: Kollektsiya "Sovershenno Secretno."

Barber, John. 1986. "The Development of Soviet Employment and Labour Policy, 1930–41." In David Lane, ed., *Labour and Employment in the USSR*. New York: New York University Press, pp. 50–68.

Bergson, Abram. 1946. *The Structure of Soviet Wages*. Cambridge, Mass.: Harvard University Press.

Boycko, M., A. Shleifer, and R. Vishny. 1995. *Privatizing Russia*. Cambridge, Mass.: MIT Press.

Brainerd, Elizabeth. 1996. "Death and the Market." Department of Economics, Harvard University, working paper.

Brainerd, Elizabeth. 1997. "Women in Transition: Changes in Gender Wage Differentials in Eastern Europe and the Former Soviet Union." Department of Economics, Harvard University, working paper.

Brainerd, Elizabeth. 1998. "Winners and Losers in Russia's Economic Transition." *American Economic Review* 88(5):1094–1116.

Braithwaite, Jeanine. 1997. "The Old and the New Poor in Russia." In Jeni Klugman, ed., *Poverty in Russia*. Washington, D.C.: World Bank.

Calvo, Guillermo. 1979. "Quasi-Walrasian Theories of Unemployment." *American Economic Review* 69(2):102–107.

Chapman, Janet G. 1970. *Wage Variation in Soviet Industry: The Impact of the 1956–1960 Wage Reform*. Santa Monica, Ca.: RAND Corporation.

Chapman, Janet G. 1991. "Recent and Prospective Trends in Soviet Wage Determination." In Guy Standing, ed., *In Search of Flexibility: The New Soviet Labour Market*. Geneva: International Labour Office, pp. 177–202.

Clarke, Simon. 1998. "Trade Unions and Nonpayment of Wages in Russia." Center for Comparative Labour Studies, University of Warwick, working paper.

Cox, Donald, Zereria Eser and Emanuel Jimenez. 1997. "Family Safety Nets during Economic Transition: A Study of Inter-Household Transfers in Russia." In Jeni Klugman, ed., *Poverty in Russia*. Washington, D.C.: World Bank.

Desai, Padma. 1989. "Perestroika, Prices, and the Ruble Problem." Harriman Institute FORUM 2(11):1–8.

Desai, Padma. 2000. "Why Did the Ruble Collapse in August 1998?" *American Economic Review Papers and Proceedings* 90(2):48–52.

Earle, John S., and Klara Sabirianova. 1998. "Understanding Wage Arrears in Russia." Stockholm Institute of Transition Economies working paper, September.

Feldstein, Martin. 1976. "Temporary Layoffs in the Theory of Unemployment." *Journal of Political Economy* 84(5):937–958.

Foley, Mark C. 1996. "Unemployment Duration in Transition Economies: Evidence from MicroData on Russia." Department of Economics, Yale University, working paper.

Foley, Mark C. 1997. "Static and Dynamic Analyses of Poverty in Russia." In Jeni Klugman, ed., *Poverty in Russia*. Washington, D.C.:World Bank.

Foley, Mark C. 1997. "Multiple Job Holding in Russia during the Transition." Department of Economics, Yale University, working paper.

Gimpelson, Vladimir, and Douglas Lippoldt. 1996. "Labour Restructuring in Russian Enterprises: A Case Study." Paris: OECD.

Glinskaya, Elena, and Thomas Mroz. 1996. "The Gender Gap in Wages in Russia from 1992 to 1995." Paper presented at the 10th ESPE Anniversary Meeting, Uppsala.

Gloeckner, Eduard. 1986. "Underemployment and Potential Unemployment of the Technical Intelligentsia: Distortions between Education and Occupation." In David Lane, ed., *Labour and Employment in the USSR*. New York: New York University Press, pp. 223–238.

Granger, C.W.J. 1969. "Investigating Causal Relations by Econometric Model and Cross-Spectral Methods." *Econometrica* 37:424–438.

Gregory, P., and J. Kohlhase. 1988. "The Earnings of Soviet Workers: Evidence from the Soviet Interview Project." *The Review of Economics and Statistics* 70(1):23–35.

Gregory, Paul. 1997. "Macroeconomic Policy, Structural Factors, and Poverty: The Russian And Ukrainian Transition." United Nations Development Programme, working paper.

Guriev, Sergei, and Barry W. Ickes. 1999. "Barter in Russian Enterprises: Myths versus Empirical Evidence." *Russian Economic Trends*, September.

Hanson, Philip. 1986. "The Serendipitous Soviet Achievement of Full Employment: Labour Shortage and Labour Hoarding in the Soviet Economy." In David Lane, ed., *Labour and Employment in the USSR*. New York: New York University Press, pp. 83–111.

Harrison, Mark. 1986. "The Development of Soviet Employment and Labour Policy, 1930–41." In David Lane, ed., *Labour and Employment in the USSR*. New York: New York University Press, pp. 69–82.

Heeringa, Steven. 1997. *Russian Longitudinal Monitoring Survey: Sample Attrition, Replenishment, and Weighting in Rounds V–VII*. Ann Arbor: Institute for Social Research, University of Michigan.

Helgeson, Ann. 1986. "Geographical Mobility—Its Implications for Employment." In David Lane, ed., *Labour and Employment in the USSR*. New York: New York University Press, pp. 145–175.

Hendley, Kathryn, Barry W. Ickes, and Randi Ryterman. 1998. "Remonetizing the Russian Economy." Department of Economics, Penn State University, working paper.

Johnson, Simon, Daniel Kaufman, and Andrei Shleifer. 1997. "The Unofficial Economy in Transition." *Brookings Papers on Economic Activity* 2:159–239.

Kanaev, Georgy. 1991. "The Future Role of Trade Unions." In Guy Standing, ed., *In Search of Flexibility: The New Soviet Labour Market*. Geneva: International Labour Office, pp. 254–274.

Katz, Katarina. 1994. "Gender Differentiation and Discrimination: A Study of Soviet Wages." Department of Economics, University of Gothenburg, manuscript.

Klugman, Jeni, ed. 1997. *Poverty in Russia: Public Policy and Private Responses*. Washington, D.C.: EDI Development Studies, World Bank.

Kostakov, Vladimir G. 1991. "Labour Surplus and Labour Shortage in the USSR." In Guy Standing, ed., *In Search of Flexibility: The New Soviet Labour Market*. Geneva: International Labour Office, pp. 81–106.

Lampert, Nick. 1986. "Job Security and the Law in the in the USSR." In David Lane, ed., *Labour and Employment in the USSR*. New York: New York University Press, pp. 256–277.

Lane, David. 1986. "The Ending of Mass Unemployment in the USSR." In David Lane, ed., *Labour and Employment in the USSR*. New York: New York University Press, pp. 1–18.

Lapidus, Gail W. 1981. "The Female Industrial Labor Force: Dilemmas, Reassessments, and Options." In Morris Bornstein, ed., *The Soviet Economy: Continuity and Change*. Boulder, Colo.: Westview Press, pp. 119–148.

Layard, Richard, and Andrea Richter. 1994. "Labor Market Adjustment in Russia." *Russian Economic Trends* 3(2):85–103.

Layard, Richard, and Andrea Richter. 1995. "How Much Unemployment is Needed for Restructuring: The Russian Experience." *Economics of Transition* 3(1):39–58.

Lehmann, Hartmut, Jonathan Wadsworth, and Alessandro Acquist. 1999. "Grime and Punishment: Job Insecurity and Wage Arrears in the Russian Federation." *Journal of Comparative Economics* 27(4):595–617.

Malle, Silvana. 1986. "Heterogeneity of the Soviet Labour Market as a Limit to a More Efficient Utilisation of Manpower." In David Lane, ed., *Labour and Employment in the USSR*. New York: New York University Press, pp. 122–144.

Marnie, Sheila. 1986. "Transition from School to Work: Satisfying Pupils' Aspirations and the Needs of the Economy." In David Lane, ed., *Labour and Employment in the USSR*. New York: New York University Press, pp. 209–222.

Marshall, Ray, and Arvil Adams. 1994. "Labor Market Flexibility and Job Security Measures in a Global Economy." World Bank, ESP (Education and Social Policy Department) Paper series, 44.

Maslova, Inga. 1991. "State Employment Programmes in the Light of the New Law on

Employment." In Guy Standing, ed., *In Search of Flexibility: The New Soviet Labour Market*. Geneva: International Labour Office, pp. 121–144.

Mikhalev, Vladimir. 1996. "Poverty Alleviation in the Course of Transition: Policy Options for Russia." European University Institute, Robert Schuman Centre, working paper.

Milanovic, Branko. 1996. *Income Inequality and Poverty during the Transition*. Washington, D.C.: World Bank.

Mroz, Thomas, and Barry Popkin. 1995. "Poverty and Economic Transition in the Russian Federation." *Economic Development and Cultural Change* 44(1):1–31.

Newell, Andrew, and Barry Reilly. 1996. "The Gender Wage Gap in Russia: Some Empirical Evidence." *Labour Economics* 3(3):337–356.

Noren, James H. 1994. "The Russian Military-Industrial Sector and Conversion." *Post-Soviet Geography*, November.

Peck, Merton J., and Thomas J. Richardson, eds. 1991. *What Is To Be Done? Proposals for the Soviet Transition to the Market*. New Haven: Yale University Press.

Pendergast, Canice, and Lars Stole. 1996. "Non-Monetary Exchange within Firms and Industry." NBER working paper 5765, September.

Pietsch, Anna-Jutta. 1986. "Shortage of Labour and Motivation Problems of Soviet Workers." In David Lane, ed., *Labour and Employment in the USSR*. New York: New York University Press, pp. 176–190.

Pindyck, Robert S., and Daniel L. Rubinfeld. 1991. *Econometric Models and Economic Forecasts*, 3rd ed. New York: McGraw Hill.

Popkin, Barry, and Tom Mroz. 1995. "Poverty and the Economic Transition in the Russian Federation." *Economic Development and Cultural Change* 44(1):1–31.

Popkin, B., M. Kosolopov, P. Kozyreva, T. Mroz, M. Swafford, N. Zohoori. 1996. "Monitoring the Economic Transition in the Russian Federation: The Russian Longitudinal Monitoring Survey." In *Economic Transformation-Households and Health*. Washington, D.C.: National Academy Press.

Powell, David, E. 1981. "Labor Turnover in the Soviet Union." In Morris Bornstein, ed., *The Soviet Economy: Continuity and Change*. Boulder, Colo.: Westview Press, pp. 101–118.

Roha, Ronaleen, and Marc Schulhof. 1996. "How Barter Saves Cash." *Kiplinger's Personal Finance Magazine* 50(2).

Romanenkova, Gortenziya. 1991. "Rural-Urban Labour Migration in the USSR: Its Role in Redistributing Population and Labour Resources." In Guy Standing, ed., *In Search of Flexibility: The New Soviet Labour Market*. Geneva: International Labour Office, pp. 165–176.

Russian Economic Trends. Working Centre for Economic Reform, Government of the Russian Federation. London, U.K.: Whurr Publishers. Various issues.

Rutkowski, Jan. 1996. "High Skills Pay Off: The Changing Wage Structure during Economic Transition In Poland." *Economics of Transition* 4(1):89–112.

Rutland, Peter. 1986. "Productivity Campaigns in Soviet Industry." In David Lane, ed., *Labour and Employment in the USSR*. New York: New York University Press, pp. 191–208.

Salop, Steven. 1979. "A Model of the Natural Rate of Unemployment." *American Economic Review* 69(1):117–125.

Shisko, Robert, and Bernard Rostker. 1976. "The Economics of Multiple Job Holding." *American Economic Review* 66(3):298–308.

Standing, Guy, ed. 1991. *In Search of Flexibility: The New Soviet Labour Market*. Geneva: International Labour Organization.

Standing, Guy. 1994a. "Employment Restructuring in Russian Industry." *World Development* 22(2):253–260.

Standing, Guy. 1994b. "Labor Market Implications of 'Privatization' in Russian Industry in 1992." *World Development* 22(2):261–270.

Standing, Guy. 1994c. "The Changing Position of Women in Russian Industry: Prospects of Marginalization." *World Development* 22(2):271–283.

Standing, Guy. 1995. "Enterprise Restructuring in Russian Industry and Mass Unemployment." ILO Labour Market Papers, no. 1. Geneva: International Labour Office.

Standing, Guy. 1996. "The Shake-out in Russian Factories: The RLFS Fifth Round, 1995." ILO Labour Market Papers, no. 14. Geneva: International Labour Office.

Stigler, George. 1969. "Reciprocity." *Antitrust Law & Economic Review,* Spring.

Tachibanaki, Toshiaki. 1987. "Labour Market Flexibility in Japan in Comparison with Europe and the U.S." *European Economic Review* 31(3):647–684.

Tompson, W. 1997. "Old Habits Die Hard: Fiscal Imperatives, State Regulation, and the Role of Russia's Banks." *Europe-Asia Studies* 49(7).

Treisman, Daniel. 1999. *After the Deluge: Regional Crisis and Political Consolidation in Russia*. Ann Arbor: University of Michigan Press.

Woodruff, David. 1999. "Barter of the Bankrupt: The Politics of Demonetization in Russia's Federal State." In Burawoy and Verdery, eds., *Uncertain Transition: Ethnographies of Change in the Postsocialist World*. Lanham, Md.: Rowman & Littlefield.

Yakovlev, Andrey. 1998. "Barter and Clearing Schemes: How to Define Basic Concepts." *Russian Economic Barometer* 7(2).

Yanowitch, Murray. 1963. "The Soviet Income Revolution." *Slavic Review* 22(2):683–697.

# Index

collective bargaining among new, 193
competition among Russian, 198
CPSU control in Soviet era, 191–92
in Czarist Russia, 191
disputes about wage nonpayment, 197–199
under Gorbachev, 192–193
under Law on Enterprises, 195
during New Economic Policy (1920s), 191–192
role of Russian, 195–197
strike committees, 197–198
Transactions. *See also* Cash transactions
inter-enterprise barter transactions, 177
in noncash money, 173–174
separation of cash and noncash, 179–181
Treisman, Daniel, 78–79
Tuleyev, Aman, 129

Unemployment
among men and women (1994–1998), 166–168, 170
during reform era (1980s), 156–157

Varov, Vladimir, 196
*Veksels*
promissory notes as noncash instruments, 178
as transferable bills of exchange, 178
Vyakhirev, Rem, 18, 36

Wage arrears. *See* Wage nonpayment/arrears
Wage debt
federal and regional governments (1997), 78
gender differences in cumulated, 164–166
value of (1994–1998), 65–67
values across occupations and industries, 66–67
Wage nonpayment/arrears. *See also* Pension nonpayment/arrears
by age, 53–54
amount and relative amount of, 49, 68
bankruptcy laws to curtail, 23
barter as response to, 187–189
from cashflow problems, 5–6
in coal industry (1990s), 123
crisis (1994–1998), 225
with cutbacks in machine and metal working firms, 42

differences by gender and occupation in incidence of, 162–164
differences by region, 1, 56–57
differences in urban centers and regions, 85t, 87–88
by educational level, 54–56
effect on Pension Fund contributions, 105
to employees in regional government, 21–22
employers' incentives to pay partial, 8, 135–136
factors easing, 226–227
family responses to, 214–220
by gender, 52–53
gender differences in cumulated wage debt, 164–166
gender differences in incidence of (1994–1998), 160–162
impact on regional voting decisions, 78–79
as implicit withholding tax, 137, 139–140
incidence among women and men (1994–1998), 158–160
incidence of, 49, 64–65, 67–68
industrial pattern of, 58–60
inequality among workers of, 137–139
interregional differences, 85t, 90
under Law on Insolvency, 31
managers' strategies to allocate, 135–147
of military personnel, 96
multivariate estimates of incidence and amounts, 60–65
occupational patterns of, 57–58
owed by regional governments, 78
poverty related to, 211–214
regional patterns in incidence and amount of, 69–75
regional patterns of, 72–74t, 82, 85–87
relation to median wage in different industries, 139–142
role of trade unions in disputes over, 197–199
Russian government response to, 195–197
during Soviet era, 10
strategies to compensate for, 2
trends in (1994–1998), 50–51
trends in sectoral (1992–1997), 47–48
Wages
decentralized setting of (1990s), 157
minimum wage established (1957), 152